Art Therapy and Dramatherapy

Masks of the Soul

of related interest

Dramatherapy with Families Groups and Individuals
Waiting in the Wings
Sue Jennings
ISBN 1 85302 144 X

Play Therapy with Abused Children
Ann Cattanach
ISBN 1 85302 193 8

Storymaking in Bereavement
Dragons Fight in the Meadow
Alida Gersie
ISBN 1 85302 176 8

Storymaking in Education and Therapy
Alida Gersie and Nancy King
ISBN 1 85302 519 4

Drama and Healing
The Roots of Drama Therapy
Roger Grainger
ISBN 1 85302 048 6

Art Therapy in Practice
Edited by Marian Liebmann
ISBN 1 85302 057 5

Art Therapy and Dramatherapy

Masks of the Soul

Sue Jennings and Åse Minde

Jessica Kingsley Publishers
London and Philadelphia

The authors and the publishers gratefully acknowledge permission to reprint extracts from the following:

Case, C. and Daley, T. (1992) *The Handbook of Art Therapy*. London: Tavistock. pp.4/122.

Hobson, R. (1985) *Forms of Feeling: The Heart of Psychotherapy*. London: Tavistock. p.20.

Landy, R. (1986) *Drama Therapy: Concepts and Practice*. New York: Charles C. Thomas. p.165.

Napier, A.D. (1986) *Masks, Transformations and Paradox*. University of California Press. p.3.c. 1986 The Regents of the University of California.

Neumann, E. (1963) *The Great Mother*. London: Routledge and Kegan Paul. pp.266–227.

Robbins, A. (1989) *The Psychoasthetic Experience: An Approach to Depth Orientated Treatment*. New York: Human Sciences Press. p.21.

Sutcliffe, F.M. (c.1880) *The Limpets*. Whotby, N. Yorkshire: The Sutcliffe Gallery. p.78.

Wilshire, B. (1982) *Role Playing and Identity: The Limits of Theatre as Metaphor*. Indiana University Press. p.32.

Winnicott, D. (1971) *Playing and Reality*. London: Routledge. pp.113/116/128/102.

First Published in the United Kingdom in 1993 by
Jessica Kingsley Publishers Ltd
116 Pentonville Road
London N1 9JB

ISBN 1 85302 027 3

British Library Cataloguing in Publication Data is available from the British Library

Printed and bound in Great Britain by
Biddles Ltd, Guildford and King's Lynn

Contents

Dedications

I dedicate this book to Henrik Bauge, the head doctor on psychiatric ward 16 at Ullevål Sykehus, Oslo, where I worked for eleven years. Not only did he teach me so very much, but he also encouraged me and supported me to develop my work as a pioneer art therapist.

Åse Minde

I must dedicate this book to Patrick de Mare, the first psychiatrist to take dramatherapy seriously at St. George's Hospital, where I worked from 1968. His breadth of vision has been a life-time of inspiration to me.

Sue Jennings

Acknowledgements

First, I must thank my patients who have given to me and taught me with such generosity, especially those who have contributed to the work of this book, especially Heidi, Sonja and Thale.

Thanks to Kaare Porsbøll and Jan Bakken for their fine photos and slides of the patients' work.

Many colleagues have been very important to my work in this field and have given inspiration, support and supervision. Special thanks to Gunvor Basberg, Srein Hangsgjerd, Eva Røine, Ingeborg Breder, Per Størksen, Murray Cox and Arthur Robbins.

Thank you.

Åse Minde

The generosity of patients and trainees with their creative work is quite overwhelming. I thank them all.

I am grateful to the following clinicians and artists for being such a staunch support, as well as creative allies and challengers, and who also taught me that confrontation can be creative and not destructive: Jean Campbell, Ann Cattanach, Murray Cox, Clare Higgins, Steve Mitchell and Derek Steinberg.

My thanks.

Sue Jennings

We would both like to thank the patience of Jessica Kingsley in waiting for this book and her faith that it would appear! The creative process of writing a joint book we will talk about later, but we would genuinely like to thank each other for the slow gestation and creative waiting that eventually gave birth to this book.

Gro Finne has contributed some inspired drawings for us and Audrey Hillyar has stage-managed the whole process, as well as assisting with final rushes!

To them all, our thanks.

Sue Jennings
Stratford-upon-Avon, UK

Åse Minde
Oslo, Norway

INTRODUCTION

Birth, Death and Cycle of the Seasons

How the story began...

We have been working together in art therapy and dramatherapy for twelve years. What started as a chance meeting at a very frustrating conference turned into a long-term friendship and working alliance. This personal and professional relationship has contained individual journeys, changes of house, births of children and deaths of parents, and has continued to deepen and expand.

Åse's perspective

I had heard about Sue – I trained in art therapy at St. Albans the year before she started the dramatherapy diploma there. I was living in a rather bleak monastery with fellow students, trying to make sense of the therapeutic use of art. Luckily for me there was a fellow Norwegian there. However, I never had the opportunity to attend any of her workshops until I went to the conference in Sweden. I went up to her and introduced myself and we started chatting as if we had always known each other. I was with other Norwegians and we decided there and then to invite her to Norway. I arranged a large seminar at a hospital in Oslo and Sue came and ran it for three days.

I attended the seminar myself, together with other colleagues, including Gunvor Basberg, Eva Røine, Tone Bjørnebo and Melinda Meyer, who are all now running courses in the arts and expressive therapies field. Who is this woman? we all thought, as we engaged with movement and fairytales and then some very deep mask-work about the self we would like to change. I remember one person who was 'locked' into a miscarriage that she had never acknowledged and she faced it through the mask and allowed herself to live again.

After that course, Sue and I worked together every year, inviting dance therapists, psychotherapists and other art therapists. However, our collaboration in art therapy and dramatherapy is the central core of our working relationship.We have been through a lot of experiences together – all of my three pregnancies for example! Sue supported and encouraged me in my own pioneering work in Norway, (even now we have very few professional art therapists). I have been introducing full professional training in Norway in various clinical and educational establishments as well as in government departments. But despite this lengthy negotiation, the training programme is still waiting to start. I find this very frustrating and, being a pioneer herself, Sue understands all of this.

I worked with her students in Greece, which was a very creative time for me. I took the whole family and we had a holiday in Athens, as well as running workshops. Years later, I had a dream about Sue and the Acropolis which we discuss in one of the chapters. We dream about each other and have an amazing sense of synchronicity in our work. I have visited her in Stratford-upon-Avon and have been to see Shakespeare plays with her.

The Summer and Autumn Schools have become something of an institution now; 1992 will be our twelfth year. I don't know what would happen if one of us left, as we have established a way of working which isn't static but continues to grow and develop as we continue to learn from each other and the participants; but in any case, it does not feel right to finish just now. We also feel it is a very good example for the students – a rôle model – showing how this work can be collaborative and not competitive. They can experience the individuation between us as well as the creative relationship; how we take it in turns to lead, often spontaneously, 'in the moment'. They also know that we do not give a primacy to our own particular art-form – we feel more that they complement each other so that each is enriched by the other's presence.

Writing of this book together has been harder than we had expected because we keep thinking of new ideas. We have changed the chapters at least three times and put things in and taken it out again. Eventually, we realised that we did not want to write another book on the history and background of the arts therapies listing all of the people who had contributed to its development and so on. We both wanted to write about the people who had been significant in our development as arts therapists and about the process of working together in this complementary way.

Quite apart from the work, Sue has re-awakened my interest in theatre again. My niece, who has completed drama training at Norway's *only* drama school, runs theatre workshops for the dramatherapy students and is now working on television and for the National Theatre of Bergen, has also stimulated my growing interest in theatre.

Sue's perspective

I was so pleased when I first met Åse – a fellow red-head and a bit crazy like me! She asked me to visit Norway to run a workshop and seemed a little surprised when I said yes without any hesitation. It was an extraordinary few days as there were some very experienced people on the course who I felt were coming along to see me try my paces! During this visit, Åse and I discovered that we spoke the same language about our work and had a fascination for what each other did. An added incentive for me was that Åse and her husband lived in a cottage in a pine forest and it was the most creative place for me to be able to think and write.

Åse was beginning to pioneer her own work in Norway, having spent a lengthy time in the USA, and her ideas were fresh and creative. I was enchanted straight away and we immediately said that we would run joint courses in the future. Åse and I have been co-working ever since the 1980 workshop, and I value her friendship as well as her professionalism enormously. I respect completely her capacity to maintain her domestic and professional boundaries and to keep the limits on her client/student relationships, which, in such a small country like Norway, is far from easy. Åse has allowed me to discover art for myself – I suppose the age of 40 was a good time to begin! As the 'dancer' in my family I was not allowed to paint and draw and I developed one picture that would fit any situation at secondary school. My personal art has always been expressed through the creation of masks in various media. Although I worked for ten years in an art college, I was still terrified of art and artists. Strange, when you are brought up to feel that there is something you know nothing about – you end up feeling you know nothing. My big breakthrough came when I was able to return to the same college and give a talk on dramatherapy using thirty or more slides of great paintings. And, of course, visiting Norway has meant that I have been able to immerse myself in Edvard Munch as well as Ibsen.

It was such a privilege to be able to see Åse and her daughter only one hour after the birth. We have seen each other through many 'women's mysteries', her several births and more than one bout of severe illness, as well as my major surgery and hospitalisation.

Although I am about to retire from The Institute of Dramatherapy to work as an actress in the professional theatre, I do not see myself just leaving the collaboration with Åse. We have already begun to plan the school which will follow the publication of this book. Åse did not know that I am planning a one-woman show on the story of the life of a medieval witch, but we happened to be discussing a patient who had said to her,

'Why are you so witchy?' and we were talking about people's 'inner witch'. She then suggested that witches could be the theme of the next seasonal school!

Art therapy and dramatherapy

For many years both the training and practice of art therapy and dramatherapy has been separate. There has been virtually no dialogue concerning their relationship, or acknowledgement of the importance of mutual exploration between artistic disciplines. Obviously we would not exclude music and dance, although, interestingly enough, there seems to be a greater understanding in this area. Might this be because drama, music and dance are all 'performance arts'? On the whole, the current position seems to be very polarised – either there is no contact and everything is treated quite separately and rigidly, or there is a desire for a total integration, resulting in a 'wishy-washy' notion of being creative, and relying on technique rather than artistic process.

Over these 14 years we have continued to discover that the more we begin to understand the others' discipline – paradoxically – the more we know about our own. Åse feels no more a dramatherapist or Sue an art therapist, yet we both feel we know and understand far more about our own practice, and about our own art form.

As we explore in the book, an artistic therapist needs to be an artist in their own right, and it is rare that two art forms can be combined in one person. However, when they work alongside each other they complement rather than compete. The same happens, for example, in the theatre when the artistic designer and the director, together with the actors bring about a true ensemble, yet each has their own role. Many artists and art therapists work with play media such as sand, sculpting and masks. These are areas of mutual technique, yet each is developed within the particular frame of the practitioner.

The moment that an art therapist 'moves' a picture they are entering into the dramatic domain and, similarly, the moment that a dramatherapist 'freezes' a scene they are entering into the artistic domain. Of course, in times of diminishing resources, it is to be expected that people become mindful of their own territory, however, there seems to have always been mistrust between art therapy and dramatherapy. It was not for nothing that the slogan was coined 'art therapists are dirty and dramatherapists are dangerous'!

It is our hope that there will increasingly be more exploration of these areas of mutual overlap, especially at student/trainee/researcher level.

It does not matter whether we describe our work as a psychotherapy or not; we are all working in a field where the artistic process is the primary means of therapy, and there is so much we do not know about each others' thinking. We have found that both at a personal and a professional level, we have made discoveries about ourselves and our work through the discipline of the other, and both of us supervise practitioners in artistic therapies other than our own.

We both feel certain that the benefits will overcome the fears and then, and only then, we will truly be able to enhance our own practice and give our clients and patients the appropriate choices in their treatment programmes.

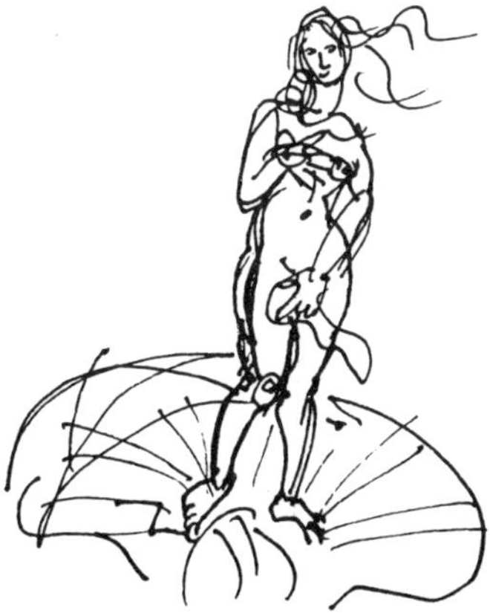

Botticelli's 'Venus' by Gro Finne

Primavera – the story of the cover of this book

Åse was waiting for Sue to send her a Jungian book called *The Pregnant Virgin* by Marion Woodman, in which the author develops and describes her process of psychological transformation. The book is written in a very personal way and illustrates the birth and journey of the book which, aptly in the beginning, had been called *Chrysalis*:

> The analogy between the virgin with child and the chrysalis with butterfly does not originate with me. In ancient Greece, the word for soul was psyche, often imaged as a butterfly. The emergence of the butterfly from the chrysalis was analogous with the birth of the soul from matter, a birth commonly identified with release, hence a symbol of immortality (Woodman 1985, p.7).

Meanwhile, Åse had a Botticelli dream in which she saw the *Primavera* picture and was inspired to go out and buy a new book – *Botticelli: Life and Work* by Ronald Lightbown (1989). The whole picture is shown on page 15, although any small reproduction cannot do justice to the magnificence of this whole work.

The content of the picture is described by Hart:

> In the universally beloved *Primavera*, we cross the portals of sleep and enter the very dream. The scene is a grove of dark orange trees, thickly

> massed. Their intertwined branches and golden fruit fill the upper portion of the picture. Between the trunks one glimpses the sky and, at one point, a hint of a distant landscape. Just off center stands a maidenly figure, one hand raised as if in benediction. At the extreme right Zephyrus, the wind god, enters the scene in pursuit of the nymph Chloris, from whose mouth issue flowers as she is transformed (according to Gombrich) into Flora, goddess of Spring. Next we see her fully metamorphosed, strewing flowers from her flower-embroidered garment upon the already flowering grass. On the left Mercury points with his caduceus at tiny clouds that drift among the golden fruit. Next to him the Three Graces dance in a ring; above, the blindfold Cupid shoots blazing golden arrows in their direction. The saintly lady in the center, so much like one of Botticelli's Madonnas, is Venus (Hart 1987, p.332).

The picture as a whole integrates so many of the themes and images that we describe in this book. It is about art and drama and dance and myth and medicine. It contains both action and stillness and illustrates healing and transformation.

> Botticelli's luxuriance of flowers may have been inspired by Politian's marvelous lines that tell how Zephyr, the soft spring wind who along of the airs of heaven is admitted into the garden, bathes the meadow with dew and with sweet scents, and clothes the ground with roses, lilies, violets, white, red and yellow hyacinths, narcissi, sunflowers, anemones, crocus, and acanthus. But the parallel is closer in spirit than in actuality, although it does suggest more poetically than literal analysis how Botticelli built up his meadow, plant by plant, using conventional models for some and blending in others flowers from one plant with leaves from another or with leaves of his own designing, but for the most part drawing from the living plant itself. Those drawn from life he must of course have worked hard on May to copy (Lightbown 1989, p.127).

Thus, the cover of this book has been inspired by Åse's dream where she 'met' Flora, and the particular detail we have chosen seems an apt metaphor for our work together. In this detail you can see Zephyr the wind god coming out of the woods in pursuit of the nymph Chloris with flowers falling from her mouth.

> Zephyr's great green-blue wing beats among the trees and his hair streams in dark tresses lit with blue. Parts of his body are flesh-colored, but most of it is also shaded pale blue. Blue, too, are his tresses and the cloak that billows up in great whorls as he descends. His brows are furrowed in the intensity of his pursuit and he gazes ardently into Chloris's eyes as he puts out his hands to take her around the waist. He is one of Botticelli's most imaginative inventions, not simply a youth of godlike beauty but, in his shadowy blues and greens as well as in his puffed cheeks, an impish spirit of the air. Before the eager breath that

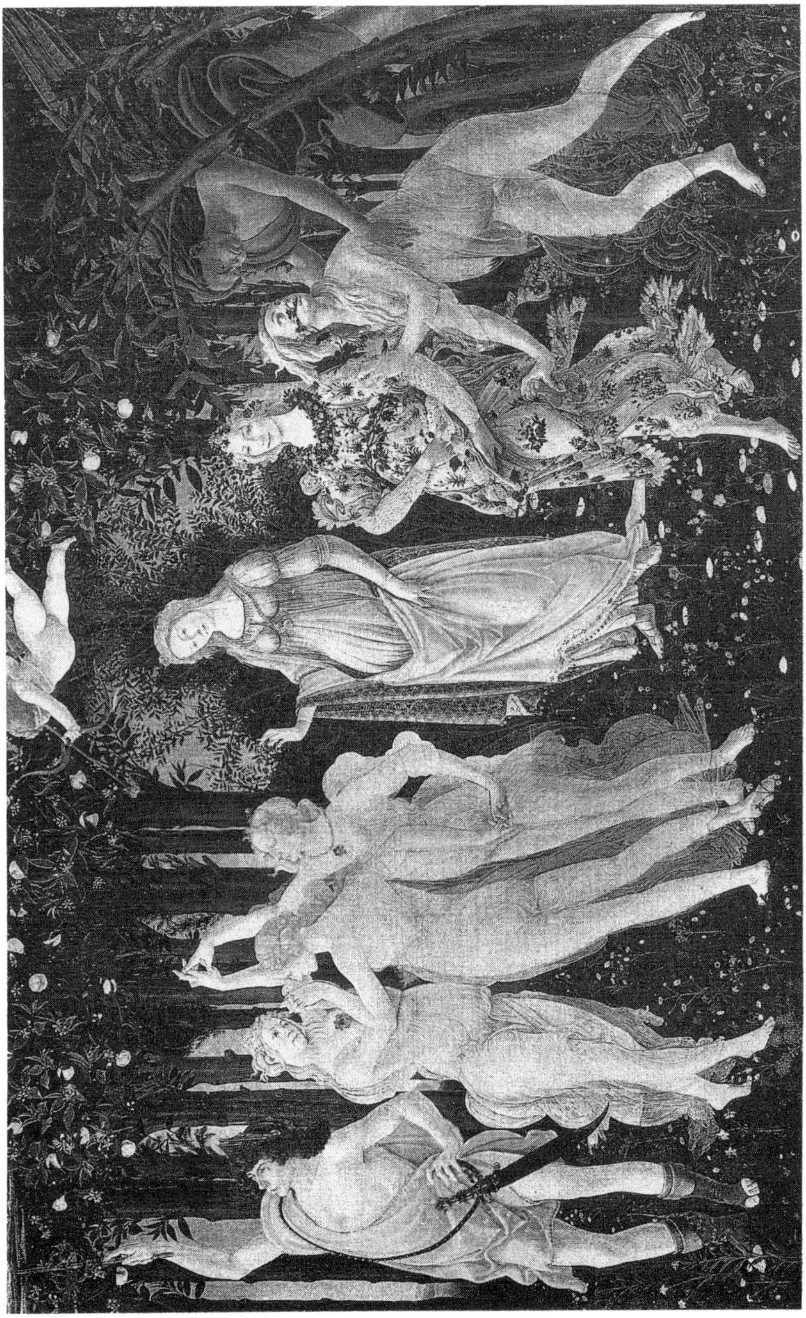

Santo Botticelli's 'Primavera'

> issues from his mouth two trees bend. They are bay laurels, not orange trees or spruce like those in the rest of the hedge (ibid, p.140).

According to Lightbown, the literary source for this scene is from Ovid's *Fasti*: 'a poetical calendar for the Roman year in which Flora tells how she became a goddess.'

> For while she was wandering in the spring, Zephyr caught sight of her. He followed, she fled, but he was the stronger. By giving her the name of wife he made amends for his violence and she has no complaint of her marriage-bed. Now she enjoys perpetual spring, the season when the year is brightest and trees have leaves and the soil, grass. In the fields that are her dowry she has a fertile garden; a breeze caresses it and a clear spring waters it (ibid, p.140).

Woodman says that Flora 'embodies the evanescent beauty of the maiden blossoming into womanhood'.

We are currently planning a workshop called 'The Garden of the Hesperides' in which these themes can be explored further, especially the relationship between healing and art and fertility, which is so strong in Botticelli's picture.

Masks of the Soul

We decided on this sub-title very recently when we realised that every time we wrote we were going beyond 'mere practice'. As Åse was reading Woodman and her references to the soul, Sue was reading Hillman's book *Healing Fiction* and was yet again inspired by his far-reaching elaboration of Jung's work. In the chapter entitled 'The Fiction of Case History' in a section headed 'Dream, Drama and Dionysos', he says:

> I believe what Jung is suggesting is this: if psychotherapy is to understand the dreaming soul from within, it had best turn to 'theatrical logic.' The nature of mind as it presents itself most immediately has a specific form: Dionysian form. Dionysos maybe the force that through the green fuse drives the flower, but this force is not dumb. It has an internal organisation. In psychology this language speaks not genetically, not biochemically in the information of DNA codes, but directly in Dionysos's own art form, theatrical poetics (Hillman 1983, p.37).

Dreams, masks and images come to life in art therapy and dramatherapy and assist in our soul-journeys.

CHAPTER 1

My Journey Into Dramatherapy

Sue Jennings

> My grief lies all within,
> And these external manner of laments
> Are merely shadows to the unseen grief
> That swells with silence in the tortured soul.
>
> (*Richard II* IV.i.295–8)

What is dramatherapy?

Dramatherapy is one of the newly-emergent arts therapies which include music, art and dance movement. It takes as its form theatre art and makes it available to clients and patients either to maintain health or to work with disorder and problems. Thus, it may be used preventatively or curatively. Dramatherapy is not new: it can be seen in ancient forms in healing rituals and theatre performances in many civilisations; however, it has re-emerged during the past thirty years as a contemporary therapeutic practice with formal training* and accreditation.† All aspects of theatre art – voice, movement, improvisation role-play‡, script work and performance – together with the use of masks, costume, lighting and staging, are necessary aspects of the dramatherapist's skills, and are made available as appropriate to clients. Just as a theatre director spends intensive and protracted time on preparation with a group of actors before

* There are several recognised training programmes in the U.K. to train dramatherapists

† In 1977, together with colleagues fromThe Dramatherapy Centre, we formed The Association for Dramatherapists, now The British Association for Dramatherapists. BADTh accredits dramatherapy courses for full membership and monitors their content and standards.

‡ Although all drama could be said to be rôle-play, the term has come to be used mainly for life and social skills work, assertion training, and so on. Although derived from the French (from the roll of paper on which was written the actor's script), it is used less in theatre where either a 'part' or a 'character' is more common. I use the word rôle in the narrower sense in this chapter.

developing a performance, so will the dramatherapist work in the early stages with body and voice before attempting more developed theatre art.

Why should theatre art be so important in this context? Why not just work on using drama as a tool for externalising people's problems? All art expresses the things we are unable to express in any other way. Through theatre we are able to express and experience what are often termed 'the mysteries of life'. The ancient Greeks thought it was possible to encounter the gods through the theatre, (the etymology of theatre is the Greek word *theatron* which has links both with *theoria* – i.e. we can understand things better through seeing them performed in the theatre – and *theos*, the word for god). We can experience feelings, emotions and actions that are not possible in ordinary life. Great plays, myths and legends contain themes that touch every individual and act as vehicles for exploring people's individual lives and families. The theatre provides a distancing process that enables the experience to be contained as well as seen in different perspectives. As Wilshire (1982) suggests, we are too close to experience to see it (we say, we cannot see the wood for the trees). The theatre enables us to have theatrical distance on the one hand and to come closer to something on the other. In other words, we are able to see things, or see them better, because *they are not there*.

> Now, what if it were the case that theatre allowed us not only to see and grasp an appearance of what something is when the actual thing is not present, but to see it better? Then theatre as that which allows us to see something done – as the etymology of the term suggests – would have been given an important and somewhat startling meaning (Wilshire 1982, p.32).

Dramatic or theatrical distancing

Both Scheff (1979) and Landy (1986) have written about the emotional distancing that is possible through the use of drama. Landy has developed his ideas particularly in relation to dramatherapy* (op.cit). I wish to look at dramatic, or theatrical, distancing, which may on the one hand enable participants or observers to have emotional distance from the dramatic material, while on the other permits a deeper experience. It is a complex process and engages the participant or viewer in multiple layers of experience, rather than the unilinear dimension implied by 'distance and closeness'.

In visual art, the viewer engages primarily with the art object – the picture or sculpture – and less directly (I think) with the creator of the art.

---

* In the USA, drama therapy as two words is established. In the UK, dramatherapy as one word is the normal term.

In the theatre, the audience are involved in a direct relationship with the actors, who themselves are in the process of creating in the moment.

> We said that Hamlet is not an art object at all, but is ourselves speaking to ourselves about our essential possibilities. For both Hamlet and ourselves our possibilities do not exist for us in our isolation, but in our relationships to others, particularly to those who are our source. (Wilshire 1982, p.94)

The creation takes place in both the literal and metaphorical space between actor and audience and varies on every night of the performance. An audience is both a group and a collection of individuals who bring with them different dynamics in terms of expectations, mood, feeling and knowledge. Both individual actors and the ensemble of actors respond to the audience variation and a system of communication is built up throughout the play. If we visit the same production on a different night, we see another unique performance. This communication is made possible by the theatrical structures and conventions used in performance. The members of the audience allow themselves to step from everyday reality into theatrical reality. Whether the communication takes place through identification with the characters and themes, or whether there is a further form of distancing through, for example, the ideas of audience alienation expressed by Brecht, however much the play may be realistic in its language and direction, it is still not 'everyday reality'.

Through the theatre convention, we allow time and distance to be compressed or speeded up, we experience a selected number of events within a scene, and we react 'as if' we are receiving truth. For example, although we know that the actor playing Lear will get up off the stage, take off his make-up and have a pint of beer before returning home, ready to play the character again the following night, it does not stop us being moved by the performance and sharing in his and his daughters' deaths at the end of the play. We know that it is not 'true' in an everyday sense, but in a good performance it is theatrically and poetically true and we respond with both thought and feeling. Now, if we work back from the moment of performance to the early work done by actors on their bodies and voices before they even attend a read-through, and the work of directors, designers and technicians that start a creative process at the beginning of rehearsals, we can begin to understand the process of dramatic art. The inspiration, creation, experiment, discarding, refining and re-creation come together, fall apart and eventually balance in a synthesis of a performance. These very processes are also the core of theatre art in the service of therapy. It is theatre art, applied in very specific ways, that is the essence of dramatherapy and its practice.

Are we, therefore, encouraging our clients to be actors? No more than art therapists are encouraging their clients to be painters in the sense of a career or profession. However, we are engaging with our clients through the processes of theatre art as actor, director and technician, i.e. the art and the craft of the theatre, with the aim that they will experience new insights, new experiences and new perspectives about the world as a whole, and their relationship with it. The client finds a greater range of expression through the development of body and voice, and within the drama is able to experience and communicate themes that were impossible before. The theatrical distancing enables this to happen in a contained way; as in the theatre, no-one is totally involved. There is always a part of ourselves watching ourselves and others; therefore we are not overwhelmed.

Dramatherapy and psychodrama

It is often asked whether dramatherapy and psychodrama are variations on a theme, or whether they are totally different. I could answer yes to both questions because each would, in part, be true. Whereas dramatherapy, for the most part, works within dramatic reality often with material from plays, legends and myths that speak for the human condition, generally speaking psychodrama works with a person's own life script – the actual events that have happened in the client's past, are happening in the present or may happen again in the future. Much of the therapeutic work in psychodrama is done through simulation, i.e. the re-creation of an episode, with different members of the group playing the roles of significant others in the scene. Many dramatic techniques are used to explore scenes in psychodrama, including those such as role-reversal and the empty chair. The individual is not distanced emotionally from his or her material unless a technique such as role-reversal is used to enable the client to play the part of the significant other.

Psychodrama is a very powerful way of working through a range of creative structures and methods, many of which were derived from the theatre by the founder of psychodrama, Jacob Moreno. Psychodrama is considered a powerful form of psychotherapy, using methods that Moreno developed from actors in professional theatre. In the literature, however, there is little attention paid to Moreno's influence, either on the theatre of his time or, indeed, on contemporary actors and directors. Hanan Sner, who has trained in both theatre and psychodrama, directed Strindberg's play *The Father* as if it were a psychodrama. The play ran for more than a year at the Habimah Theatre in Tel Aviv and illustrated how the combined power of the two structures heightened the dramatic process of this play.

In Moreno's *Theatre of Spontaneity* which led him into psychodrama, we can observe a process of revolution in the arts, as he talks about the creation of a theatre without playwrights, in which the audience and actor become the only actors, and

> The old stage has disappeared, in its place steps the open stage, the space-stage, the open space, the space of life, life itself. (Moreno 1947, p.a)

Although Moreno has strong links with the theatre, it is also evident that he wished to break down the borders between theatre and life which has been the task of many theatre directors, especially Stanislavski (1980). However, the more the psychotherapist makes use of the theatre as a metaphor for life, or translates the language and structure of the theatre into the everyday, the further he or she moves away from the inherent healing which is in theatre art and dramatherapy.

There are other action-based methods which make use of dramatic techniques, such as Gestalt Therapy, NLP and, of course, Transactional Analysis (TA). The last, at times, comes very close to some aspects of dramatherapy with its use of scripts and roles, and some dramatherapists incorporate a TA approach into their working frame. However, there is still an intrinsic difference between a therapy which makes use of action methods and one which acknowledges the artistry in the therapeutic process. Dramatherapists would acknowledge the creativity and influence that all these forms have in therapeutic practice, but would suggest that there are strong differences as well as similarities. At another level they are all variations on a theme – an attempt to relieve some of the human distress that affects large numbers of the population.

I said at the beginning of this chapter that dramatherapy is one of the newly-emergent arts therapies (or 'creative arts therapies' or 'artistic therapies' or 'expressive therapies') but that it has an ancient history. If we look across the world at any culture, in both recent history as well as in ancient times, we find that 'theatre' (which includes drama) is part of the life of the society and the individuals within it, and that it both vocalises themes for change as well as being a part of that change. Theatre enables growth and change to take place. Any history of the theatre charts the revolutions and upheavals, the life-cycle and the healing, and dramatic ritual; from where we stand now, we could call much of this therapeutic in the contemporary sense of the word. This theme is developed further in Chapter 3.

In dramatherapy, the dramatic art is the therapeutic form and content. Thus, in a feed-back time at the end of a group, as much time is spent on reflection on the drama itself – whether it 'worked' as a piece of dramatic art – as on the feelings of the participants themselves.

> Is it not monstrous that this player here,
> But in a fiction, in a dream of passion,
>
> (*Hamlet* II.ii.548–9)

Hamlet expresses the dilemma of all of us in his attempts to understand the dramatic process of the actor. What is the reality of the actor's experience when he or she portrays emotions? Philosophers, theatre artists, anthropologists, psychologists, drama teachers and now dramatherapists have continued the struggle to understand the artistic form of the theatre and its relationship to society, healing and therapeutic practice. Drama and theatre have been part of religious practice and have also been thrown out on the streets; actors have been revered and have been treated like vagabonds. How can we begin to understand drama and theatre and its relationship to therapeutic intervention?

Human background

Human beings are essentially dramatic in their development (Jennings, 1987), commencing their response to the world around them at a few weeks old. Infants move and sound in rhythm, make marks and imitate, even before they can walk. By eighteen months, they are dramatising scenes with imagined others – toys and people – and are capable of role-reversal, i.e. an infant will talk to a toy and then answer on its behalf. Play becomes increasingly dramatic in form through puppets or families of dolls: stories are re-created or invented. By the age of seven, a child is participating in drama rather than dramatic play.

Our early experience in drama is an important part of social and psychological development, as the plethora of research into the play of children has shown. We need to be able to play a wide range of roles in life, manage different scenes in appropriate ways and participate in celebratory rituals. Writers such as Goffman (1969) have shown us how human interactive behaviour follows certain dramatic rules. Role-play is used as a means of learning social skills, assertiveness, business acumen; what I would term 'the drama of everyday life'.

We now realise that we dream in dramatic form (Jennings 1987). Our dreams are like miniature private theatres where we are either actor or observer. McDougall (1986, 1989) has described in her excellent books *Theaters of the Mind* and *Theaters of the Body* case history material on psychosomatic disorder. She has developed her way of describing what happens to the 'theatre owner', i.e. the patient, through the extensive use of theatre structure and metaphor.

> Why 'Theaters of the Body' as a title? While writing *Theaters of the Mind* [McDougall 1982a], I slowly became aware, as so often happens when one is writing, that a further book was developing out of the one in which I was involved. In choosing the theater as a metaphor for psychic reality, I was perhaps following in the steps of Anna O who, at the turn of the century, referred to her free associations during her therapy with Breuer (Breuer and Freud 1893–1895), as her 'private theater (McDougall 1989, p.1).

This is what I would term 'the drama of our inner life'.

Theatre art and dramatherapy

What is so often neglected in our consideration of drama is its essential importance in our creative development, in the development of our imagination and other right-hemisphere functions.

> *Drama, as an art-form in which we are participant as actor, technician, director and audience, is crucial for survival. If we do not have the opportunity to participate in 'the drama that is larger than life', then maybe we will create dramas that are larger than life in more destructive ways.*

Dramatic ritual, one of the oldest forms of drama, gives societies opportunities for affirming belief and relationships, for exploring themes of good and evil and for experiencing dominant symbols, images and metaphors which affect both the individual and group in multi-layered ways. The powerful nature of the drama has often caused concern. Plato vilified the person and nature of the actor and said that the art of acting could be morally damaging.

Plato's injunction is a reminder not only of the power of drama / theatre dynamics, but also of our ambivalence towards it. Dramatic process is often dismissed as 'only acting', or 'pretending', or the 'false self'. It is easier to focus on the drama of everyday life, which can be monitored and assessed in task-orientated programmes, or to apply the images and metaphors of theatre to life phenomena. In the mid-nineteenth century, for example, superintendents of large mental asylums were preoccupied with the character of Ophelia (Jennings 1990b) and would coach their female patients in her mad scenes. They would then take photographs of these patients in their white hospital gowns, bedecked with flowers, and use them to illustrate madness in textbooks for medical students (Showalter 1985) – a complete absorption of a stage character from a play into the clinical concepts in medical practice. A good example of what Åse and I refer to as taking the arts into clinics and making patients ill!

Just as Hamlet reflects on the process of the actor and asks how it was possible for an actor to portray real emotions for no cause –

> For Hecuba!
> What's Hecuba to him, or he to her,
> That he should weep for her?
>
> (*Hamlet* II.ii, 555–7)

and suggests that if the actor had the depth of Hamlet's emotions

> He would drown the stage with tears
> And cleave the general ear with horrid speech
>
> (II.ii, 559–60)

It is also a challenge for us to accept that the re-creation of the human condition through theatre art can lead us into a greater depth of experience than life events themselves.

The reason that theatre art has continued to exist, despite struggles with the Church and State, is that it is able to express important truths that cannot be expressed in any other way. With the combination of distancing and closeness, of universal and individual themes and its unique propensity to present life to us in a myriad different forms, it is an essential part of our survival.

While our societies move ever closer towards 'high tech', and technology and science are given priority in school curricula, it seems difficult to demonstrate this essential nature of 'theatre art for survival'. It is too easy for people to say that theatre has nothing to do with the 'real' world, or that it is just pretending, or that it is 'only play'. I have written elsewhere (Jennings 1992b) on the importance of the essentially human capacity to both accept as well as create what is essentially 'not there'; what Napier (1986) refers to as 'our ability to recognise illusion' and 'the skill of make-believe':

> Our ability to recognise illusion depends upon the extent to which we accept some method of apprehending it. Such a statement sounds self-evident, yet what is called for is basically paradoxical: the acceptance of what empirically is not. This is the skill of make-believe; in science it is the very nature of hypothesizing. Pretending, whether it be something

> about ourselves or about the outside world, is basic to our apprehension of change (Napier 1986, p.3).

The human capacity not only to accept but also to create what is not actually there through fictive drama lies at the very core of our understanding of dramatherapy. It is the most fundamental principle of the efficacy of dramatherapy, whether it is being applied in a preventative or a curative context.

> Thus, the recognition of illusion is the single pre-requisite for understanding something that seems self-contradictory -in other words, for recognizing paradox – and the recognition of change is possible only with this understanding: that something may appear to be something else. (ibid)

Rather than viewing drama as less to human life than relevant because 'it is only acting' or 'it is only playing' or 'it is not real', we can begin to see how relevant it is precisely because it *is* acting, playing and unreal.

The Speech of the High One

I know I hung on that windy tree,
Swung there for nine long nights,
Wounded by my own blade,
Bloodied for Odin,
Myself an offering to myself:
Bound to the tree
That no man knows
Whither the roots of it run.

None gave me bread,
None gave me drink.
Down to the deepest depths I peered
Until I spied the Runes.
With a roaring cry I seized them up,
Then dizzy and fainting, I fell.

Well-being I won
And wisdom too.
From a word to a word
I was led to a word,
From a deed to another deed.

(From the Old Norse,
'The Poetic Edda' AD 1200, Hollander 1962)

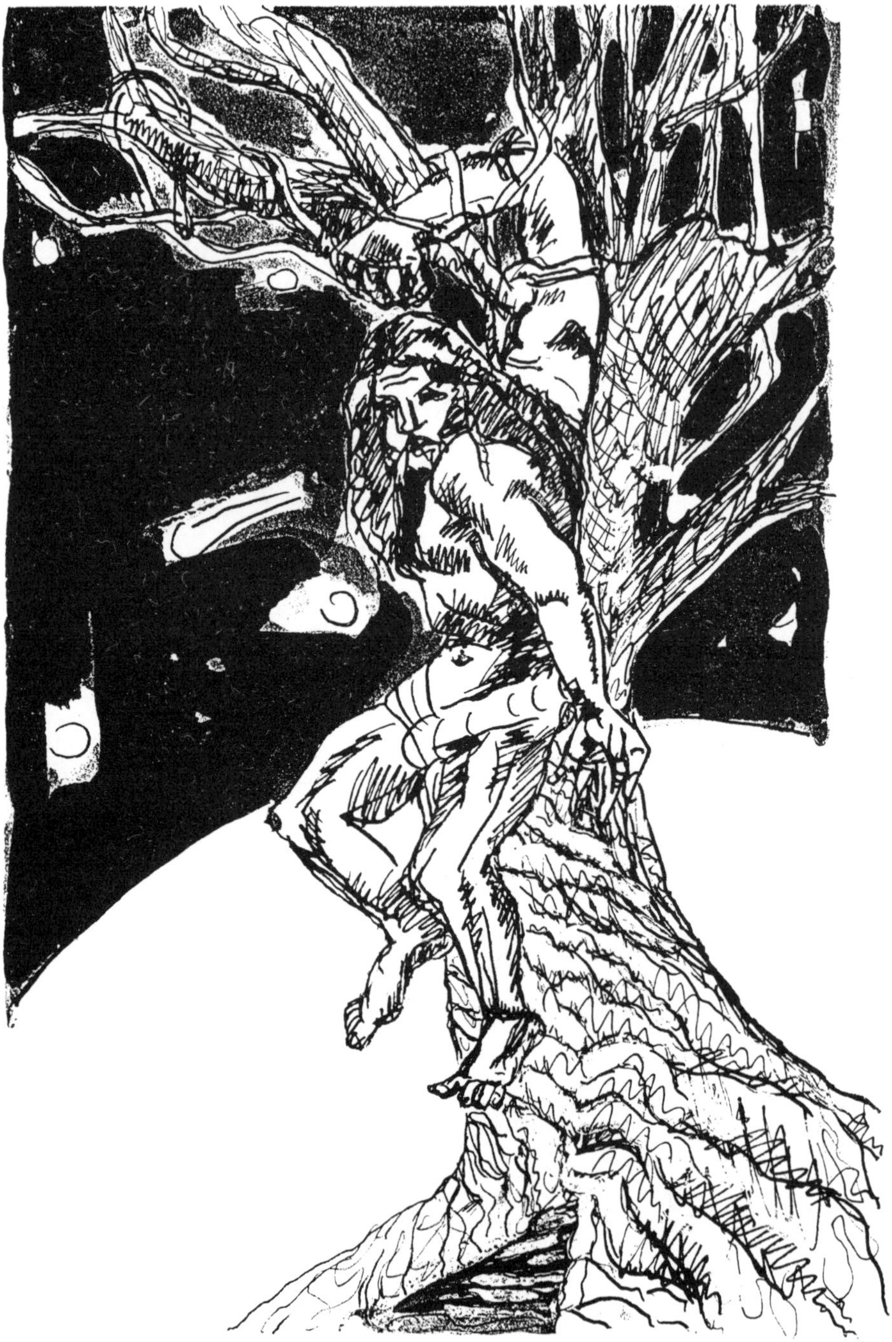

Yggdrasil (by Gro Finne)

In the beginning was the Word, and the Word
was with God, and the Word was God.'

(*John* 1.i)

Theatre art and theatre-and-dramatherapy are concerned with thoughts, feelings, ideas and images being formulated and expressed through words and deeds. '*Through acting, we are empowered to act*' (Jennings 1992), and, indeed, to become resolute. Through the structure of theatre plays, rituals and myths, we are able to engage with dominant symbols and archetypes which link our inner and outer world experience. These structures safely contain our experiences, while exploration and possible change is taking place.* The content expressed through dominant symbols and archetypes, and the multiple layered dramatic metaphor, allows us to come face-to-face with the unfaceable; to look at our own darknesses and the shadows of others in a variety of constellations. The word and the deed enable movement of several kinds – movement of perception as well as movement of body.

A recurring theme in much of my own dramatherapy work is the dominant symbol of Tree and Forest. If you ask someone to describe what sort of tree they would be, they are always able to answer the question. Although I use a variety of landscapes (see also Chapter 9 on Creative Journeys), the one involving trees seems to 'work' both for me and the dramatherapy groups and individuals. People will describe barren landscapes in relation to trees – 'where the last tree has died and I can find no rest' (a patient with fertility problems).

I use the theme of creating 'The Forest of the Group' when involved in team-building and staff consultancy, and again, no-one ever misunderstands, yet not everyone carries the same image, so the forest may have trees of all types – standing alone and standing in groups aged from days old to a million years.

What, therefore, is my own affinity with trees and forests? Why are trees and forests dominant symbols in my dramatherapy work and what does this say about both my own rootedness and my wandering?

Inevitably, I take a backwards glance and consider the various influences from as far back as I can remember. As one of the 'second wave' of children in my family, my parents were rather elderly when I was born. In my own case – a not unusual one, I think – I was left to my own devices and spent lengthy solitary periods where I created imaginary worlds through stories and pictures, especially in the garden shed. I learnt to read

* I do not feel we should assume that change is the aim of therapy; growth, yes – but people also need to know what life choices they may have.

early and consumed books by the day. Most fairy stories, myths and children's adventure books present woods and forests as mysterious, dark places which can be both exciting and dangerous. Witches, trolls, as well as big bad wolves, live in woods, yet Peter Rabbit and his family lived there quite happily and only got into trouble when he went into Mr. McGregor's garden.

We moved house very often – nine times before I was ten years old – so 'home' became what you took with you rather than where you stayed. However, my brothers and sisters, as adults, have settled in very long-term homes, or at least places, whereas I have continued to wander happily through the length and breadth of England as well as overseas, although very recently I have re-discovered the 'special place' of my childhood – famous both for Shakespeare as well as for very old trees!

Many of the houses where I lived as a child were in the countryside ('Then the enemy can't see us,' I was told; a constant reminder that it was war-time), so we were surrounded by woods, copses, orchards. Trees became places to climb and hide in (although that meant one was a tom-boy) – and especially to smell. I vividly remember the smell of my two favourite trees in the orchard when I was nine: a huge walnut tree under which I would lie and be overwhelmed by the green ceiling of leaves as well as intrigued by the brown stains from the nuts themselves, and also a very old willow tree which served as a 'useful place to put things in'. I have planted a willow tree in the garden of every house I have lived in.

When the time came, as an adult, or rather as a grown-up child, to undertake a major journey as an anthropologist on field-work, there was no doubt about my choice to go and live in the tropical rain-forest in Malaysia, (though it is perhaps curious that I felt I had few choices in my life until my own three children were growing up). Despite the snakes and scorpions and the lack of food, the monsoons and the unbearable heat, the hepatitis and ringworms and roundworms, it was as if I had really been given the opportunity to fulfil a childhood dream – to actually visit THE FOREST. There was never any doubt in my own mind that I would study a forest people,* and the lengthy stay for me and the children in a bamboo stilt-house on the banks of a river in a village in the forest has proved a major landmark in my life. I am writing about this experience elsewhere,† but it is important to state here that the actual journey to the

* I mean here a forest people as contrasted with a desert people. The Temiar themselves do not see themselves as *forest* people, rather people who live in villages that happen to be in the forest.

† *Drama, Ritual & Transformation* (in press), Routledge (1993).

forest, with the opportunity to study the dance, drama and healing rituals of a very special tribe, expanded my experience and perception – paradoxically, while living in a very focused and narrow way.

I learned an enormous amount about trees and forests from the Senoi Temiar tribe. The forest as a whole is a dangerous place to be, especially deep forest, and there are individual trees that are 'demonic' and others that cause illness. The seasonal fruit trees are, quite literally, 'family trees', and families trace their ancestry through the fruit trees planted by generations of relatives. The fruit of these trees belongs to the 'relatives' while it is still on the tree, and is anybody's once it falls to the ground. My own children were always amazed at the capacity of the Temiar children to hear the sound of a durian fruit hitting the ground at 100 yards!

Another important element and archetype is water and, again, one that I often use in my work. Although I do not like being in water, whether baths or swimming, I feel at my most content when I am near water. The stilt-house where we lived in the forest was on the banks of a large river and the sound of running water ever present. For years after returning to the UK, I would wake up and realise that I could not hear the river. One of the most beautiful sights engraved on my memory is a log-boat journey into the deep forest where the trees met overhead and I was journeying through this immense green tunnel.

How do I integrate these experiences into the way I work as a dramatherapist? It is important for me to realise that I can reject the persuasive suggestion that the rain-forest journey was an avoidance of my personal journey into my own dark regions. I acknowledge that the actual journey brought about a far more raw confrontation with self, and the experience reaches aspects of myself that mere words cannot touch. It also affirms my understanding of the core importance of ritual dramas in preventative and curative practices. The dominant symbols of water and forest, as well as their 'signposts' in terms of how people 'map' their lives, stay with me in my work. However, something crucial that I learned from the tribe is that the reality and the metaphor work in parallel. Although water and trees are important symbols, they are also important in day-to-day reality. A Temiar can recognise a map of the terrain simply by looking at the configuration of the rivers. If a Temiar becomes unaware of where there is a river, he or she becomes very disorientated, confused and anxious. Conversely, once a (not 'the') river is re-discovered, the anxiety disappears and they literally 'know where they are'.

Creating the forest of the group

The 'Tree of Life' exercise is a useful way into people's tree images, and warms up the body for creativity. People stand in a circle with enough space between them to move their arms and with their feet a shoulder-width apart and parallel.

Stretch the body and relax several times, ending in the curled up position. Slowly grow into a tree, feeling your roots going into the centre of the earth from the soles of your feet and the sap gradually infusing all your limbs. Slowly grow towards the sky with the sap reaching into your finger-tips and the whole of your tree growing outwards and upwards.

(*Teaching point:* This whole group exercise guides people through the ritual-risk structure of dramatherapy. On the one hand, it allows and builds the basic security of the roots, and on the other, 'seeds in' the idea of growth.)

With crayons, felt-tips, finger and/or brush paints, members of the group are invited to create a tree. You may begin this with a guided imagination exercise, where people imagine a landscape or a garden with trees and choose one for themselves, or suggest they create a tree that they remember as very special from their lives, imaginations or dreams, or ask them if they could be a tree and what sort of tree they would be. You can also work with actual pictures of trees, providing there is a wide variety of choice, through postcards and photographs (see also Chapters 4 and 5 for further art therapy and dramatherapy structures with the theme of trees).*

Imagine you are the tree, and write about yourself in the first person. Include how old you are and where this tree is located; what type of landscape; how near are other trees. Then, share this with other trees that you think are similar to yours. (People make small groups of three or four trees that are similar. If there are people with 'unique' trees, suggest that they make a group of trees that are different).

Stand in a line behind each other, based on the age of your tree. (In a recent workshop, the age ranged from 'new born' to a million years' old; however, it was noticed that, apart from the new born and an infant tree, all the trees were over a hundred years old. This led on to statements such as 'we need new growth in this forest,' and, 'where are the young branches,' and, 'I feel too old'.)

(*Teaching point:* Dramatherapy used in this way provides the dramatic distance through the metaphor of the trees, and a safe container for the expression of thoughts and feelings that hitherto have been unexpressed. However, it is

---

* Åse Minde and I are writing a book on dominant symbols and archetypes in *Art Therapy and Dramatherapy.*

important to stay within the metaphor and not to change the goal-posts with questions like, 'Is this significant in the life of your department?' unless of course there is an agreed brief to explore the group dynamics in a direct way, in which case the contract with all members of the group will be different.

The above allows for insight and understanding within the safety of the dramatic structure and metaphor.)

Place all the trees in relation to each other to create a forest: it may take some time to be clear where you feel your tree is growing. Try different constellations, until you feel your tree is placed in the right position. Explore the spaces between the trees (one group had a clearing in the middle which was thought to have either a lake in it – or a witch!).

In small groups, create and then enact the story of the forest. The richness of the forest is then experienced as several groups contribute varying stories about life in the forest.

Using 'junk' brought by people in the group (boxes, old material, wire, newspaper, wool, string, and so on), create one tree. This really becomes a time to see whether a group can work together for the sake of the tree and, in my experience, they do. Often, they sub-group and create different aspects, and roots, trunk, branches, leaves, birds and nests, all come together in a giant tree.

Ask people to place themselves where they feel they belong in the tree. Usually there is a spread between the roots, trunk and branches. If there is an extreme disproportion, this can be acknowledged: people may want to re-position themselves.

(*Teaching point*: In the first image, 'The Tree of Life', where I spoke of people expressing both their rootedness as well as their growth, I want to emphasise the importance of establishing the 'safety of growth'. It is difficult for us to grow unless we have roots – yet roots provide stability, and growth implies change. Hence the paradox of the drama.)

When I have plucked thy rose,
I cannot give it vital growth again,
It needs must wither. I'll smell it on the tree.

(*Othello* V.ii.13)

There are many ways of working in dramatherapy with the image of a tree, and I am also reminded of how Virginia Oaklander works with children in the drawing of a rosebush (Oaklander 1978). It is important to be able to work flexibly with 'tree in movement', through drawing and dramatisation.

The above description of a dramatherapy sequence illustrates the dramatherapy developmental paradigm of embodiment/projection/role (EPR). In this session, the participants in the group *embodied* the tree, then drew it *projectively* before leading into dramatised stories in *rôle* – thus working through a developmental dramatic structure applicable in most dramatherapeutic practice. As I said at the beginning of this chapter, too often our experience is too close to us to see it – we cannot see the wood for the trees. Working with trees in dramatherapy, we can see the wood *and* the trees.

The dramatherapy space

The space for theatre art is space set apart, within which the transition is made from everyday reality into dramatic or theatrical reality. In many cultures it is considered a magical or holy space where the dramatic ritual or performance can bring about change. We discuss the spaces in sand-trays and houses and mazes in subsequent chapters because they are 'spaces within the space'. Here I am considering the dramatherapy space itself.

The dramatherapy room, like a theatre, needs to be used solely for that purpose. It can vary in size from the large studio room to a small theatre, depending on the milieu in which it is situated. In my own work, it felt like a watershed when I acquired a small fringe theatre, the Onstage Theatre, for a couple of years. It was particularly important because it made a statement about dramatherapy taking place in a theatre to which both trainees and clients came, instead of them attending a clinic. Unlike Moreno, when he made theatre into an 'open space', I was very much aware of keeping it a designated theatre space with all the possibilities it gave to us.

The dramatherapy room needs to be warm and to have a floor-covering where people can lie down or sit without getting chilled (cork tile or wood plank/block is ideal, otherwise a composition coating is fine providing it is not placed directly onto concrete!) The space needs to be adaptable so that different levels can be used; large building cubes and rostra are very practical, as is the frame ladder used by lighting technicians.

The space should have a small lighting board with a choice of lights (floods and spots) as well as dimmer switches. I have worked in this way with patients themselves creating the right ambience for a piece of drama through changing the lights. Some people may choose to work in shadow or in muted light.

Vignette

I asked a patient whether they wanted to move into the spotlight for the character they wanted to explore.

Patient Do you think this person is in the spotlight?

Therapist Do you think the spotlight is on this person?

Patient Let me stay in the shadows first and then we'll see.

Therapist Let the character stay in the shadow for the moment.

Patient Right – but will you still be able to see me?

Therapist I can see you and the character in the shadow.

Dramatherapy equipment needs to include basic art materials and a collection of music and sound instruments – a tape and record-deck with good speakers, floor cushions and blankets, and a dressing-up box with varied 'props', as well as more elaborate costumes.

When people are conversant with theatre convention we encourage them to wear clothes that can be adapted. For example, they may come to the group in tracksuits and T-shirts on which a costume can be built if necessary. Mask-making materials and a collection of pre-formed masks are also necessary. If the main capital expenditure is on the flexibility of the space itself, much of the consumables can be improvised from 'junk'.

Åse and I wrote our individual chapters (1 and 2) separately and then gave them to each other to read. We are amused that both of us refer to being creative with waste – for me it is 'junk' and for her it is 'trash'! As we quote from *Peer Gynt* in a later chapter:

Our gold may seem scrap to you.
You may think each crystal window-pane
Is just a fistful of socks and rags.

(Ibsen, *Peer Gynt* p.62)

In my meeting with Åse Minde and her culture, I must stress my early exposure to Nordic influences. The very first book I received as a gift (and I still have it) is *Tales from the Norse* (Nelson), and we shall include some of these stories in therapeutic material in subsequent chapters. In talking about tree images, I must not forget 'Yggdrasil', a sacrificial tree that stands at the centre of the three cosmic regions – 'The Tree of the World'. It was here that the Nordic god Odin hung for nine days and nights in a sacrifice of the self in order to gain wisdom. When we are engaged in pioneering work, and indeed pioneering something as consuming as dramatherapy, there has to be major sacrifice, and 'nine days and nights' is symbolic time for the rest of eternity.

CHAPTER 2

My Journey Into Art Therapy
Trash Texture and Timing

Åse Minde

> When creative energy is satisfied, it becomes a reliable support, giving comforting nutrition in dark moments and paves the way towards health. (Hill 1945)

> Look, inner man, at your inner girl. The deepest experience of the creative artist is feminine, for it is an experience of conceiving and giving birth. The poet Obstfelder once wrote, speaking of the face of a stranger: 'When he began to speak, it was as though a *woman* had taken a seat within him.' It seems to me that every poet has had that experience in beginning to speak.
>
> (Rainer Maria Rilke, to a 'young woman', in Mitchell 1989, p.337.)

Since the dawn of human history, art has been used both as a means of communication and for healing purposes.

Since the beginning of psychiatry, art has been used in institutions, originally with the main purpose of passing time, but later for more recreational purposes, which developed into occupational therapy (Reisby 1981). The interest of psychiatrists in the artwork and psychopathology of patients and famous artists was the very beginning of art therapy, but not until later did they understand the value of using art in therapy – that it could actively be used, not just for psychopathological reasons. Case and Dalley (1992) write that

> Many writers have explored different relationships between art and psychoanalysis and how the practice of art therapy has evolved to incorporate both. Edwards (1989), traces differing models of art therapy and attitudes towards art and psychoanalysis back to their origins some 200 years ago. By describing attitudes towards art and madness in the eighteenth and nineteenth centuries, Edwards demonstrates how ideas from other areas of enquiry, such as the use of art in rituals, religious

> customs and anthropology, form a 'more elaborate and enduring context ' for art therapy that was in existence well in advance of its establishment as a discrete profession. Art history and the history of psychiatry have given rise to certain models of art therapy practice and Edwards postulates that the roots of codified, diagnostic attitude towards imagery are in the eighteenth-century neoclassicism, and in their 'rational' belief that a person's state of mind could be read from a picture (Case & Dalley 1992 p.4).

The first that is known of art being used as therapy comes from just before World War II, when a group artists and psychiatrists in the United States and England started to get interested in the more therapeutic use of art.

Adrian Hill, a British artist who, during World War II spent time convalescing at a sanatorium, turned to painting to relieve his boredom. Other patients became interested and started to paint, using their paintings as a way to talk about their fears and feelings. Hill later worked hard to bring art into the hospitals and has written two books about this (Hill 1945; 1951).

In the early years of the development of art therapy, there were clear parallels with art teaching. Nevertheless, the differences between the teacher's rôle and that of the therapist began to emerge as art therapy theory, and the practice developed gradually in the direction of psychotherapy throughout the 1970s (Waller 1984). However, despite this development, and despite the increasing literature on the subject, art therapy is still considered a new discipline.

> Work of the eye is done, now
> go and do the heart-work
> on all the images imprisoned within you;
> for you overpowered them: but even now
> you don't know them,
> Learn, inner man, to look on your inner
> woman,
> the one attained from a thousand natures,
> the merely attained but not yet beloved
> from.
>
> (Rainer Maria Rilke, 'Turning Point'
> in Mitchell 1989, p.135)

My own journey

As far back as I can remember, I have been interested in communication – language has always been to me much more than verbal. From a background in textile art, I moved on to the areas of psychology and art therapy. I remember, when I was young, finding work with textiles very calming when I was upset; I enjoyed weaving because the technique is based on certain rules which have been established for generations, yet there are great possibilities to explore and build in one's own colours and forms. The images imprisoned within me were starting to take form and colour.

As a child I always travelled a lot in my fantasies. Since then, I have done much 'real' travelling and have married cross-culturally and I find it interesting to think of all the journeys I have made to become what I am: much of my work is about journeys.

Sue and I met on a journey and since then have made many more together. I feel that our whole life is a journey, consisting of many smaller journeys. As an art therapist, one has to be able to travel on others' journeys, visiting many different worlds, but at the same time, remaining in your own.

One expression often used about the different art therapies is the 'non-verbal' therapies. Personally, I do not feel comfortable with this expression because it can so easily lead to misinterpretation. Some might assume that arts therapists do not believe in traditional verbal therapy, or that they believe that language is not important. I do not want to be a carrier for such assumption because I find language extremely important. However, art often helps people to experience the world in different ways and therefore helps to give more substance to words, which makes the words more *alive*.

> When I speak of aesthetics, I am referring to making the inanimate, animate; giving form to diffuse energy or ideas, breathing life into sterile communication. Communication is a key word here, for a complete work of any medium becomes art only when it touches us as a living truth. This happens when it is an authentic expression of the artist, and more often it involves an integration of polarities (Robbins 1989, p.44).

I have seen how art has helped me to look at language in a different way. It has helped me to listen more to the ways in which things are expressed; the sub-text of what is said rather than in what dialect they are spoken.

In my first years as an art therapist, I remember how it seemed very natural to try to understand therapeutic process by seeking answers in psychology. Throughout the years, I have, of course, developed both through experience and increased theoretical knowledge and I now find myself seeking answers to and understanding of therapeutic journeys from literature and philosophy.

What is art therapy?

Art therapy derives from two main areas, art and psychology, but other closely-related areas have also been important for its development. Art Therapy literally means using art in a therapeutic way. Patients are asked to express their feelings, dreams and inner experiences through different art media, such as painting, clay and other visual media. The art-work is considered to be a representation of the object world, but the person who creates the object projects parts of him or herself into the work; thus the art-work itself contains a representation both of the self and the object.

In creative art there will always be a meeting; the artists meet the landscapes, ideas or inner visions they want to create. While creating, they become absorbed into the landscapes and become a part of the art-work, but, at the same time, they come out of it and try to see it from different perspectives. This process, I believe, from my eighteen years as a practising art therapist, is what makes art therapy so valuable. The possibility of

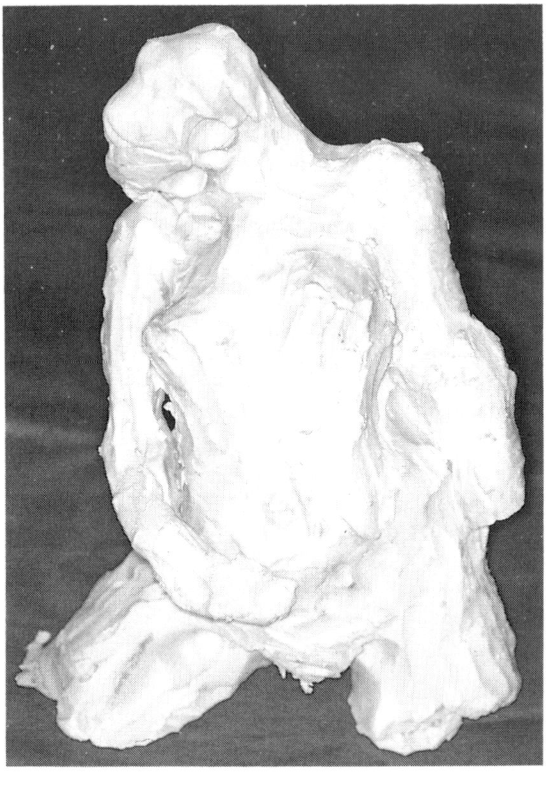

interaction between the inner and outer world; to be a part of, and yet outside.

> Now, when I have made this little idea out from the clay and I am holding it in my hand, I can turn it, see it from underside, see it from different angles, hold it up towards the sky, pretend that it has the sizes I wish, and really be in control nearly like when God creates something (Henry Moore, quoted in Nielsen, 1988).

The art-work also becomes a meeting place or a bridge between the therapist and patient where they can meet on a common ground or a transitional space. Arthur Robbins, in his book, *The Artist as Therapist* (1987), says:

> In therapy, patients and therapist alike are engaged in finding the artist within themselves. The therapeutic process for the patients is an on-going struggle to discover true inner representations and symbols and gives them form in terms of developing richer, more congruent living realities. Therapists tap the artist within in the on-going process

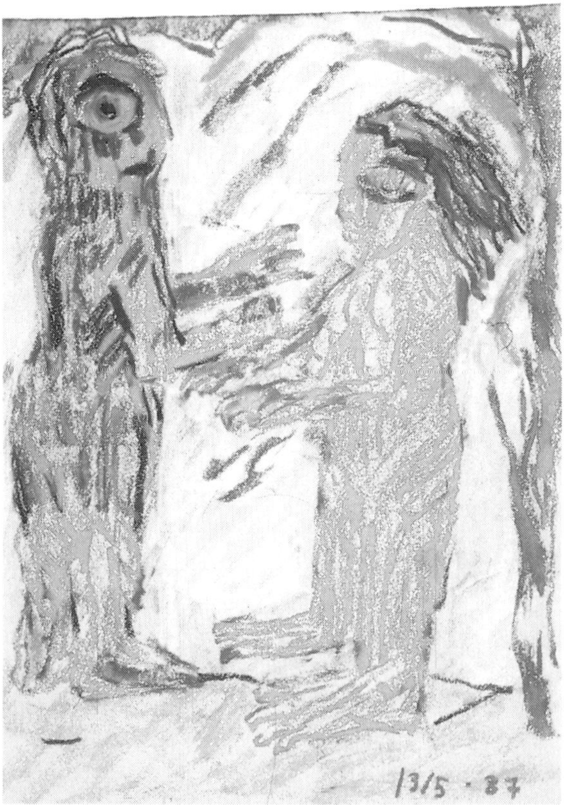

Meeting between therapist and patient

> of maintaining the individual holding environments that will provide the space, energy and impetus for patients to change.
>
> Together, patient and therapist create a matrix where verbal and non-verbal communication comes alive, as both parties are touched by common experiences. This complicated mode of interaction takes on a form similar to a symphony or a work of art, where multiple levels of consciousness and meaning exist simultaneously the therapeutic and creative processes clearly have many parallels here. (Robbins 1987, p.21).

The picture on the next page made by a female patient shows her relationship with her father. In this room she, as a child, is next to her father and one feels that both nothing and everything is said. Looking back on this picture years after ending therapy and a few months after having lost her father, when I talked to her about using some of this picture in this book, she said that it depicted much anger, hate and love, and other non-verbal communication which never came alive.

At a later stage in the same patient's therapy, she made this picture and said it was to do with the fear of being rejected. Looking back on it many years afterwards, she said, 'I did not realise at that time that this really is reaching out for my unreasonable mother: it still makes me freeze when I look back at it.' In this picture, 'mother' is almost like some dark shadowy monster, so that the patient does not recognise it as 'mother'.

Murray Cox says the following about metaphors:

> Metaphor exerts its mutative effect by energizing alternative perspectival aspects of experience. This means that material which the patient has endeavoured to relinquish, avoid, or deny so that it is 'safely' classified, categorized and 'filed away', appears again in the 'pending action' file. And this inevitably has a startling effect upon the patient. This may take the form of 'surprised relief' because the presumed intolerable was found to be acceptable. On the other hand, the discovery that there is still fire in affect embers can indicate that material, previously regarded as 'de-fused' and safe, has once again become disconcertingly insistent (Cox & Theilgaard 1987 p.99).

My patient, who had undergone five years of therapy, came back to me six years later at a time when she was pregnant and had recently lost her father. When looking at this picture she experienced a reactivation of some of her earlier symptoms, i.e. fear of rejection.

> It is much more difficult to kill an old spirit than reality (Virginia Woolf quoted in *Woolf* 1991, p.1).

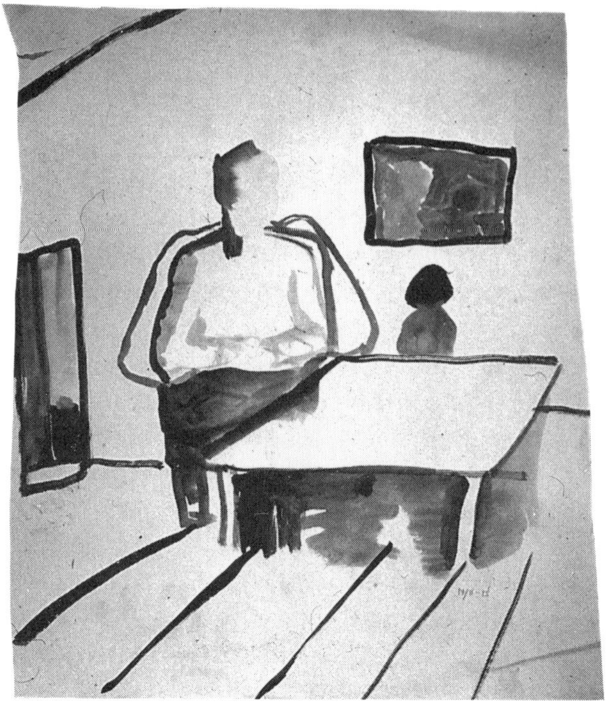

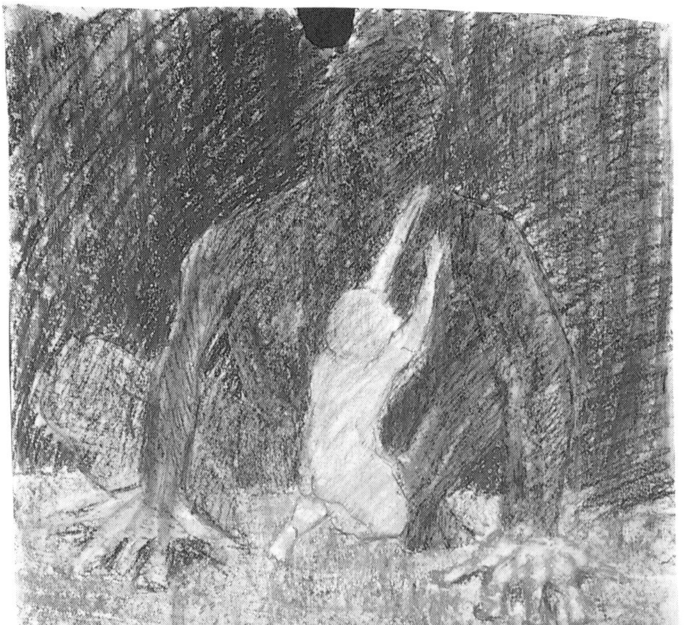

Visual art

All visual art is about room. How I use the room depends both on how I subjectively experience the room inside me and how I see the room objectively outside me.

Immanuel Kant said that it is not only we who experience the world without; the world, at the same time, forms itself through our ways of perceiving it (quoted in May 1975, p.122). The art-work itself, therefore, becomes a meeting between the inner subjective way of seeing and experiencing the world, and the outside object itself.

The different art medias have their own structures and limits. Therefore, when used in therapeutic situations, the various materials themselves become crucial to how a patient, for example, can give external order to inner fears and chaos.

Artist as therapist

When using art in therapy, the merging of two main processes is very important – the creative process and the therapeutic process.

The artist observes what is happening in the creative act – the different layers in each picture, how the artistic technique is used to get a special effect or to hide materials not yet ready to take form. The artist *senses* the forms and colours; the visual symbolic language. The artist has an inner dialogue with the therapist who is there to structure a safe environment to contain what is expressed both verbally and non-verbally, and at times to be the navigator. However, it is important that the therapist does not fully take over the ship and navigate for his or her own needs. This, I think, often happens when the ship might be in stormy waters and the therapist needs to steer towards quiet waters because of personal fears. The opposite can also happen – the therapist feels the ship is moving too quietly and prematurely pushes the client into more dramatic situations. Navigation means that there may be times when the therapist needs to point out to the client that there are other possible directions to choose than the one they have chosen.

Leonardo da Vinci said, 'In life the beauty goes under, but not in the art' (quoted in Nielsen, 1988). I have worked with people who have been stuck in the mud or got lost in the dark, but the human capacity for transforming chaos into beauty has never stopped amazing me.

Vignette

In an art therapy session, a patient was making a clay figure of herself carrying a huge backpack, much bigger than herself, filled with burdens.

She said, 'I do not have the strength to go on any more' and did not see any possibility of putting the backpack with the burdens down, or looking into what she was carrying. However, I was sitting opposite to her, and from my perspective the figure looked very different – it looked like a small tree with very big roots growing out of a solid ground (the backpack). She had for a long time in the therapy been involved with all the burdens she had to carry.

This was a woman who never asked for help, and the fear of receiving it she found even more difficult. When she told me about her sculpture, I asked her to turn it around so that I could see what she was talking about. I said to her, 'Now I can see what you are talking about. From my perspective, it looked so different.'

She then started to look at the figure from the perspective I had seen it (upside down). She was quiet for a long time; then she said that it looked like a small bush growing up from the earth: 'You know, I never thought I could grow from my burdens.' She literally changed in front of me when she said it. Her back stretched out from the stopped position and she gave a light smile.

My navigation had just been to try to see her sculpture from a different perspective, which in this case helped her to move from a blocked situation which she had been in for a long time. This was an individual piece of navigation for this particular patient – with others it may well be different.

The importance of colours and different art materials in art therapy

Our whole daily life, from when we are born, is a changing season of colours. For thousands of years, human beings have clothed themselves in colours. Colours are used in all cultures and in many cultures have very specific meanings. Certain colours are used with death and mourning; others for celebrations, and so on.When I look at modern architecture, it seems as if the world around us is turning quite grey. Goethe has said that 'Colour is the speech of the Soul of Nature' (quoted in Shindler 1970, p.5). I remember, as a little girl, when I travelled by 'bus to the countryside to visit my grandparents on their farm, I was preoccupied with how colourless all the farmers' wives were. They were all dressed very similarly in a blue-grey colour that made them nearly invisible and their own individual colours of light and darkness were by no means expressed. I was later reminded of this episode when reading a sentence from a book about the Goddess Innana:

> The woman I needed to call my mother was silent before I was born (Rich, quoted in Perera 1981, p.7).

I believe that a part of Norwegian culture called the 'Jante Law' in expressing the attitude 'You shall never think you are any better than the others', is the influence leading to the blue-grey colourlessness of the farmers' wives.* Even as a child I was aware of this, and developed my own little game, trying to find the inner colour hidden behind the blue-grey. When working with patients in art therapy, I have found that each individual has their own very special meaning of colour. How colours are used together – dominating colours, missing colours, colours to hide another colour – provides necessary information for the therapist. Sometimes the therapist, having learned and developed the knowledge of technique from the artist within, will ask a patient to work with a specific colour in order to navigate the therapeutic situation in an important direction.

The same thing occurs with the use of other art materials, of which some are more structured than others. In working with patients, I find it very important to use a whole range of art materials. Most of the time, patients are free to make a choice depending on what they feel; but it can sometimes be very important to move them out of a situation in which they are stuck, or to give them materials that can help them to build more structure around themselves in order to reduce the chaos and vulnerability surrounding them. Some people might think this is structuring too much and hindering spontaneity. I believe that this structuring provides the form in the art work, and structure gives our daily life a form. I have seen too many art teachers and art therapists fearing to interfere with the spontaneity of their student or patient and, in their failure to navigate, creating chaos. Rollo May says:

> The form itself always remains as long as the creativity force exists. If the form should disappear, so should the spontaneity. (May 1975, p.110)

How does the art therapist work?

The art therapist works in a studio. The room and the environment are, of course, very important, and in my work as an art therapist in England, the USA and Norway, room and space in most institutions is a problem. Usually, the art therapist is given rooms that others have found they could not use and one learns to make the best of the situation! When thinking about room space, I realise it has always been important. It is important

* 'Jante Law' is a social concept developed by the author Aksel Sandemose in his book *En Flykltning Krysser sitt Spor* which postulates ten rules of typical Norwegian behaviour in the same form as the ten commandments.

that the art work can be created at a table, as well as on the floor, or the wall, or a scaffold. However, the most important aspect is creating a safe, holding, environment, where each patient can be free to express him or herself.

> Psychotherapy takes place in the overlap of the two areas of playing, that of the patient and that of the therapist. Psychotherapy has to do with two people playing together (Winnicott 1988, p.44).

In order to make the patient feel safe enough to play and to create, I find it important to have a room which has corners and places to hide and move and which is, at the same time, holding.

Art therapists work with both groups and individuals. The way of working with either is dependent on particular patients, the ethos of the institution and the concentration of the therapist. Many people ask me, 'How do you get patients to paint?'

There are many techniques which can be used to get patients to paint, or to take the risk. In the art room, I like to have lots of materials available – paints, different crayons, clay, bits and pieces of material – to build and sculpt with. I also have a sandtray with many small toys, animals and figures which I have collected on my journeys. It is important that the therapist feels able to tune in to patients' needs. Very often patients come up with clear metaphors, which are like gifts, to developed further. For example, (patient): 'I am stuck with my life, I have so many problems.' the therapist picks up this metaphor, asking: 'How stuck? Are you frozen – unable to move? What kind of texture does it have? Is it like glue?'

One of the pioneers in art therapy in the USA, psychoanalytically-orientated art therapist Margreth Naumberg, said:

> The technique of art therapy is based on the knowledge that every individual, whether trained or untrained in art, has a latent capacity to project his inner conflicts into a visual art form. As patients' pictures search inner experiences, it frequently happens that they become more verbally articulate (Naumberg 1958, p.511).

Edith Kramer, an art therapist who worked extensively with children in the USA, describes the process involved in art activity as having inherent healing properties which show their usefulness in therapy. Art is a means of widening a range of human experiences by creating *equivalents for such experiences*. It is an area where experience can be chosen, varied and repeated at will. In the creative act, conflicts are re-experienced, resolved and integrated.

Ullman and Dachinger (1975) say that most art therapists probably believe in the importance of both these views. I also believe this to be true.

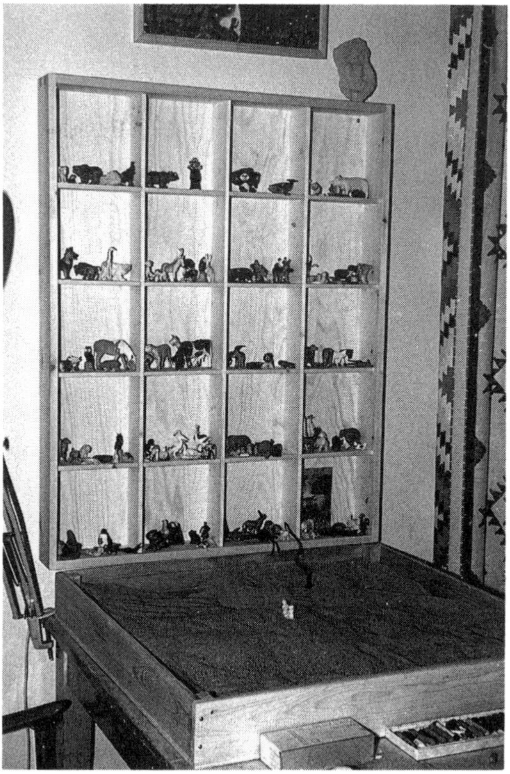

The sandtray in the art therapy room

I believe that the focus on what is happening during the creative process is very important in art therapy now, but it is not enough alone; the therapist and patient must together try to understand the art process and product and work through what comes out of the art product. The working through in different ways verbally and non-verbally after the creative act itself is also important.

The importance of texture

The different texture of art materials can be of great importance because often they bring the patients in touch with different feelings. Some materials may be cold and hard, others soft and warm; others might be very flexible, while some have very little flexibility. I find that some patients, out of fear, stick to the same material even if they do not like it, because they feel familiar with it. In therapy situations, people often say: 'I do not know anything about myself. I don't know how to paint.' They need help in navigation to find out what is there already.

One exercise I use with groups is to ask the participants to find a piece of cloth or material that they can identify with. What is the texture? Is it a loose-weave or hard? Is it soft, elastic? – and so on. Lots of people find this a very helpful way of starting to think about how they see themselves.

One patient brought an elastic band to the group and said that she had the tendency to stretch too much and that she felt very tired of stretching. When asked how far she would stretch before she managed to find a limit for herself, she let the whole group pull the elastic around so that it was almost stretched out. Another patient, who had isolated herself for a long time, said that she did not have any materials that she could use at home, so she went to several different material stores and negotiated with the sales assistant to find the right material: she knew exactly how it should be. This patient had said many times, 'I do not know who I am or what I want with my life.'

I have developed this exercise in many different ways. People can be asked to bring something to every group, like pictures of fruit or places (see Chapter 8 on Doors). Having collected different things, they can use them to make a collage or build a sculpture and, little by little, they will create a form with which they can identify.

Trash

Sometimes the patients will destroy their art-work in anger, or they will throw it away because they censure it as not being good enough, or being too threatening. I will not stop this action, but I usually give them a trash-bag and ask them to save it while they are in therapy, because maybe one day they will find that they can use the trash. One woman I was working with was very upset and angry one day when she came to a session. She said, 'Nobody understands me', and was upset with the whole world. I gave her some clay in which to try to express her anger. She was complaining and working with the clay for twenty minutes when she suddenly pressed it together and said, 'This is ridiculous! I am sitting here, building castles out of air for you. It does not help me to come here.' Before she left, she wanted to throw away the clay, but I stopped her and gave her a trash-bag to keep it in. 'That is nothing', she said; 'Why do you want to save it?' 'Maybe you can do something with it later', I said. One week later she wanted this clay and said, 'It felt so good that you could contain my anger.' Out of the clay was born a woman – a beautiful figure, yet very vulnerable. I can think back to many incidents like this, when people actually could go back and look at what they wanted to get rid of and transform it into something else.

> This 'taking life heavily' that my books are filled with...means nothing (don't you agree?) but a taking according to true weight, and thus according to truth: an attempt to weigh Things by the carat of the heart, instead of by suspicion, happiness, or chance.
>
> Rainer Maria Rilke to Rudolf Bodländer, March 13, 1922 (Mitchell 1989 p.342)

Timing

Listen to the raindrops of your soul.

In thinking about concrete examples on why timing is so important in the therapeutic situation, this sentence just came to me. Timing has much to do with using the sensitivity of the artist and giving a therapeutic structure at the right moment, but I believe that the most important thing is to travel at the same speed as the patient. In art therapy sessions I often bring up this question of how fast the patient wants to move. I ask them to think about whether they like walking, going by boat, train, plane, and so forth. I often also ask them to think about finding a safe place to come back to, allow them to play like a child – leave mummy, run backwards and forwards, play peek-a-boo. I have, in many situations, found it extremely useful to have created a safe place as a metaphor or symbolic place.

Sue and I were free-associating on images of ourselves as therapists. One was a storehouse (more than a container) – the fertility goddess Innana is a goddess of storehouses; another was a train with many wagons, filled with different things, that can move fast or slow or stop. This seemed to complement the storehouse: the storehouse and the train – stillness and movement. The storehouse can contain, as well as using any equipment available in the different rooms, art materials, literature, philosophy, and so on.

I once worked with a young woman who had, for about nine years, been struggling with eating disorders. To begin with, she had suffered from anorexia, which had later developed into bulimia. During the three years I worked with her, she would still have anorectic periods. In one session, during one of these periods, she was deeply depressed. She made a picture of herself walking on a narrow road. On each side was a steep drop down to a landscape filled with black holes. To me, it looked as if the road went on like this for miles. She said to me, 'You know, I have to walk on this road until earth and heaven meet, until I have enough balance in myself to leave you.' I then thought, 'Well, that road is so long that it might take years.' Something within the situation made me feel uncomfortable. I took the picture home with me and that night it was the last thing I thought about before falling asleep. There was something I had not picked up. That night, I had a dream about myself, walking along that road, and in my dream there was a clear struggle between life and death.

I brought the patient's picture to my supervisor and said, 'Can you help me? What message have I failed to see?' We were sitting on either side of his office, and he said, 'Can you see that the road goes on for miles and miles?' 'Yes', I said, 'Can you?' 'From my perspective, it looks as if the road is ending in a cliff,' he said. When I looked again, I saw that it could look as if the road ended in a cliff. 'Well, maybe she is telling you she is falling,' he said to me. This felt to me as if it could be correct. I never told the patient this episode but sent her a card painted by the Norwegian painter Kai Fjell of a mother with a baby in her arms and reminded her of our next session. This was a thing I did not usually do, but my intuition told me that in this situation it would be correct. She never mentioned the card until four months later when she said, 'Do you remember the card you sent me of a mother and child? When you sent that to me I was feeling as if I could not go on, but the card told me that you would be there to help me along the road.' I believe this is a good example of timing – the postcard arrived at the right moment: in one of my storage rooms, Kai Fjell with his painting appeared and helped me to make a statement which at that moment gave enough nourishment to move on.

Distancing in art therapy

One of the advantages of using art in therapy is that, in a unique way, it allows the individual to distance themselves from what they are working with: they can leave the art-work, but it will always be there to come back to.

Many of the people that I have worked with throughout the years find it difficult to find words for their inner feelings, fears and experiences. The art-work becomes a symbolic language for their inner feelings and helps them to make a bridge between the inner and outer reality. For example, if you ask a person to paint a house, most people will manage to paint a house. What they choose to emphasise in the house, however, will show some of their personality: it might be a house without windows, doors or roof. Very often, when working like that, the patient will suddenly say something like, 'When I am describing this house, it sounds as if I am talking about myself' – what Sue and I call the 'Aha experience'.

For instance, in working with drug-abusers, I often use this method of distancing in order to move closer. If a young person is asked to sit down and say something about themself, they often feel very afraid and say that that is stupid; but when using metaphors which allow distancing, they feel safer and more able to expose their fears and feelings. At times in a therapy situation, the patient might also find the material they are working with is too dangerous – they may feel very vulnerable at what is beginning to surface.

I was once working with a young psychotic man who had a very difficult relationship with his mother. Before being admitted to hospital, he had attempted to rape several young women. For a period I saw him both in individual therapy and group therapy. A male psychiatrist was my co-leader in the group. The patient, in very indirect ways, expressed jealousy in the group at having to share me with others. He had also started to become interested in my private life. I had told him I was married and in the session after this he painted a picture of two men and cut their heads off. I interpreted this to be his feeling about sharing me with the psychiatrist and my husband. However, I brought the picture with me to a treatment meeting, and one of my colleagues there – a psychologist – said, 'But I feel he is saying he is losing his head.' We concluded that I should have another staff member with me in the sessions with this patient, but I said, 'I want to have one more session alone with him to prepare him for that.' My art therapy room was located in the basement and at that time I did not even have a bleep: it was quite isolated from the rest of the ward.

The next session, the patient started to draw the school he first went to as a child. He said, 'My mother always held my arm very tight when we walked into the schoolyard. I felt so humiliated by this.' Then, he suddenly painted the school as being on fire. I was sitting across the table from him and watched him sweat and struggle with his anger and feelings of humiliation. He then got up from his chair, folded back his shirt-sleeves, and took off his ring and watch. I do not know what I was thinking, but I remember being afraid. In one way I felt paralysed. He said, 'I have to go to the toilet.' I still felt afraid, but remember thinking that I could not run away because that would be untherapeutic. I hung his painting on the blackboard on the other side of the room and when I heard him flush the toilet I went to meet him at the door, remembering my colleague's interpretation about him losing his head. I gripped my arm firmly around his shoulder and said, 'I hung your picture up far from where you are sitting so that you can distance yourself from it. Because I believe that this

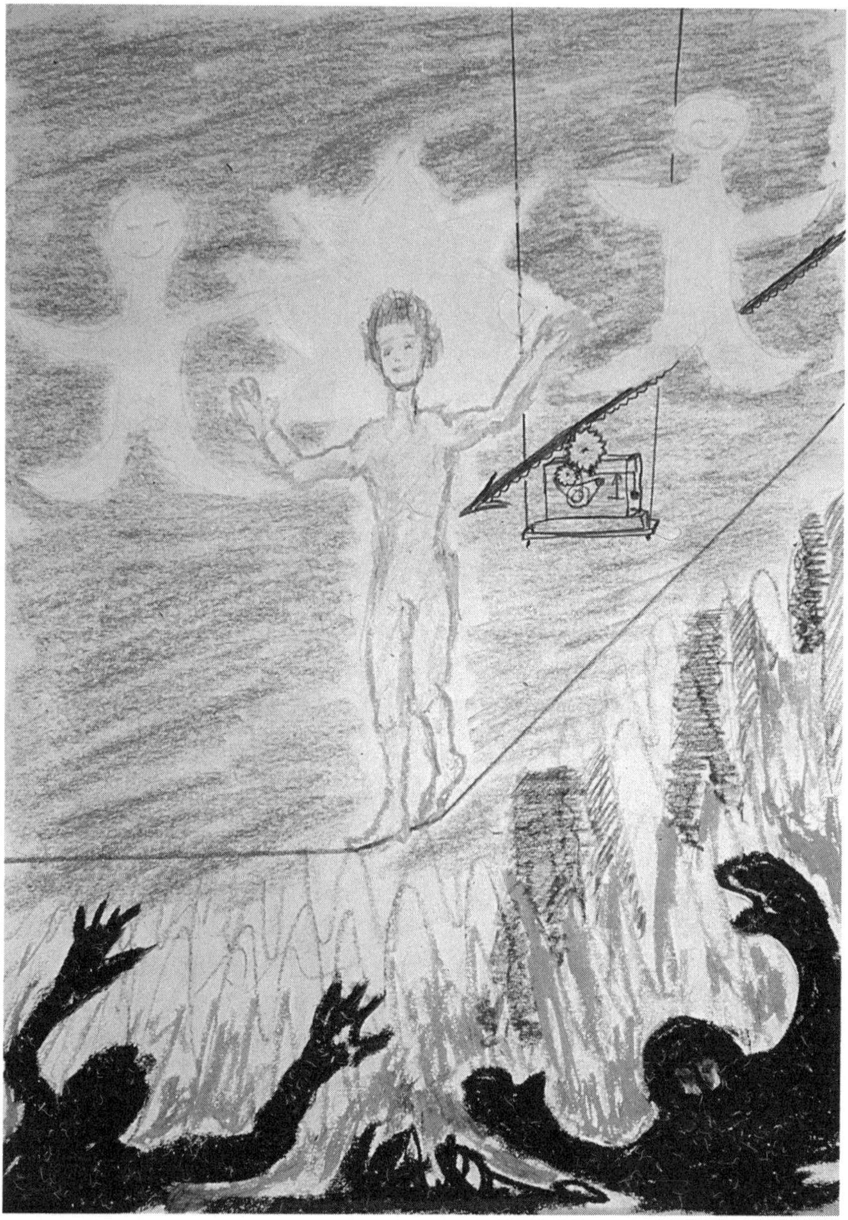

Balancing act. 'I am always playing with my life, not able to make a choice. I want everything and risk everything'

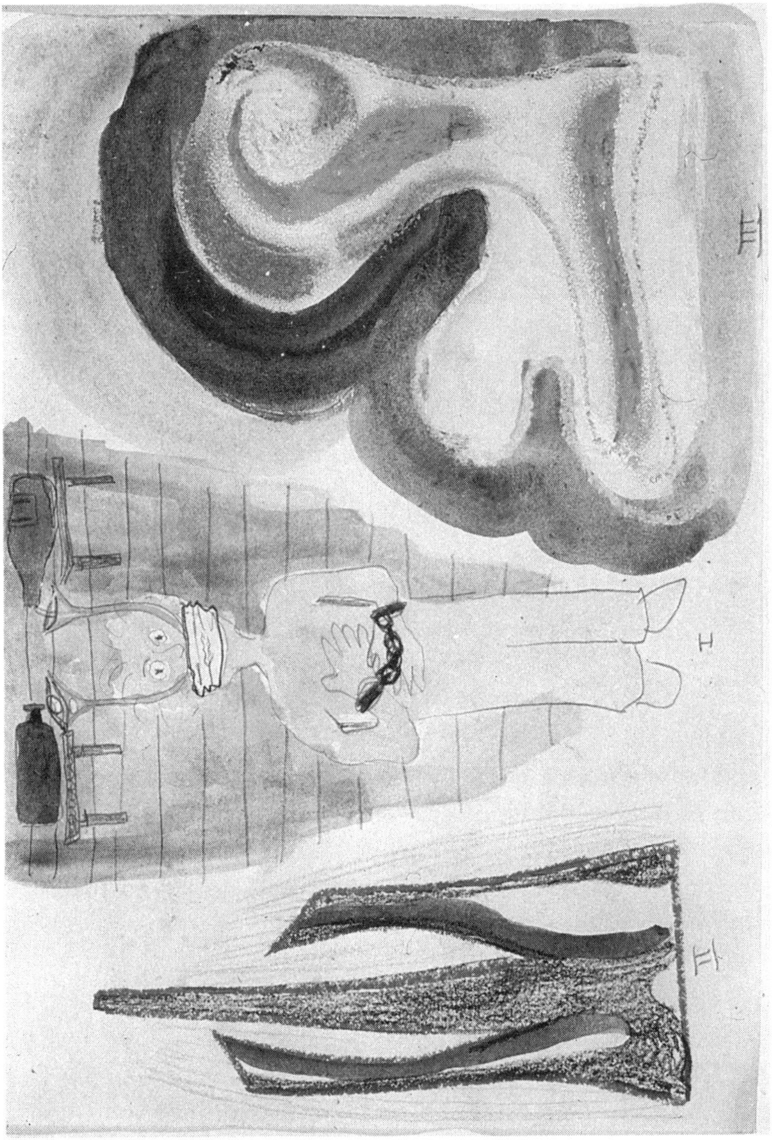

'It is hard to integrate the masculine and feminine sides of me. I am split in between. I drug myself and feel paralysed in the situation.'

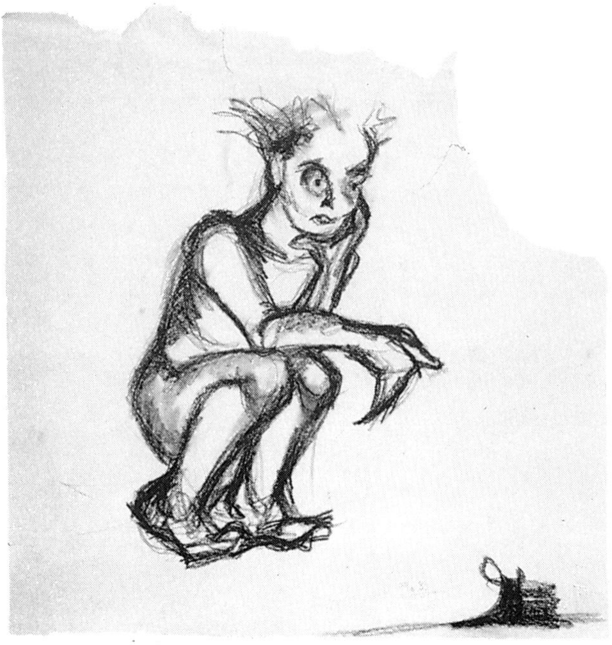

Fear, anxiety

is so difficult for you to face, it will be better to put it away for some time.' He looked at me and said with a very calm voice, 'At last you are saying something reasonable.' Later, in therapy, he could come back to this, but at that moment he was not ready. The art-work was there, stored, to return to – his picture was in the storehouse.

Art therapy versus other art media

During the years I have worked as an art therapist, I have co-led groups and worked closely with several dance therapists, dramatherapists and psychodrama leaders. This has been an important influence on how I work as an art therapist. I have always been very involved with how people communicate and express themselves; therefore movement from, for example, bodywork to artwork or drama or psychodrama, has been very natural. It can be used both ways: starting out in art, moving to drama, or starting out in drama, moving to art. I still think of myself as

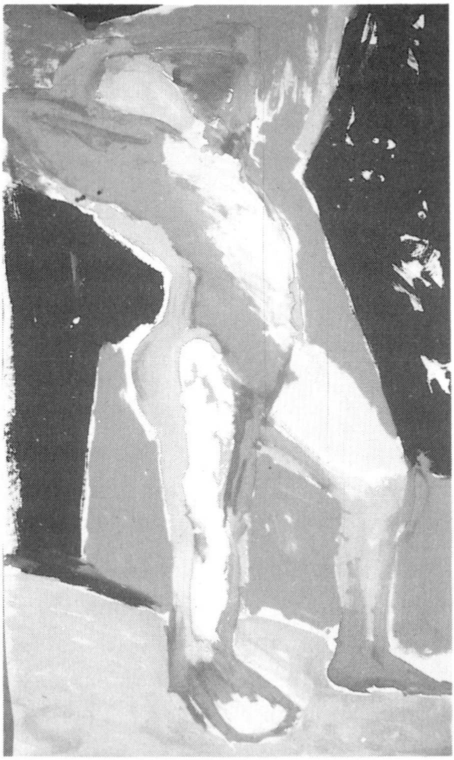

'I have finally found my strength.' When the patient saw this picture some years after ending therapy, she said 'Do you remember how I had trouble with my breathing? I felt my throat was blocked when I wanted to express myself. It is threatening, in a way, to see one's strength, one's good and bad sides.'

an art therapist and my strengths are the visual arts, but learning from dance and drama has given me new tools which I can use when I am in the process of the art-work. I can ask a patient to dramatise their work instead of just talking about it, if it seems appropriate. In working with groups, the changing from one media to another can be of great value.

In the last few years while working in hospitals I have worked a lot with staff in different wards, and with internal conflicts in different settings. Together with a psychiatrist, I was asked to work on staff development on a somatic ward. There were many problems of communication on the ward. As is usual with communication problems, it was not easy to see what was causing them, but what was quite clear on this ward was that a lot of the problems were focused on a very demanding and difficult patient. He had become a scapegoat and a lot that had nothing to do with him was being blamed on him.

The staff were asked to choose different play animals which they felt represented both the strongest and most negative sides of their job. Having worked with this in many different ways, they were divided up into small groups, creating a landscape which those animals felt good in. Having shared these with the group, we introduced a new animal for them – one which was very different from all their own. This animal was sick and needed help, and if they could not find help in their own community, they were asked to negotiate with other communities to help the newcomer and outsider. They were asked to draw some things on how they would travel to the other community. Some had trains, boats or planes, but there was one group that made a spaceship – they said they felt they were on another planet; they let their newcomer die because they did not know how to ask for help. What became clear here was that this group consisted also of the people who felt most outside on the ward. It is a good example of how art and drama can be combined and used on many different levels. The excellent thing about using art in therapy is that it allows people to play and try out situations. Very often, when there are problems of communication, these are due to not feeling safe enough to open up or clearly state what one actually means. In dealing with this problem through art, it becomes very clear what is the problem, but most of all it allows for playing and moving closer to colleagues in a safe way.

Conclusion

I have briefly described the background of art therapy and its underlying principles. I have shared some of my own processes which have contributed to my development as an art therapist. The emphasis in art therapy is placed on the fact that the art-work helps the patient to express their inner feelings and experiences through art. The art often helps the individual to find new solutions and gives life to dead energy to enable them to communicate their inner feelings and experiences to the outer world. The art-work is always there. They can distance from it and it will always be theirs to come back to and perhaps to discover that it is possible to see it from a different angle, a different perspective. It is possible to transform destructive form into constructive form.

> And the rumor that there was someone
> who knew how to look,
> stirred those less
> visible creatures: ...
>
> (Rainer Maria Rilke, 'Turning Point' in Mitchell 1989)

Appendix

I have worked in this field for many years and for the last twelve have been pioneering such work in Norway. Since I studied and worked as an art therapist both in England and the USA, it has been natural for me, in planning the training of art therapy in Norway, to compare it with developments in those countries.

In developing a study plan for starting a two-year full-time postgraduate training programme in art therapy.

The committee I worked with wrote to twenty-five different universities and assessed their programmes and the evaluations from both staff and students. As a result, I believe we have got a good quality training programme. One of the problems in this work, has been the ten years spent dealing with the Norwegian authorities and trying to make them understand that art therapy has developed into its own profession and has its own language and philosophy. They wanted to think of it as an extension to occupational therapy or a psychological technique. To me, art therapy has its own philosophy, and training cannot be based on an artist who studies some psychology or a psychologist who learns art, as we call it. The training of students, therefore, may contain a programme consisting of many levels.

CHAPTER 3

The Storehouse

HILDE [*stopping and looking at him*]: Have you got several nurseries?

SOLNESS: There are three nurseries in the house.

HILDE: That's a lot. So I suppose you've a good many children?

SOLNESS: No. We've no children. But now *you* can be our child for the present.

(Ibsen *The Master Builder* p.144)

By the word of the LORD
the heavens were made,
And all the host of them
by the breath of His
mouth. Gen. 2:1 [Job 26:13]
He gathers the waters of
the sea together as a
heap;
He lays up the deep in
storehouses

(Psalm 33)

JUNO: Honour, riches, marriage blessing,
Long continuance, and increasing,
Hourly joys be still upon you!
Juno sings her blessings on you.

CERES: Earth's increase, foison plenty,
Barns and garners never empty,
Vines with clust'ring bunches growing,
Plants with goodly burden bowing

(*The Tempest*, IV.1. 106–113)

In this chapter we attempt to share with you the contents of our storehouses that occur to us as we write. We have tried not to control the writing, but to allow the images to surface of their own accord. They have taken us through our own therapeutic, artistic and aesthetic experiences in a variety of media as well as recalling meaningful interactions.

In the writing of this book, we have been aware of certain dominant images and roles that keep re-presenting themselves in our dreams, our discussions and our day-to-day clinical practice. The titles of later chapters demonstrate the importance of the relationship between stasis and metastasis – the therapeutic capacity to regulate stillness and movement. Although 'stasis' is also considered to mean 'equilibrium' (OED), in our view it has to be in conjunction with the transformative potential of metastasis. Therefore 'The Body' (Chapter 6) is followed by 'Transitions' (Chapter 7); 'Doors' (Chapter 8) is followed by 'Journeys' (Chapter 9). In 'Mask' (Chapter 10) we consider a bringing together of the stasis and metastasis in the multi-layered image and role of masks. However, we wish to point out that this process only became apparent in the writing of the book and it is significant that this Chapter in which we describe the various contents of this 'storehouse' before leading into the metastasis of the 'Kettle of Transformation' (Chapter 4), is the last to be written.

Although we have both written in the first two chapters of our own journeys into art therapy and dramatherapy, it is as if we have always been in a process of almost 'moving to a new house' since we are starting to 'unpack' the experience, exposure and education that we feel contributes to these storehouses. We deliberately use the present tense since this is a process that continues and the rooms becomes replenished in so many different ways.

> My spontaneous view of Åse's storehouse is this vital small person, with a Norwegian knapsack on her back, which has the most incredible abundance inside.
>
> My immediate view of Sue's storehouse is her enormous capacity to find the right 'story' at the right moment.

We are very aware of the fact that when discussing the various influences that have formed and shaped us, we do not immediately discuss psychoanalysis. Where then, in this many-roomed house, is it stored away?

> Of course, thanks to the house, a great many of our memories are housed, and if the house is a bit elaborate, if it has a cellar and a garret, nooks and corridors, our memories have refuges that are all the more clearly delineated. All our lives we come back to them in our daydreams (Bachelard 1964, p.8).

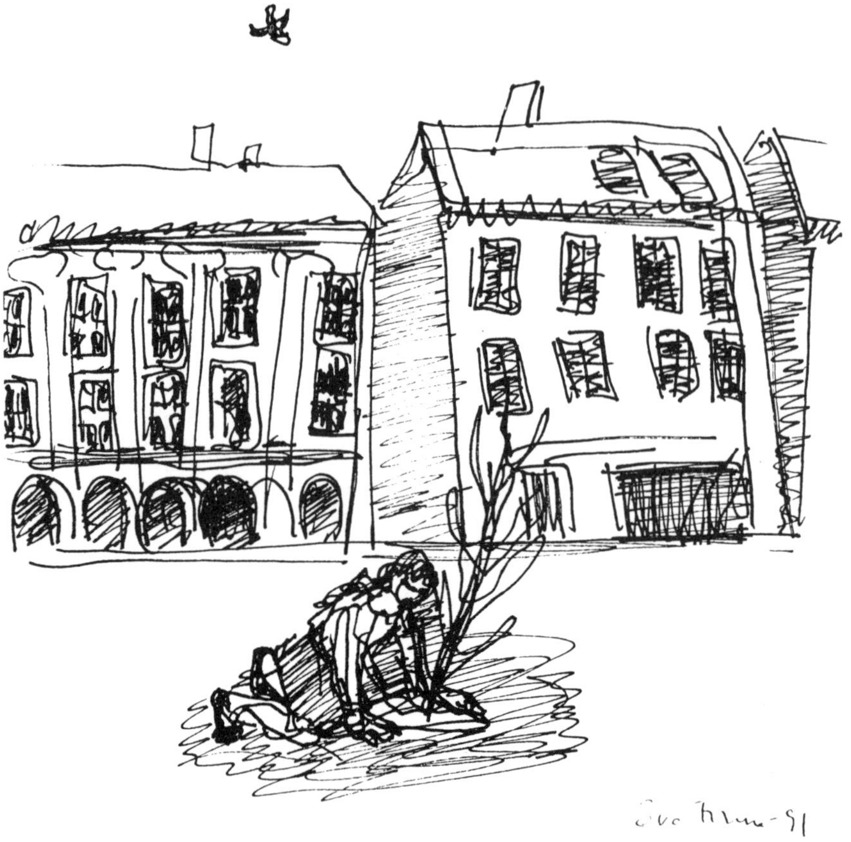

The storehouse (by Gro Finne)

So where do we put our 'objects' – in the cellar or in the attic? There is no doubt that both of us have stored away our object-relations influence as part of the wider theoretical story within which we work. Psychoanalysis is a frame within which disparate images and themes may be understood, however, we feel it is important to acknowledge that there are several interconnecting frames or doors or rooms.

Sue: I had a lengthy Freudian analysis and group analysis during my transition from the professional theatre to dramatherapy; interior journeys which culminated in the 'real-world' journey to Malaysia to research tribal ritual and drama.* It was after field-work experience that an anthropological understanding of dramatherapy began to surface in

* This family journey to the tropical rain forest where I took my three children aged 7, 12 and 14 as well as my 14-year-old foster child, had a profound effect on us all.

relation to ritual drama and symbolism, heavily influenced by the work of Victor Turner (1968) and Gilbert Lewis (1982). I was able to make a bridge back into (or forward into) a Jungian perspective through a greater understanding of dominant symbols and archetypes. In recent years I have felt that there has been a resolution of these formative influences in my adult life, so that they can all exist in my storehouse and not be banished or locked away. It is not always easy, having been a pioneer of dramatherapy training, not to have had this training myself. It is a synthesis of these many experiences that have brought together theory, education and practice.

Åse: I have experienced a growing alliance between art, aesthetics and various psychoanalytic theories. After many years of clinical practice and a gradual understanding of psychoanalysis, it is more and more clear that I am talking about an alliance between creative and therapeutic processes. I am reluctant to use the word 'integration' as it has become very popular and is often misused, and I would be careful to ensure that in this 'alliance', I am talking about a relationship; i.e. the interconnecting doors that help us to expand our understanding of ourselves, our clients and our practice.

In *Structuring the Therapeutic Process*, Murray Cox (1988) talks about the experience of becoming a therapist and quotes Conrad from *Heart of Darkness* where he says:

> 'He resembled a pilot, which to a seaman is trustworthiness personified. It was difficult to realize his work was not out there in the luminous estuary, but behind him, within the brooding gloom.'
>
> In this brief passage, Conrad has caught several aspects of the experience of becoming a therapist. The analogy of the pilot speaks for itself. He is not the captain of the ship, but may facilitate the captain's negotiations of unknown and treacherous waters. One of the skills which the therapist can never fully master is that of discerning *the* moment (*kairos*) or turning point during sequential psychotherapy sessions, from the moment (*chronos*) which may not be a turning point.
>
> The patient may need to turn from free-association about the pathogenic past (the brooding gloom) to exploratory free-association about what he might become, as he is caught up in the expanding flow of his personal life in relationship to others (the luminous estuary) (Cox 1988, p.89).

In art therapy the 'turning point' may be easier to capture because it has been given form and visualised. However, it often occurs that even if the patient gives form to something, it may still not be consciously 'seen'; i.e.

it may still be an unconscious process. It is of major importance that the therapist does not 'move ahead' of the patient, which is what the essence of empathy is about, as well as the 'fine tuning' of the therapeutic relationship. The therapist may see a 'clever interpretation' that is to do with his or her needs rather than the patients'. It may also be that the therapist finds the 'creative waiting' that is to do with the therapist's need rather than the patients'. It may also be that the therapist finds the 'creative waiting' or 'hovering attentiveness' (Cox and Theilgaard 1987) hard to bear. Nevertheless, there is a right moment for the therapist to intervene; when the 'brooding gloom' of an individual patient, an individual in a group or the group as a whole moves towards unhelpful destructiveness. This also requires the 'fine tuning' of the therapist's senses.

In preparing this book, we discussed the internal states of the art therapist and dramatherapist.

Sue: When we are talking about this storehouse and all the experiences that are there, do you find you consider them in the same way?

Åse: You mean, does the same person have the key to all the rooms?

Sue: Exactly. I know we can have this storehouse but how do we get access to it…who has the key…or keys?

Åse: After many years of experience I have learned to listen and to trust the artist within me and the therapist within me. So the artist and the therapist both have keys….

Sue: So they are both in dialogue – as internal roles. I want to add to that the internal patient. Our 'internal patient' makes connections with clients and patients that would not otherwise be made – so there is a special key there…

Åse: Then, of course, there must be an internal supervisor… what about the internal artist in the dramatherapist?

Sue: I wrote about this…the four internal states of the dramatherapist: the therapist, artist, patient and supervisor…and the dialogue that goes on between them. However I think it should be 'artiste' – we talk about a 'theatre artiste'.*

Åse: And they all have access to the storehouse in different ways and at different times. The creative waiting

* When I first played with this idea, I used a group of trainees to play the different internal roles of the dramatherapist – there were three – the patient, therapist and supervisor. I later realised that the internal artiste had been directing the play!

informs this doesn't it? How do we know the right moment...we don't always get it right do we?

Sue: I think there is a major sensory element here...we know through our bodies because our senses have informed us. We don't just hear or see we *feel* what is going on...it smells right...now I'm using senses metaphorically as well as in reality.

Åse: The Siamese twin example (see below) was a sensory experience: I knew it was appropriate in my body. I mean we don't always share this type of disclosure with a patient...but in the moment it felt appropriate and it was exactly the right image for her.

Sue: And it had occurred to you while you were relaxing and thinking about something else...

Åse: So we are saying that there are many keys to this storehouse and different people...roles...can open them at the right moment.

Sue: Something like that. This storehouse is such a precious thing. Even while writing this book we have both recovered dreams and images and memories that were stored away. I mean, in the introduction you had seen the Botticelli picture before and it came unbidden into your consciousness.

Åse: And the dream about meeting you on the Acropolis. And then of course I talk later about the sculpture of my father's hand and his recent death and the need to move on.

Sue: I had a dream when writing Chapter 4 when we talk about the sand tray and the sea shore. I remembered a book that I read when I was about ten years old called '*John Halifax, Gentleman*' and a particular few lines in it when John is being taught to write as an adult:

> A thought struck me. 'John, hand me the stick, and I'll give you your first writing lesson'. So there on the smooth gravel, and with the rose-stem for a pen, I taught him how to form the letters of the alphabet and join them together. He learned them very quickly – so quickly, that in a little while the simple, copy-book that Mother Earth obliged us with was covered in all directions with 'JOHN – John'. (Craik 1857)

I had not thought of that book for years – certainly all my adult life and there was the earth as we've talked about before, being used as a transitionary space between two adults…

Åse: And its also about someone learning to write – and that's what we are doing. It's not that we can't write as such…but it has taken a long time to write about this process that no-one has written about before; and mother earth occurring yet again as a symbol – like with Moomintroll….

Sue: Learning to write and 'Mother Earth' giving the copybook. And I suppose with mothers again we talk about object relations. I wish people would talk about 'human objects' more and use more accessible language…I have yet to find a simple definition of object relations….

Åse: Maybe the problem is that many people think there is one key, The Key, rather than several keys…even in the object relations writings there are several definitions.

When we talk about the various psychoanalytic and psychotherapeutic theories that form part of our storehouse we are aware of the fact that we are eclectic – and rightly so! For example, there is not a problem with the co-existence of an instinctual 'pleasure principle' of ego psychology as well as (not instead of) the 'human relations principle' of object-relations theory. The former emphasises the drive of the individual and its needs, and the latter the urge to maintain and have ties to others. Many theorists have contributed to the evolution of object-relations theory*, however, all of them put emphasis on the importance of the early maternal tie as being the first 'object relationship'.

Both of us agree that these early experiences are important and may well be the form and content that is expressed through an artistic therapy. However, if we also make the connection with the Jungian perspective, we are able to work with a richer perspective which also acknowledges the importance of the artistic process. If we had continued the above dialogue it would include our disquiet about the sublimation view of artists and actors expressed by Freud and, indeed held by many clinicians even now. As quoted in an earlier piece of writing†, there is an assumption that artists come into therapy because of their art; as one psychoanalyst

* For an excellent discussion and historical overview, see Kernberg (1984).

† This is discussed at greater length in *Shakespeare Comes to Broadmoor* (Cox 1992b).

asked, 'Why do actors make such bad patients?' Is it still the equation with Dionysus that assumes the hysterical nature of the actor, that provokes clinicians to dismiss the theatre artist or, indeed, the dramatherapist?

However it is interesting to record what Jung says in relation to 'theatre' and to 'dreams'. Whereas many clinicians make use of the theatre as a metaphor* for life itself, as well as for therapy, Jung attempts to integrate certain aspects of the process of theatre art into his understanding of the dream process. He suggests a dramatic structure for dreams (1960) which although is notional rather than actual, nevertheless introduces the idea of theatre into a process that is usually considered to do with images. Perhaps the dream is a combined process of drama and image, taking place within the internal theatre of the individual.

Patsy Nowell Hall† is an art therapist with whom we have both worked and whose capacity to work with combined disciplines of arts therapies stimulated us both. Having died prematurely, Patsy has left a legacy of work in her Jungian approach to art therapy. In her chapter 'A Way of Healing the Split' (1987) she discusses the duality of knowledge expressed by Jung; 'the way of creative formulation' such as art, dreams and symbols, and 'the way of understanding' such as intellectual understanding and abstractions and so on. In fact, she expresses through Jung's perspective, an attempt to reconcile the two brain hemispheres and their particular human functioning. The right hemisphere of the brain is where images, intuition, metaphors arise, whereas the left hemisphere is connected with logic, facts and numeracy, for example. Is this just another metaphor which attempts to integrate the ancient division between thought and feeling, between science and art, between medicine and artistic healing?

Hall goes on to say:

> Jung believed that symbols are a natural mode of psychic expression, and the natural language of the unconscious (as opposed to the Freudian idea of 'manifest content' which conceals talent or repressed desires.

---

* Shakespeare of course is the prime genius of the theatrical metaphor since he uses it within the play which always gives it an additional frisson. I have written elsewhere (1992b) on the use (maybe overuse) of theatre as a metaphor in therapy. I have expressed before a personal view that dramatherapy represents, for many psychotherapists, the Dionysian position, which arouses many fears and fantasies. Apollo is denied a role in the theatre, yet so often the Apollonean role is taken by the Chorus, which is a very effective dramatherapeutic device.

† We wish this chapter to be our own personal tribute to Patsy Nowell Hall with whom we have both worked. Sue recalls very special moments when working together at Turvey Monastery, Cumberland Lodge and the Greek Dramatherapy Institute. Patsy had a capacity, we both feel, to work across disciplines and not feel threatened by other arts therapies.

> Symbols arise spontaneously – they cannot be produced intentionally. He recognised the living quality of symbols and symbol-making. Symbols are living and personified aspects of the psyche. They are charged with psychic energy – with numinosity – and are thus dynamic, have driving power, and will produce consequences (op cit).

Rycroft suggests that Freud had a real conflict concerning the role of the scientist and the role of the healer; the person who on the one hand observed and recorded meticulously, at least in theory, and yet on the other hand talked about 'free-floating attention', when he advised his students about practice.

> What I am suggesting is that one of the unresolved contradictions in Freud's thinking is between psychoanalysis conceived of as a natural science – objective, detached and intellectual – and psychoanalysis conceived of as an intuitive, receptive mode of relating to others; and that awareness of this contradiction combined with failure to resolve it is part of the contemporary 'malaise' of psychoanalysis (Rycroft 1985, p.57).

We could suggest that the arts therapies continue to struggle with this very issue. Are we talking about a focus of art or of science? Are we talking about artistic processes or psychotherapeutic processes? Are the arts therapies in the mainstream of psychological treatment with roots in the psychoanalytic or related field? Or are they closer to the shamans' practice, to 'native medicine', to the long history of 'healing' which began before the establishment of Western medical models?

Is the arts therapist 'centre stage' and thus in the mainstream of established therapeutic practice together with medicine and psychoanalysis, or is the position on the margins, inhabited by the shaman and native healer and itinerant artists as well?

Our own thoughts on this subject are that the 'politics of therapy', in terms of acceptance, recognition, formalised training, pay scales and referral networks is one debate in relation to the therapeutic and healing professions as whole. The debate is usually governed by budgetry resources – especially at the moment with the move into being 'providers' and 'customers' or 'users' – and is not the basis of developing a theoretical basis for art therapy or dramatherapy. However, it may well be a political statement to 'prove' that arts therapies fit neatly into established clinical theories in order to argue for recognition and mainstream activity.

This is a separate topic; the politics and economics of artistic therapies as contrasted with their history and sociology. We do not intend to develop these themes at length in this book, but to draw the reader's attention to the seeming need to invent histories. Jean Duvignaud (1972) challenged various assumptions about the history of artistic expression in his book *The Sociology of Art*. He suggests there is a fashion, or even mania, for explaining things by their distant origins, stimulated in particular by the popularization of prehistory and archaeology.

He says that the preoccupation with 'origins' – closely tied to evolutionary theories in natural sciences, paleontology and physiology – takes for granted three unfounded premises. He says:

> These propositions are as follows:
>
> i. that simplicity and primitiveness merge the closer one gets to the origins of mankind
>
> ii. that the complexity of present-day conditions results from a progressive combination of simple elements already present at the beginning of human history
>
> iii. in spite of the disruptions which have occurred, the evolution of creative activity is continuous.
>
> According to these, therefore, the complexity of modern life can be understood in relation to the simplicity of primitive societies (Duvignaud 1972, p.27).

Duvignaud's critique of this approach is that it both separates artistic expression from real experience and gives it a particular kind of existence; one that is pure and natural.

> It is modern writers, and only modern writers who try to 'give a purer meaning to the words of the tribe' (ibid, p.28).

It is paradoxical that the view that Duvignaud is challenging is one which separates art from 'real' experiences and then suggests it is more real!

Duvignaud's hypothesis of the relationship between artists of all kinds and societies needs to be studied in itself, but our reason to include him here is to arrest the slide into the various myths on the origins not only of artistic expression, but also artistic therapeutic expression. As society itself grows and develops, its response to the arts will continue to move. Grotowski (1968) captures something of this when he talks about the organic nature of dramatic expression. Duvignaud says that he is trying to prevent reductionism of works of art to 'mere biography' or vice versa, and to understand the latent meaning of the themes 'in the light of the success or otherwise of the attempt to exteriorise and objectify them' (op cit, p.49). One more quotation must suffice in relation to his view on drama and theatre:

> In a sociology of art, we define drama as a combination of behaviour, emotions, attitudes, idealogies, actions and creations which, for the creative individual, crystallizes the whole of society and places the genesis of a work of art within the complex of those contradictory forms which make up collective life (op cit, p.49).

In our eclectic approach to theory and practice, we feel the journey is a spiral one in which we touch on the various experiences of our own lives as well as those we have ingested from others. There is a movement as the more we discover, the more we discover. It may take many years for some parts of the storehouse to be accessible to us in the now, such as in the John Halifax quotation above. We keep meeting in different forms and constellations and, of course, the meetings create new images and drama.

What continues to surprise us in our work is the recurrence in many different structures, forms, symbols and themes that have existed across time. In concordance with Duvignaud, we would not wish to create a 'primitive link' in a mythic past which really does not explain anything. We would rather suggest that there is a mythic present, which draws on a large stock of symbols, images and stories that have this numinous quality to illuminate. However, we would emphasise the importance of arts therapists having a full and varied storehouse from all the arts and literature.

Let us return to the artistic rooms in the storehouses which contain both our own artistic experiences as well as those we have gleaned from the storehouses of others – in particular the art gallery and the theatre.

Åse: Some of my art therapy journey has undoubtedly been growing from the impact that the French impressionists made on me. A lot of their art-work led me towards peoples' souls and my interest in the human psyche. Edvard Munch, the Norwegian artist, has always spoken for me, especially when he says 'I should not like to be without suffering, how much of my art I owe to suffering'.

Sue: It is similar to my interest in the work of Antonin Artaud, whose work was a strong reaction against the formal French theatre. He had a series of breakdowns and spent many years in institutions. However, he also says that his illness is a political act. His work on solar and lunar drama* is very interesting in terms of splits.

* Grotowski, of course, says that Artaud is impossible to perform! However, apart from his interesting solar-lunar opposition, I find his use of larger than life effigies to express metaphysical truths, an interesting concept and also a very useful way of working in therapy.

Åse: I could have echoed Munch's words myself, so much of my own creativity has grown out of my suffering. Part of that is this book – feeling so stuck and frustrated – and perhaps being afraid to give form to all the different images that I have collected over the years.

Sue: As the designated dancer in the family, my art education was pretty stifled; people thought that I should be given Degas ballet pictures!

Åse: My mother remembers how I used to get on a chair and perform for guests, yet I remember myself as quite shy. Years of personal therapy and supervision have allowed me to be in touch with both those sides of myself.

Sue: That's very interesting because my mother remembers me as the extrovert and I felt myself to be painfully shy! In my very first performance on stage at the age of three, I rushed off crying into her skirts. Which reminds me of your new book again – I had to be a 'baby butterfly' and, you see, I hadn't had time to be a chrysalis. But I was much much older before I became aware – before I could allow myself to 'see' works of art.

Åse: I have always been a collector and have amassed over 30,000 pictures in the storehouse, collecting metaphors and images as I go. I have never been in doubt that what I do has value, but I have had fears about putting it into form. It now feels quite natural to be completing a book on these processes, and I have been able to get in touch with that part of me that likes to be seen and heard.

Sue: My first real visual art experience was with the Cycladic art forms that I spent a lot of time with in Greece. Twenty years ago I felt an attraction to these marble forms and when I went to Athens spent my free time at the museum*. I am a collector too, and have several dozen of these figures as well as fertility figures from other cultures. And, of course, I have quite a lot of cows! Two of the stories I use (The Laidley Worm and The Lady from the Stars)† have a central image of cows and milk!

---

* The marble cycladic female figures are still an archeological mystery. Thought to be grave idols – possibly for fertility – they demonstrate how flexible the sculptors were. When a mistake was made, it was incorporated into the statue instead of being scrapped.

† The Lady from the Stars is a fascinating story from South Africa re-told by Lawrence Van der Post in *Heart of the Hunter* (1961)

Åse: Through my own art-work and that of patients, as well as famous artists, I have learned that aesthetic is about bringing beauty out of ugliness. Many years ago when working with Arthur Robbins, whom we have referred to several times in this book, I made a clay figure of my father's hand; it was a very strong hand and the actual making of the sculpture made me aware how well this hand had become internalised in me. While working on this book my father died; a few weeks later I met Arthur again and he reminded me about the sculpture. I need to finish this book now and move onto the next one.

Sue: When my father died, my mother thought I should have his umbrella so that it would always protect me; 'so you are always under your father's umbrella'. This felt like being too much in his shadow so I bought myself a Shakespeare umbrella which I alternate with an Ibsen one!

Åse: So much of what we are writing about has female images; fertility pictures, containers, houses...but we also write about male influences and have case histories of male patients too. However, other writers say how most art therapy work is being done by women.

Sue: It is the same in dramatherapy. It is very rare to have an equal number of men and women on courses and workshops. And of course the Cycladic art is primarily about female forms. But my next big influence was Munch so perhaps it is more balanced...

In these Cycladic images, the female form goes from the very simple – the so called 'violin figure' – to the more complex. There is no written history in these figures, but the suggestion is that they represent various processes of pregnancy, so that in the picture we can see a non-pregnant figure, a pregnant one and then a 'post-partum' figure, indicated by the horizontal 'stretch marks'.

Many artists have been influenced by this art form, including Henry Moore. What interests me is that these people gave themselves such hard materials to work with – this marble makes it a long and arduous task; every figure follows exact proportions, so that these artists ranging from the first to the third millennia BC had a measuring system. I am also impressed by the way they incorporate mistakes into the sculptures, so that if a leg breaks, the figure ends up with shorter legs! It is suggested that the 'folded arm' variety came about to simplify the carving; there is a consistency in almost all the sculptures of the left hand being folded above the right.

It is suggested that these figures are grave goddesses from a fertility cult, however, some have been found that are life-size and almost all of them have pointed feet, which suggests that they should be lying down. There are male figures too (although very few) and they include musicians – a harpist and a pipe player, as well as a family group.

> *Vignette*
>
> When I was working with a group on landscapes, they were invited to go on an imaginary journey to a landscape and to discover an image. Over half the group 'brought back' violin figures which took up a large space in the landscape. The participants had never consciously seen any of this art, and were somewhat bemused as to where the images came from. However, they proved to be dominant symbols for the individuals in the group to work with, and provided a transition for them to create individual hero's journeys (see Chapter 9). It would seem that these images from an ancient culture served as a metaphor for entering therapeutic work.

The journeys that they chose to take were ancient journeys taken by well-known heroes. In one case the image created for Jason's search for the golden fleece turned out to be a placenta hung on a tree and the person cried and said it was the current struggle between herself and her husband. She was so desperate to have a child that she would go anywhere or do anything to achieve this.

Her desperation regarding childbirth was the focus of both the battle between the couple and her feelings of neglect because he did not appear to want children as much as she did. The placenta-on-the-tree image became a very powerful motive for the group and was later developed in work on 'preparing the fertile ground'. Åse and I did an extended version of this workshop recently in Norway, called 'Bearing Fruit', where we looked at the harvesting of what we had planted through the tree image and also the fruit that did not ripen. We worked with Robbins on this particular workshop and he reminded us that not only is there the fruit which is abundant and the fruit that does not develop – there is also the fruit that is wasted.

> When a picture is made in therapy it may 'uncloak' an image of which the artist was previously unconscious. Once such an image is pictured it is 'out there' rather than internal; it can be seen and this effects a change

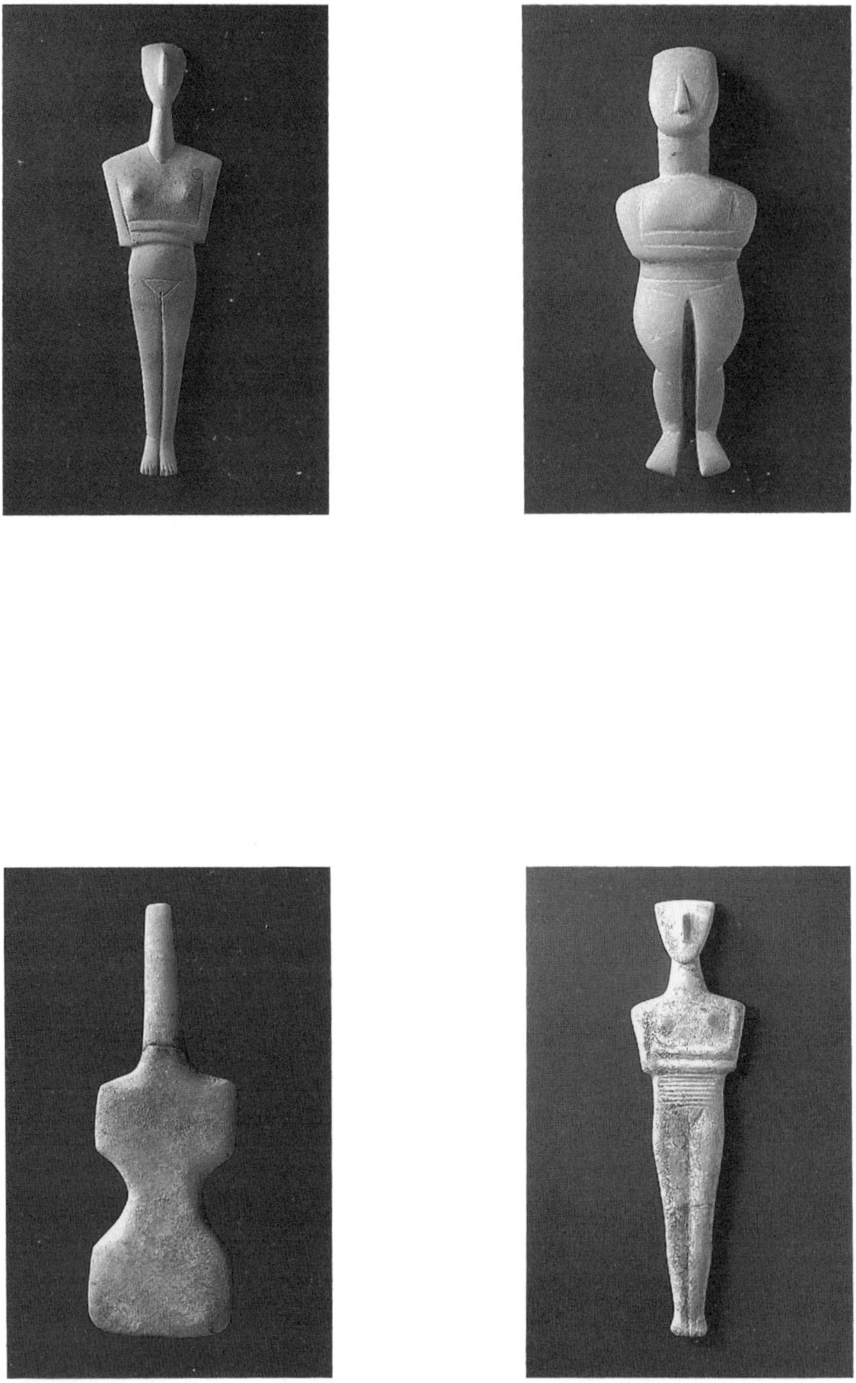

'Cycladic figures'

> from an unconscious state, in the artist, to a more conscious one. As a result of this, even without verbal interpretation, a transformation begins to take place in the inner world of the artist (Schaverien 1992, p.7).

We have also thought about the importance not only of an image being able to be 'uncloaked', but also of the times when an image or role needs to be 'cloaked'. In the various stories we describe, you will notice that people acquire cloaks – of wisdom, for example – in order to be able to finish their journey.

In discussing in brief some of our visual artistic influences, we must mention again that Åse worked in textile art and weaving before training as an art therapist more than 20 years ago. Her weaving continues to be such a creative part of her that Sue decided to give her the gift of an ancient image. Neumann (1963) has much to say about the Great Mother, and the connections with weaving and of course spiders' webs are very strong. The spider's web contains many associations. It can trap us as well as being able to heal – as we know from country folk remedies. The story of Arachne is told by Ovid: a Lydian girl challenged Athene to a tapestry-weaving contest, and when the goddess destroyed what she had done, she tried to kill herself and was changed into a spider.

> The dependency of all the luminous bodies, of all the heavenly powers and gods, on the Great Mother, their rise and fall, their birth and death, their transformation and renewal, are among the most profound experiences of mankind. Not only the alternation of day and night but also the changes in the months, seasons, and years are subordinated to the all-powerful will of the Great Mother. And that is why, not only as the Mesopotamian Tiamat, but throughout the world, she holds the tables of fate, the all-determining constellations of heaven, which is herself. And accordingly the Great Mother, adorned with the moon and the starry cloak of night, is the goddess of destiny, weaving life as she weaves fate (Neumann 1963, p.226).

> The primordial mystery of weaving and spinning has also been experienced in projection upon the Great Mother who weaves the web of life and spins the threads of fate, regardless whether she appears as one Great Spinstress or, as so frequently, in a lunar triad. It is not by accident that *we speak of the body's 'tissues'* for the tissue woven by the Feminine in the cosmos and in the uterus of woman is life and destiny. And astrology, the study of a destiny governed by the stars, teaches that both begin at once, at the temporal moment of birth.
>
> Thus the Great Goddesses are weavers, in Egypt as in Greece, among the Germanic peoples and the Mayans. And because 'reality' is wrought by the Great Weavers, all such activities as plaiting, weaving, and knotting belong to the fate-governing activity of the woman, who, as Bachofen

> discovered, is a spinner and weaver in her natural aspect (ibid. p.227 [our emphasis]).

As soon as we start to talk about 'plaiting, weaving and knotting' it opens up yet further imagery that leads us forward in our therapeutic work. The Queen Mab speech, from Shakespeare's *Romeo and Juliet* (reproduced in the appendix) contains the most superb 'plaiting' metaphors, as well as being an interesting image for what happens in dreams. The speech is spoken by Mercutio – a hot headed, impetuous friend who dies early in the play, trying to defend his friend's honour.

Sue: Shakespeare forms the bridge back again in terms of the theatre rooms in my storehouse to which we have not yet referred, being preoccupied with the process of discovering the hitherto hidden artistic and literary spaces. These spaces are very exciting and, of course, connected with the dramatic or sacred space. There was a time when theatrical, sacred and healing space was the same, and the three processes interconnected. Now the theatre, the church and the hospital are separate institutions and each is thereby weaker.

Separate and special 'space set apart' is a necessary prerequisite for the act of theatre or dramatherapy to take place. My experiences of theatre space started very early because I was taken to see classical ballet from the age of six and then took myself to Shakespeare from the age of eleven. I was fortunate to live for part of my childhood near Stratford-upon-Avon and to have the opportunity to immerse myself in the plays as well as the performances. My theatrical career lasted a few years, as a chorus dancer and then repertory actress, which encompassed a wide variety of roles especially in Shakespeare and Shaw – Puck, Maria, Nerissa, Jessica, understudy of Lady Macbeth and later Queen Margaret in Henry VI. All these plays in themselves (as well as the experience of playing parts in them) enriched my earlier life in ways that I am still discovering. It was a 'turning point' for me when I realised that extensive therapy did not 'cure' me of my wish to act; it rather allowed sufficient interior space for the acting to be able to function. Years ago, there seemed little enough of me to go round but now the storehouse feels full, with some reserve when stocks run low.

The act of theatre happens 'in the moment' and is therefore elusive and transitory. Although its effect may be lasting on observer or participant, the art form itself, unless captured on video or film, ends with the ending of the play or the scene. Traces linger both consciously and unconsciously; the inner-space is jostled so that the pieces form in different clusters

– maybe something has moved that has not moved before; we may not be aware of it, it may be just a sensation. A fleeting moment, a bird's wing against the cheek.

In the storehouse there is also the room with the tools or skills. The classes in movement and dance and voice, the sessions of improvisation and text work, the repeated attempts to 're-work' a line, a word, an inflection...it is to do with the capacity to 'stay with the experience' and to know when it is appropriate to move on. One of the misconceptions in both drama and dramatherapy is that it is a question of a roomful of techniques and games, rather than a creative and therapeutic process that engages with both individuals and groups.

I have learned much from the theatre director who insists on 'working through' at peak moments in the dramatic scene or text, compared with the extensive time spent in attempting 'working through' peak moments in my own therapy. Playing Queen Margaret, and even being the understudy of Lady Macbeth, showed me my own violence in epic form and both enabled me to understand myself a little more and to communicate these 'dramatic truths' to the assembled audience.

I also remember other types of 'truth'; for example, on a schools tour of *A Midsummer Night's Dream*, the lovers are finally asleep in the forest and Puck is going to put everything right again. Two boys in the front row said to each other, 'Are they dead?' 'Poke 'em and see' came the hissed reply. Whereupon Lysander was reduced to shaking silent laughter as a mucky finger jabbed him in the ribs. The shaking was infectious and all four lovers were quaking. Meanwhile, as Puck, I am waiting to do my bit – my voice comes out more like Joyce Grenfell than a forest sprite in an attempt not to corpse – there is another hiss, 'Told you they weren't dead, they're just ill'.'

Yet again, we have come back to forests and the stories that inhabit the storehouse in abundance. Stories and myths from many cultures and societies, the ancient as well as the new. How important it is to have feminist fairy stories as well as traditional tales and to be able to go beyond the obvious: to allow the contents of the storehouse to take on their own meanings and associations, once they are 'out there'. If we anticipate explanations and interpretations or force the material into certain theories, then our patients and clients are only there to service our needs and reinforce our identity.

We should continue to develop our languages through as wide a range of artistic experiences as possible as well as extending our own vocal capacity in its range and nuance. We need to be aware of when we are speaking the language of science and when we are trying to communicate in the language of art.

Robert Hobson, the distinguished psychotherapist, puts it this way:

> The language of the world of things is literal and discursive whereas person-talk calls for a 'language of the heart', which I term feeling-language. In order to 'disclose' to someone what I mean by 'I love you', I would have to tell stories: first one story, then another story, and another, and another, until the 'ice breaks' or 'the penny drops'. The 'disclosure' or 'discernment' calls for a language which is more akin to an art form, with symbols which do not merely point to discrete things, but rather 'present' a mode of being. A language not of 'facts' but of feeling (Hobson 1985, p.20).

The next chapter takes us into the movement in the storehouse, or cauldron; in particular the sea and sand images that we both find permeate our work. Meanwhile, the following quotations will, we hope, keep the creativity of thinking and feeling that these processes are engendering.

> Why does the aesthetic moment evoke in us a deep conviction that we have been in rapport with a sacred object? What is the foundation for this belief? It occurs, in part, because we experience this uncanny moment as an event that is partially sponsored by the object. Further, we cannot calculate when we will have an aesthetic experience. It is almost inevitably a surprise. This surprise, complemented by an experience of fusion with the object (icon, poem, musical sound, landscape, etc.), of feeling held by the object's spirit (Bollas 1987, p.31).

> All science is an attempt to cover with explanatory devices – and thereby to obscure – the vast darkness of the subject. It is a game in which the scientist uses his explanatory principles according to certain rules to see if these principles can be stretched to cover the vast darkness. But the rules of the stretching are rigorous, and the purpose of the whole operation is really to discover what parts of the darkness still remain uncovered by explanation (Bateson 1958, p.280).

CHAPTER 4

The Kettle of Transformation

Play and Paradox

WANGEL: I've just been up to see her, and she seemed quite calm. But underneath all her moods, there's something that I simply can't fathom – something hidden, that makes her so changeable all of a sudden, so unstable, so capricious.

ARNHOLM: That's only natural in her morbid state of mind.

WANGEL: It's not just that. Fundamentally, it's something that was born in her. The trouble is that Ellida comes of seafaring stock.

ARNHOLM: My dear Doctor, what exactly do you mean by that?

WANGEL: Haven't you ever noticed that the people who live by the open sea are like a race apart? It's almost as if the sea were a part of their lives; there are surges – yes, and ebbs and flows too – in all their thoughts and feelings. They can never bear to be separated from it – oh, I should have thought about that before. It was really a crime against Ellida to take her from out there and bring her here.

(Ibsen, *The Lady from the Sea*, p.298)

On the shores below, the ice-floes
crashed and splintered, yet no murmur
reached us, only swirling mist-shapes
leapt like dancers, weaving - singing -
round about our eyes and ears.

(Ibsen, *Peer Gynt*, p.25)

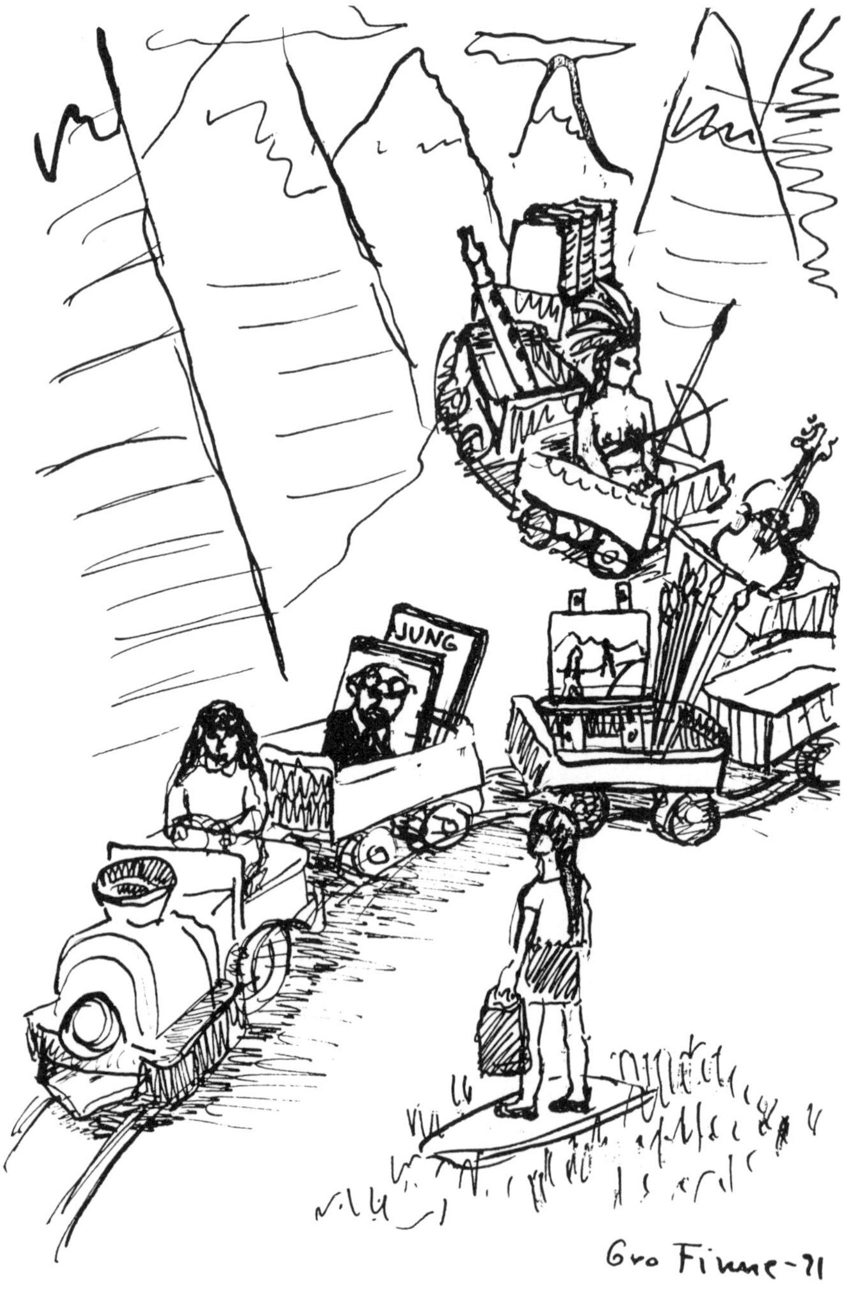

The therapist driving the train (by Gro Finne)

GONZOLO: Now would I give a thousand
furlongs of sea for an acre of barren
ground. Long heath, brown furze, anything.
The wills be done, but I would fain
die a dry death.

(*The Tempest*, I.i.61)

In Chapters 1 and 2 we introduced our individual work in dramatherapy and art therapy and discussed the formative influences in theory and practice that shaped our own work both in the early years and more recently. To put it another way, up until now we have been discussing our maps and signposts before commencing the joint voyage of our work together.

This chapter is concerned with the themes of paradox and transformation which take place in the art therapy and dramatherapy experience. Indeed, these themes have become part of the guiding light which steered us through our continuing joint exploration. Between the land-voyage and the sea-voyage is the sea-shore (or river-bank) – an in-between space where transformation can take place. We have both been preoccupied as children, and indeed as adults, with the invitation to play that the sea-shore always gives.*

Sue: Just as I described the fertility clinic where I work as a sea-shore on which a variety of human flotsam and jetsam is washed by the tide, similarly, art therapists and dramatherapists can be likened to beach-combers who inhabit this marginal space and search for treasures. The sea-shore is a meeting place of worlds where ships and people leave and arrive and boundaries are drawn. Different flowers grow in sand-dunes from those which grow further inland, or from even the seaweed itself.

Pirates, poets, explorers and sailors all have an intimate knowledge of the sea and the sand and the travels beyond their horizons and depths. Farmers, troubadours, artists, mountaineers and soldiers all have a similar knowledge of the land, the sand, the cross-country travels and the depths of Mother Earth. The land has layers; from the highest mountain to the deepest crevasse, as well as the caves, the tunnels and the whole of the subterranean world. The sea goes ever deeper as we voyage further; with terror when we cannot see the land in any direction and relief when the first tree-top is espied.

People create and paint and build with sand and are fascinated by the transitory nature of their creation as the sea comes and washes it away. The Navaho Indians create ritual sand-pictures and the Bavenda

* We both live in countries where there is substantial quantity of sea and a rich variety of stories of expeditions across the sea or treasures that arrived from the sea.

virgins form python coils with their movements on the soil in a fertility dance (though both of these rituals take place inland rather than on the sea-shore). Play therapists, art therapists and dramatherapists assist their patients in re-creating miniature sea-shores in the sandtrays in their therapy and playrooms.

The sandtray provides the opportunity for both children and adults to explore texture, substance and form through dry, damp and 'sloppy' sand (Mr Jeremy Fisher's larder was 'all slippy sloppy')*; by building castles, mountains, tunnels and caves; by creating shapes and patterns with stones and shells – and then wiping the slate clean with a single stroke.

> Timon hath made his everlasting mansion
> Upon the beachèd verge of the salt flood,
> Who once a day with his embossèd froth
> The turbulent surge shall cover.
>
> (*Timon of Athens*, V.i.213)

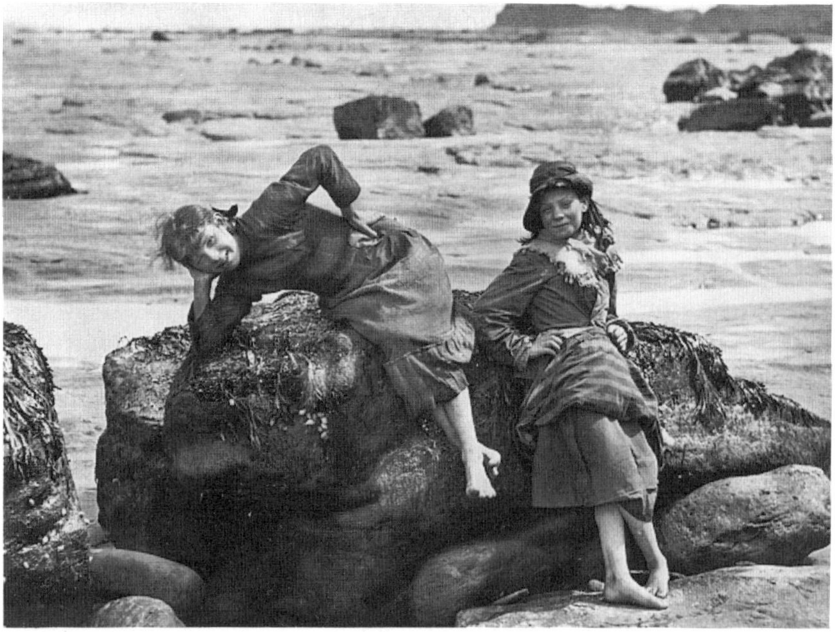

'Limpets', Frank Meadow Sutcliffe (1880)

* The sounds of these words are remembered from the Beatrix Potter books, even when the story becomes hazy to an adult; another example is 'pit-pat waddle pat' of Jemima Puddleduck in *The Tale of Tom Kitten.*

Playtherapy literature is beginning to multiply; 1992 may well be remembered as the year of Playtherapy (or Play Therapy). There are now six new books by five different publishers* and professional training for playtherapists is now established in the U.K. and Greece as a discipline in its own right. In fact, most artistic therapists acknowledge that the roots of their work have their beginnings in childhood play, and some incorporate sandplay and its variations into work with children and adults. There is also a growing number of people who work as 'sandplay therapists', most of whom pay allegiance to Jung.

> The world technique, like the extended dramatisation, involves a dramatic representation of self, family and community. Unlike the extended dramatization though, the world technique proceeds through small objects which represent one's inner vision of the world. As one projects his image of self, family, and community onto the objects, manipulating them through free play, he enacts a drama in the presence of the therapist (Landy 1986, p.165).

> He stood staring at the tray for a while and then ran his hands into the sand. He caressed it, felt it, ran his hands through it as though discovering the texture of sand for the first time in his life. Just having his hands in it seemed to satisfy some hunger (Weinrib 1983, p.45).

> The child experiences, quite unconsciously, what I call a free, and at the same time, a protected space (Kalff 1980, p.39).

> The children who work in the sandtray come in direct contact with some of the universal symbols and have a chance to understand their lives in terms of these symbols. Regardless of whether te individual understands the significance of the symbols, by using the sand tray he seems to fell liberated as the more painful, angry and confusing parts of himself surface, at last communicating had been locked inside. Symbolically, a bridge is laid between fantasy and reality. In fact, a miniature of a bridge is a frequently used miniature once a person starts to reach out to life. As a transition and a communication tool, the bridge is often a connection to life itself (Dundas 1978, p.6).

> World can be static or dynamic and it is this second possibility which is of such value with children. The life of a child both externally and interiorly, is one of action. Their own experiences and those of the constituent world around them are seen by children as stories: stories which can be endlessly repeated or varied and whose endings on one occasion, even if this ending be total destruction of all constituents, have

* The following Playtherapy books were all published in 1992–1993
Ann Cattanach, *Play Therapy with Abused Children*
Sue Jennings *Play Therapy with Children*
Joel Ryce Menuhin *Jungian Sandplay*
Levret McMahon *Handbook of Play Therapy*
Janet West *Child-centred Play Therapy*
Shlomo Ariel *Strategic Family Play Therapy*

> no effect upon the next beginning. These can be directly represented in the World tray, played out, analysed with the therapist, and the contents realised as they appear in endless repetitions (Lowenfeld 1979, p.14).

Lowenfeld says that for the World technique, the therapist needs a vast array of toys and objects in order for the child to have choices in the worlds that they create. As with journey boxes (Jennings, 1993b), the toys in sandplay allow for the child's imagination and, in my own experience, a range of toys that includes a variety of materials – pottery, wood, durable plastic, cloth and so on, rather than enormous numbers of the same type of toy – can well serve the person's imagined worlds. Some people prefer to work with 'natural' objects, as described above, and also experiment with painting the sand.

Above all, the importance of the sandplay, as with the sea-shore, is that it is at the margins and borders of our experience which ebbs and flows in and out of life's experience. Both of us make use of sandplay in our work in art therapy and dramatherapy, both as a bridge into 'larger' work and also in itself, if that is where the patient guides us. One thing we are both firm on is that the toys we use are very good quality. The pottery figures mentioned in Chapter 5 provide a range of family and work-roles, including three-generational families, which people are drawn to and identify with very easily.

Åse: In the art therapy work room, I am usually seated by the big wooden table where the sandtray is placed, next to the shelves holding all the small animals, and objects and, of course, paints, crayons, clay and other materials. I often find the animals provide a starting point for patients at the beginning of therapy; they will say something like 'I used to have a cat' or 'I never was allowed to have a pet', so being prompted to begin their story.

Clinical Example

A psychotic young man, twenty-five years old was referred for art therapy. He was extremely paranoid and always 'on guard'. He came into the art therapy room like a shadow, looked around briefly and then went to sit at the sandtray. I sat across from him and he started to play with the sand. He asked me:

Patient: Do you know how it feels to walk on sand?

Therapist: I like to walk barefoot on a beach. What about you?

Patient: I don't like the sand in my shoes. It gets everywhere, between my toes and I can't get rid of it. It gets to you. Sand, sand, SAND. Maybe I'll build a castle in sand.

Next session he went back to the sandtray:

Therapist: Do you want to build a castle in sand?

He built a castle on top of a mountain with a moat surrounding it.

Patient: Up there no-one can see me. There are seven gates into my castle made out of iron. You will have to cross the moat by boat and then climb the mountain before you start on the gates.

Therapist: Do you feel lonely in the castle?

Patient: Well, at least she won't get to me there — my mother.

Later he revealed that he and his mother had lived together in an incestuous relationship.

I worked with this patient for two years before he was discharged to a halfway house. For several months the therapy sessions took place in the sandtray. His first metaphor of the castle stayed with him for a long time. I felt I had to be very careful with my 'moves'; it was like a game of chess between us. After eight months his hand touched mine in the sand and he said:

Patient: Do you know that words in the sand get washed away but buried in the sea. My wounds might be wiped away but buried inside me.

This example clearly illustrates how art therapy and dramatherapy meet. As an art therapist I use different media in order to reach the patient on different levels. I believe that to meet the needs of clients we need to know that we can cross each others borders. Some practitioners no doubt would call the sandtray work playtherapy, but for me it is clearly art therapy. Whereas I use the metaphor of a game of chess, Robbins (1989) likens it to a dance, or 'an art therapeutic diptych'.

> Throughout this dance, a variety of images between therapist and patient interplay on both a conscious and unconscious level and create a dynamic interactive art form, or what I call the art therapeutic diptych. When working, the ongoing sessions have an aliveness, integrity, authenticity, and rhythm or balance. Each session becomes a work of art with a theme, the theme weaving in and out of any number of sessions. Just as any artist faces blocks or becomes stale and repetitive, however, so, too, do therapist and patient become lost in the evolving therapeutic process. Stagnation arises from the homeostatic forces within the patient or therapist struggling against the counter-forces toward change. The traditional interpretations that normally bring patient and therapist back

in sync with one another do not seem to help. While both parties can equally resist the call for change, it is hoped that the therapist is more in touch with his or her resistance to the unknown, and consciously works to master them (Robbins 1989, p.10–11).

Sue: In my room at the London Hospital Medical College, I have a variety of toys and small objects and also a collection of different containers with various objects inside them. These include small painted boxes, tins with story pictures and woven baskets, from sizes that can be held in the hand to those than can be held on the knee. These provide starting points for certain clients. A colour or shape or scene seems to arrest their attention and the drama unfolds.

Clinical Example

A young man was referred for therapy shortly after he married because he was unable to have sexual intercourse with his wife. They were both Jewish and wanted to have children straight away. He felt it would be a total disgrace if he did not produce children. After the first consultation he said that he wanted to come and see me again on his own.

He picked up the various containers and found one with 'monster toys' inside.

Patient: That's me. All monstrous and horrible. I feel such a bad person.

I suggested he created a sculpture of himself, using different animals and objects to portray the different sides of himself. He built a heap of the monsters – dinosaurs, snakes, and wild 'cats' and behind them placed a 'wobbly jelly' animal that looks formless and above that he placed a furry octopus that he spread to make it look quite menacing.

(*Teaching Point* – In sandtray and small animal work, it facilitates the process if you have different levels – not just under the sand, I use a small set of shelves which enables different perspectives.)

Patient: That's me – all those nasty monsters and a disgusting weak thing hiding behind. And this (indicating the octopus) is waiting and watching all the time.

Rather than attempt any interpretation of the above, I asked him if there was anything else he would like to put in the picture – perhaps something he was in the past or that he would like to be in the future. He did not talk but went through all the animals and then placed a lamb and an elephant by the 'jelly' creature.

Although he stayed in therapy for several years, his potency returned in a few months. The main story that he worked with in therapy was of early homosexual play with other children, and then of accompanying the leader of expeditions to public lavatories to wait for men. This period of his life had lasted about a year when he was ten, but the effect had been to make him feel, in his own words, utterly 'disgusting and filthy', with the fear that he could damage or pollute his wife.

We have both built up a large collection of animals and objects to use in our work and also acquired the special trays that printshops use for different type-faces, that have lots of small compartments. These can be hung on the wall to house a selection of small animals and people. It looks like a many-roomed house and can be a stimulus for people to see that things can break out of an ordinary pattern i.e. the toys don't have to be grouped 'like with like'.

In my work with drug abusers, I find that many of them have difficulty talking about themselves and are also very ambivalent about receiving therapy in the first place. The animals provide helpful metaphors that are sufficiently distanced for them to be able to come closer. A starting point can be the choice of two animals and then an invitation to write a story, or create an environment for the animals to feel safe in. This type of story is deliberately in the third person in order to maintain the distance.

Clinical Example

One man in a group took a lamb and a woodpecker. He painted a picture of the lamb with the woodpecker on its back.

He said that the lamb was very kind and tolerant and did not complain about the woodpecker sitting on his back and pecking him until he bleeds.

In his second picture the lamb is biting the woodpecker's neck. The lamb had lost patience and was going to try and kill the woodpecker. He then went on to say that the two animals are himself when he needs drugs.

Patient: The lamb is standing still. The woodpecker in me makes me move and get somewhere in life but then the lamb stops me. The woodpecker needs the lamb as without the lamb it will not find rest.

Within the context of transformations it is important to pay some attention here to the phenomenon of transference and counter-transference. Therapists generally now recognise that transference happens in daily life in all kinds of situations and can become the focus of therapy. When the art therapist or dramatherapist enters the media with the client, he or she needs to be aware that that media creates other transferential themes that within, say, classical psychoanalysis are kept con-

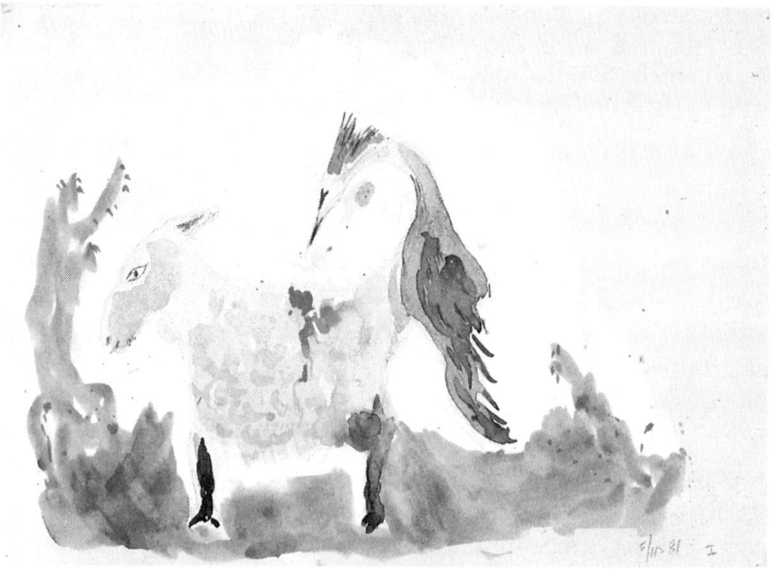

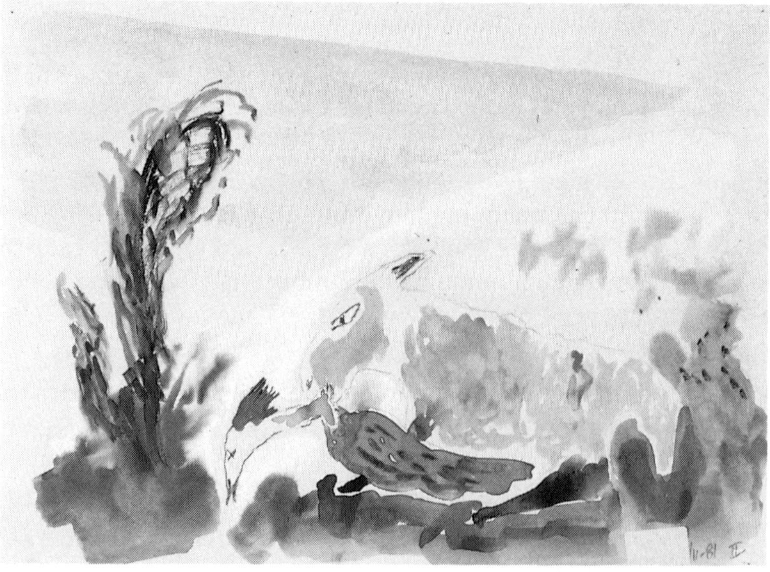

stant. The client is able to project a vast range of fantasy onto the therapist if they maintain, as far as possible, a neutral stance (see Read Johnson 1992), however direct engagement *with* the client through art or drama often means that the transferential relationship is being addressed in the here and now. For example, when Mike came to a therapy session and asked if he could check the times and dates of the next two sessions, he went on to being very angry with the women in his life. Having created the safety of his sessions, he was able to begin to verbally attack me in terms of 'you are all the same you women'. We set up a series of vignettes where he put me into role as women from his childhood (he had been surrounded by elderly female relatives) and he was able to express his feelings of being trapped and smothered.

As I have written elsewhere (Jennings 1986b, 1987);(see also Landy 1986, 1992), transference is a dramatic act. We behave towards other 'as if' they are significant others in our lives, and although the material thus expressed is usually unconscious, to create the transferential scene can move blocked experiences further on. So many people when they attend therapy have become stuck in a circular relationship or set of relationships that repeat themselves in destructive ways. Also, we find that people relate to the unacknowledged, especially idealised part of themselves. For example, the young impotent man described above saw his wife as the lamb he had put in the sculpture (remembering also the pascal lamb and the connection between goodness and sacrifice). He said how good and pure she was and how vile and destructive he was.

Landy suggests that most dramatherapy transference is conscious because of the 'casting in role' of the other. However, he goes on to say that unconscious transference themes do arise as follows:

> ...in dramatherapy transference, transference is overt. Both client and therapist, by definition, cast each other into alternative roles. It is a healthy act rather than a neurotic one. However within the imaginative act of transference, an unconscious component might arise, as for instance, the client attributes an excessive amount of energy to a role enacted by the therapist (Landy 1992, p.104).

In effect, what I think is being said is that the act of drama in itself, by casting others into roles, can bring about unconscious material in the dramatherapy; thus the consciously played out piece of theatre leads into an unconscious dramatic scene. Landy goes on to say:

> Dramatic transference becomes most pronounced when the client (or the therapist, in the sense of counter-transference), chronically casts the other in the same role (ibid).

This is exactly what happened with Mike and his many women. Having illustrated through the vignettes the issue of the many elderly female relatives, I moved the situation into a greater distancing to work with fairy stories and good and bad witches. This eventually enabled some internalisation of these projected roles, as well as reconciling the 'good and evil old woman' of his transference.

Transference and counter-transference in art therapy

Åse: During art therapy patients start to give form to their feelings, which have often lain within them for a long time. These feelings are transferred to a piece of art by the patient and, when the therapist 'meets' this artistic expression, the feelings can be transformed.

The phenomenon of transference occurs between the patient and the therapist at the time in hand, but naturally aspects of the patient's former life and relationships are also involved. The therapeutic use of transference is to interpret these earlier experiences and to understand and integrate them so that they become a part of the *conscious* ego-controlled content of the patient's psychic life.

> In art therapy the image often becomes the focus through which the transference relationship is explored (Case and Dalley 1992, pp.60–62).

It is of great importance, therefore, that the art therapist is able to express to the patient that they are strong enough to contain the material that the patient is ready to expose.

During the years of working as an art therapist, my own development, including supervision, on both a professional and a personal level has made it easier to be a container for the many different and sometimes very heavy transferences from patients. I feel the subject of supervision is taken far too lightly by many therapists; it is extremely important in order to achieve 'containerability' and to be able to 'see through' the patient's 'mirror'. It is all too easy to blend in aspects of one's own personal scenario so that the therapy reflects, for example, not only the patient's mother, but the mother of the therapist and the therapist as a mother too!

Even so, I have sometimes found my own counter-transference on a patient to be useful: information and help for a therapeutic situation has come to me through my dreams, for example.

> *Vignette*
>
> I was once the therapist for an anorexic patient and had been working on her mixed feelings towards her mother. For a long time only feelings of anger and hate had been in focus.
>
> Just before a session with this patient, I was having a teabreak in the staffroom of the psychiatric ward where I worked and, glancing through a women's magazine, began to read an article about a pair of Siamese twins who had lived for more than twenty years with their heads grown together at the forehead. I was horrified, and thought: 'Can this be possible?'
>
> Later, during the session, the patient became full of anger and talked and talked:
>
> 'I have no money (she said); the social security doesn't give me enough. Last night my mother came to see me in my flat and she had to spend the night in my bed because I wasn't given enough money to buy a guestbed. We had to share the same pillow.'
>
> As she was talking she had been drawing a picture of her and her mother's head lying on the same pillow but, at the forehead, the heads were joined. I was amazed, having so recently seen a picture of Siamese twins, and chose to share my thoughts with her.
>
> I told the patient what I had seen in the magazine and how I could not rid myself of the feeling of how painful it must be to be two different persons with different personalities, yet joined together.
>
> The patient looked at me with eyes full of tears and said, 'That's right, it is so painful: I realised last night just how stuck I have been with my mother; but I also felt, for the first time in my life, that I was able to understand her and that life has not been easy for her either.'

There have been many similar situations during sessions where metaphors from the patient or from my own life have been helpful in the therapeutic process.

> However sad, mad, or bad children may have felt themselves to be, creative art and activities have enabled change to come about. Inner worlds have been expressed; fantasies and feelings have taken shape and colour in the magic play of art. The 'Wendy' house has been a sanctum – a house within a room; a stage-set for a drama, which I could either watch or share – or a wholly secret place (Halliday 1987, p.128).

We have both been drawn time and again in both our clinical work and our teaching to the story of 'The Invisible Child' told by Tove Jansson in '*Tales from Moominvalley*', which concerns a small child who is 'made invisible' through the harshness and sarcasm of her aunt. (We mention this story in Chapter 6 when discussing the work we are doing in relation to artistic therapy and the body). 'The Invisible Child' is often a relevant story for people with eating disorders because so often they have a feeling of either not being seen or of being seen in a negative way. This genre of story, like the sandtray or the journey box, can be used as a space to play in – or a playpen – with an extensive range of methods and techniques.

Another example is Alice in Wonderland (Carroll 1865), in which Alice says to the Caterpillar when he asks her who she is that she does not know because she isn't herself:

> 'Who are *you*?' said the Caterpillar.
>
> This was not an encouraging opening for a conversation. Alice replied, rather shyly, 'I – I hardly know, sir, just at present – at least I know who I *was* when I got up this morning, but I think I must have been changed several times since then.'
>
> 'What do you mean by that?' said the Caterpillar sternly. 'Explain yourself!'
>
> 'I can't explain *myself*, I'm afraid, sir,' said Alice, 'because I'm not myself, you see.'
>
> (Lewis Carroll 1865, *Alice's Adventures in Wonderland)*

Similarly, people who come into therapy feel that 'they are not themselves' or that they are 'beside themselves'. The process of transformation can allow people to 'find themselves'.

The story 'The Invisible Child' opens with the aunt, a kind of messenger character, arriving at the Moomintrolls' house to hand over the invisible child. The family are engaged in a very homely and creative activity of peeling mushrooms. A summary of the story is as follows:

> *'The Invisible Child' in* ***Tales from Moominvalley*** *by Tove Jansson*
>
> This short story, about a child, contains psychological undertones, although it is written as a children's tale depicting imaginary characters.
>
> Ninny has been repressed and treated with sarcasm by those nearest to her; she reacts by becoming invisible and it is not until she is welcomed into the warmth of the Moomin family that she begins to feel safe enough to express her own personality and thus become visible again. Grandmother's old recipe book is a starting point for Moomintroll Mama's attempt to allow her to be visible again.
>
> At first, Ninny finds it difficult to be childlike – she is insecure and unable to show her emotions except by retreating into an invisible world where

she cannot be seen to be hurt. Even spontaneous play, which is natural to most children, she finds almost impossible.

'Run, run, can't you!' My cried, 'Or can't you even jump?' Ninny's thin legs dutifully ran and jumped.

'She can't play', mumbled Moomintroll.

'She can't get angry' little My said, 'That's what's wrong with her...You'll never have a face of your own until you've learned to fight. Believe me.'

Gradually, however, Ninny's confidence is built up, particularly by Moominmama's small attentions, for she recognises Ninny as a real person and finds time for her as an individual. Moominmama makes the child a pretty dress from her own rose-pink shawl, she follows little bedtime rituals and shows humour, patience and understanding. When Ninny has an accident with the jar containing apple cheese and it breaks, Moominmama reassures her with a positive and perceptive comment:

'And Granny always said that if you want the earth to grow something for you, then you have to give it a present in the autumn.'

Symbolically, if a child is to develop, then the child must be nurtured.

Slowly Ninny begins to make an impact on the family so that the whole family unit benefits from the increased 'communication'. Moominpapa clears his throat:

'We're happy to see' he started, 'that we see more of Ninny today. The more we see the happier we are.'

The breakthrough for Ninny's true personality occurs when Moominpapa playfully attempts to push Moominmama into the water from the landing stage. Because of Moominmama's continuing caring concern for her, Ninny's growing loyal affection comes to the fore and in defence of Moominmama she bites Moominpapa's tail.

This is the catalyst for the release of Ninny's inhibitions and as she feels free to burst into laughter for the first time, her whole personality comes to life and she finally becomes completely visible to those around her.

If you read the story to a group there are certain images that immediately stand out. They usually are:

1. The pile of mushrooms of different sorts on the table.
2. The invisible child with a bell round her neck.
3. Grandmother's recipe book.
4. The child's brown paws appearing as the first thing visible.
5. Mother saying 'And Granny always said that if you want the earth to grow something for you then you have to give it a present in the autumn.'

6. Ninny biting Moominpapa in anger and then laughing.

If we look at these images, they actually provide a structure for exploring the whole story. Each of them may be painted, modelled, or acted, or created in a combination of media. We have both found that the beginning, with the family around the table sorting mushrooms, provides an earthy, growing metaphor as well as one of fine variety in the delicate variations of different types of mushrooms (the good food contrasted with the deadly poison).

The arrival of the messenger aunt, 'the rescuer', is a role that many people identify with and can be explored through an enactment of the first scene.

In workshops we often ask people to keep a diary to record their experiences. As an alternative, in one workshop we asked a group to create a recipe book. They started off with sayings, ideas and 'recipes' that they could remember from their childhood. During the workshop they were asked to create different 'recipes' to address problems that needed a resolution.

We also explored the transformation of mother's shawl into the red dress for the child – the people in the group considered whether there was anything from their parents that they would like to change into something for themselves; (compare this with the Inanna story in Chapter 9 where people removed 'symbolic garments' that had come from their parents and that they did not want).

We have developed the scene where the whole family is picking apples in the orchard and Ninny drops the apple cheese in various improvisations. The saying of Grandmother's about giving a present to the earth as a contrast to the sarcasm of the aunt proved a tearful moment for many people. They were reminded of the sarcasm and ridicule that they had suffered as children and how difficult it is for a child to find an advocate.

> The scorn and abuse directed at the helpless child as well as the suppression of vitality, creativity, and feeling in the child and in oneself permeate so many areas of our life that we hardly notice it anymore. Almost everywhere we find the effort, marked by varying degrees of intensity and by the use of various coercive measures, to rid ourselves as quickly as possible of the child within us – i.e., the weak, helpless, dependent creature – in order to become an independent, competent adult deserving of respect (Miller, 1987, p.58).

However, the final scene, in which Ninny is able to express her anger, is perhaps the most important. This scene is very relevant, especially to many women who have grown up trying to control their anger but who have responded by crying instead. For the theme of this chapter, it is significant that the final scene of transformation – of the family being able to see Ninny for the first time – takes place on the sea-shore while the family are having a picnic.

The sub-title of this chapter is 'Play and Paradox' and we perhaps need to make some additional reference, especially as the word 'paradox' is in regular usage in our language now, especially in therapy. According to the dictionary, it has been in little use since the seventeenth-century, but several meanings are given:

1. A statement or tenet contrary to received opinion or belief.
2. A statement seemingly self-contradictory or absurd, though possibly well-founded or essentially true.
3. A phenomenon that exhibits some conflict with preconceived notions of what is reasonable or possible: a person of perplexingly inconsistent life or behaviour.

Oxford Concise Dictionary

> Ay, truly. For the power of beauty will sooner transform honesty from what it is to a bawd than the force of honesty can translate beauty into his likeness. This was sometime a paradox, but now the time gives it proof. I did love you once.
>
> (*Hamlet*, III.i.115)

We consider Napier (1986) is helpful for therapists when he says:

> A paradox is something that appears self-contradictory, a thing that at some time, or from a particular point of view, appears to be what it is not. Logically, paradoxes appear to infringe upon the law of contradiction, upon the logical prohibition against being and not being at the same time...
>
> We know what things look like and recognize specific change because we are aware that something is no longer what it was. Our awareness of change is, thus, essential for resolving the ambiguity that is basic to paradox (ibid, p.1).

Cox and Theilgaard (1987) talk about the paradox of the Aeolian Mode (drawn from poiesis rather than poetry), to be both supportive and confrontational simultaneously. Their book, *Mutative Metaphors in Psychotherapy* is essential for all artistic therapists engaged in understanding symbolic and metaphorical worlds, especially the chapter entitled 'The

Listening Landscape' (p.123). However, in the previous chapter, in the discussion of metaphors and their capacity to be mutative, they say:

> We have given many examples of the way in which metaphor can serve as a container for feelings which are too overwhelming to be tolerated. We have also shown how it can prove to be a vehicle for carrying, mobilizing, expressing, and integrating affect and cognition in furthering the therapeutic process. Metaphor exerts its mutative effect by energising alternative perspectival aspects of experience (ibid, p.99)

The above describes the essence of the paradox that is inherent not only in poiesis but also in artistic therapies. What we term 'the healing metaphor'* is paradoxical in nature and therefore has the possibility of transforming our experience. This leads us into the main title of this chapter, 'The Transformative Kettle' – an expression which we first discovered in the work of Eric Neumann in *The Great Mother*. He says:

> The kettle of transformation is identical with the Øsacrificial blood bowl whose content the priestess requires in order to achieve her magical purpose...it 'contains' the soul... The necessity of its use rests on the matriarchal belief that even in the womb no life can be built up without blood. For this reason the kettles of Mexico, the bloodbowls, like the cauldrons of the underworld, are vessels of transformation on which depend fertility, light, and transformation (Neumann 1955, p.288)

The recurring image in this chapter is that of the therapeutic container that can 'hold' the patient while transformation is possible. Within artistic therapy, this holding factor is not only the therapist in person, but also the medium through which they are working. So the sea-shore or the sand-tray, the sculpture, the picture, the scene and the play, the fairytale, the myth and the mask are all containers – as well as the therapeutic room itself.

Sue: In our developing relationship and artistic exploration, we have both been aware not only of the development of our own artistry, which we discuss in the next chapter, but also the larger 'frame' within which both of our therapies are housed. It was not until I worked in Scandinavia that I began to fully appreciate the art of the painter Edvard Munch. His popular 'Scream' is copied and quoted in so much literature that it obscures for the non-specialist in art the amazing range of his life and work. I had not known that he knew Stanislavski and had completed some designs for the theatre. I find his images of illness and depression as well as the pictures which depict women as well as sperm, healing metaphors which speak right to the heart of my own work as well as

* *Metaphor and Healing* is the title of a book being written by Dr Mooli Lahad on his work with damaged children . Like my term 'The Theatre of Healing', it is an attempt to convey the complexity of the process inherent in this therapy.

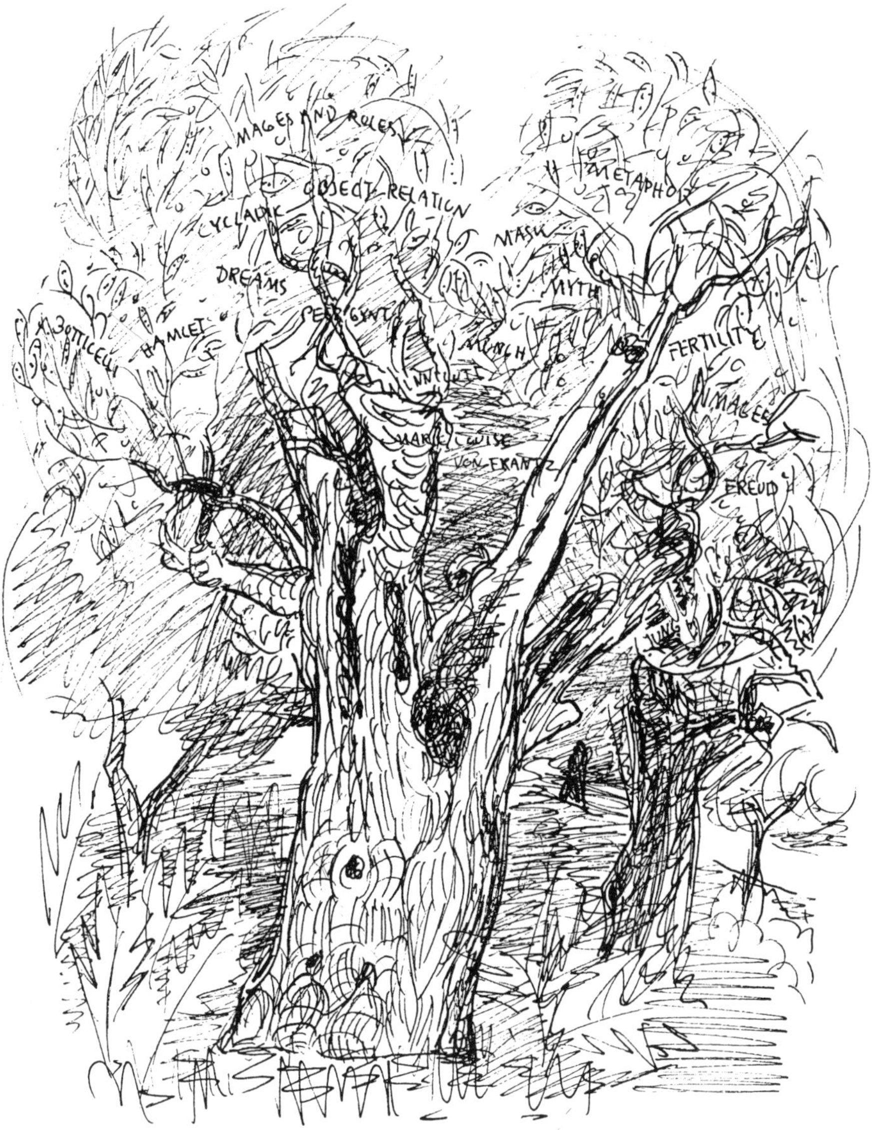

The therapist's tree

into myself. Similarly, when Åse came with me to The Royal Shakespeare Company to see 'Pericles' – not one of Shakespeare's most accessible plays – she found a voyage of discovery which incorporated all of human experience as well as therapeutic and healing journeys. We have often discussed how dramatherapy also needs the phrase 'theatre-art' in order to incorporate the very form from which it has grown over time. In pre-great theatre times when theatre forms were ritualistic and religious in nature, many of them were performed for preventative or curative purposes. The circular shapes that we refer to in later chapters were once the sacred spaces that contained the healing theatre. Performances of the ancient Greek theatre were also held for 'therapeutic reasons', as mentioned in Chapter 1. The two words 'drama' and 'theatre', are needed to encompass the vastness of the form. Similarly, 'art' as a word is used in the general sense to cover several art-forms and needs to be qualified as visual art. Why, then, is not all art visual, we might ask?

Having worked in several cultures as an anthropologist, I can see that the strict borders that we place in the West between the several art-forms, do not necessarily apply cross-culturally. For example, the healing dramas performed by the Temiar in Malaysia incorporate music, singing, dance as well as drama; there are 'ritual objects' created for the specific performance – head-dresses, whisks and fans. The healing dramas integrate all of what we in the West would call 'the arts' (Jennings, 1993) and, furthermore, they are often prompted by people's dreams or else their illnesses. Finally, the Temiar themselves refer to these sessions as playing – not to mean that they are not serious, but usually to indicate that deep trance and contact with more dangerous spirits will not take place.

> ELLIDA: No fascination and no terror. I could have faced it – become a part of it – if I had only wished to. Now that I could choose it, I could also reject it.
>
> WANGEL: I'm slowly beginning to understand you. You think and reason in pictures – in visual images. This longing of yours – this yearning for the sea, and the fascination that *he* – this stranger – had for you, were really only the expression of a new and growing urge in you for freedom.
> ...That's all.

(Ibsen, *The Lady from the Sea*, p.328)

CHAPTER 5

The Fertile Relationship

GREENCLAD ONE: Well, there's one thing you must remember.
That is the way of the mountain people.
Everything there has another meaning.
If you come to my father's house, you may easily think
You're just in an ugly heap of stones.

PEER: Well now, it's exactly the same with us.
Our gold may seem scrap to you
You may think each crystal window-pane
Is just a fistful of socks and rags.

GREENCLAD ONE: Black seems white and ugly seems fair.

PEER: Great seems little and foul seems clean.

GREENCLAD ONE: O, Peer! I see it! We were made for each other!

(Ibsen, *'Peer Gynt'*, p.62)

In this chapter, we attempt to articulate in greater depth the way that we work and play, despite the fact that we are unable to spend protracted periods of time together.

Sue: During the first few years of the Summer and Autumn Schools, apart from telephone conversations and letters, we met only once a year. It is only since 1988 that I have been visiting Norway to run the Oslo dramatherapy training programme on behalf of The Institute of Dramatherapy*, allowing Åse and I to spend more time together, largely in the planning and discussions for this book. Both of us have major commitments in our work and private lives and undertake frequent travelling to other countries for both work and family. However, there has always been a curious kind of synchronicity in the way we plan and work together.

---

* The Institute of Dramatherapy (see Appendix) runs professional training courses in Oslo, Norway, as well as other countries.

Sometimes this can be quite disturbing for students – on several occasions we have opened our mouths at the same time and said the same thing in chorus! Such an example was during the use of the Moomintroll story of 'The Invisible Child' (see Chapter 4), when we said to the group at the same time:

> It is important to connect with our grandmothers and their recipe books of wisdom.

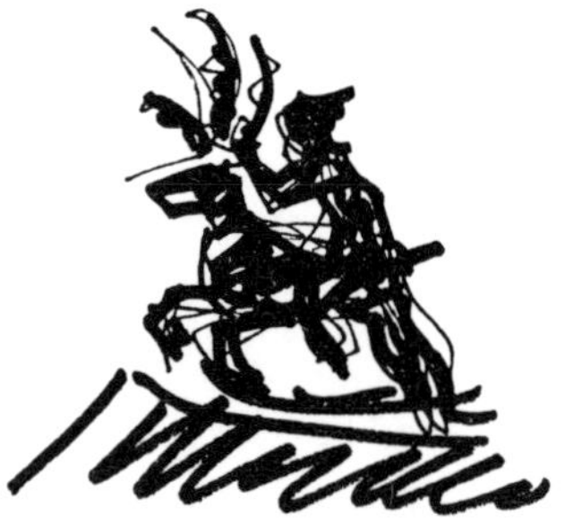

Peer Gynt by Gro Finne

The students often think we have planned a meticulous script in advance and so it is partly for them that we are trying to understand this collaborative creative process that is paradoxically so similar and yet so different. This co-thinking and co-feeling started many years ago – the following is an apt example.

Åse, supported by The British Council, was visiting the UK to conduct a survey of different art therapy training programmes. It was at a particularly busy time in both our lives and we only had time for a brief meeting in London in a little café near Euston Station. Åse greeted me with a hug, and said 'I have brought you two more figures for your sculpting and playtherapy work'* as she gave me a small packet. I opened it and said 'How clever of you to choose exactly the appropriate figures.'

'What do you mean?', said Åse, 'I just took two that I didn't think you had.' 'Well' I replied, 'one is of a woman holding a new baby and the other is a patient undergoing surgery: you are just about to have your first baby, and I am convalescing after surgery!'

Part of this process comes from a total trust in the creativity and person of the other; even if we do not understand what the other person is doing, we can both trust each other enough to go with it, as we illustrate later in this chapter. We are also intrigued by each other's work and, although neither of us would feel either confident enough to train in the other's

---

* Dramatherapists use the term 'sculpting' to describe a particular kind of projective technique. People re-create their worlds – their family, their life as a whole and so on – through small toys and objects (mini and macro sculpting), chairs, people (life-size sculpting), large objects, ladders, platforms, people standing on chairs and so on (larger-than-life and epic sculpting). The sculpt that is used in dramatherapy can be moved and changed back to how it was before. See Jennings (1990) for more detailed descriptions of sculpting methods.

discipline or even that it would be appropriate, nevertheless we both feel we have learned in a unique way from each other's work.

> The imagination of the actor adorns the text of the play with fanciful patterns and colours from his own invisible palette (Stanislavski 1937).

The following telephone conversation took place in November 1983 after we had been collaborating for five years.

Åse: Sue? This is Åse ... (pleasantries about weather, children and parents). The summer seminar? I've been thinking about possible themes and talking with Gunvor. Have you any thoughts?

Sue: I'd like to work with houses. I've been collecting pictures of houses and doors and working with models. What about you?

Åse: Oh Sue, I love that theme. It's funny that you bring that up because lately I have been thinking so much about house shelters. Gunvor and I actually did some work on the room inside and the room outside; building pyramids; keeping inside your inner private feelings, outside what you want to share with others.

Sue: We could build houses and shelters, small ones and big ones.

Åse: Let's start with some claywork, focusing on them as a way of projecting feelings about their own bodies; then we can create a shelter for the clay figure, a symbolic place they can go to be safe if they feel uncertain in the group...

Sue: What about the dance and movement, especially as we are working with a dance therapist?

Åse: If we work with the projected body feelings then before that, Gunvor could start in movement and dance for people to get into their own bodies.

We feel that the process of our relationship is rather like a marriage, where we need to be aware of each other's vulnerable areas as well as being open and honest about potential feelings of competitiveness: do we need to 'show off' to each other with a 'clever' technique, which can get in the way of the work on the 'process'? Of course, we do not always work in synchronicity and there are times when one of us goes off at a tangent and the other stays with it.

The following is a list of themes that we have addressed together, both in discussion and through our art-forms:

1. The overlap in the media we use. The developmental paradigm* can reflect both the visual art process and the dramatic art process. These processes meet in the mask (see Chapter 10), which integrates both art therapy and dramatherapy in a fixed form and which has multiple layers of experience and meaning.
2. We monitor each other's timing of intervention and trust each other to intervene if there is a sense of getting lost or diffuse. We also monitor each other's use of language (especially as we both have different ones!) and will elaborate for each other. The workshops are run in a mixture of English and Norwegian.
3. We spend enough time on de-roling and de-briefing. We share fears, fantasies and counter-transferences. In other words, we deal with our own feelings; about the group itself, the session that we have conducted, and also, of course, about each other.
4. It is also important that we are able to be objective towards each other and give evaluative feedback – both positive and negative – without feeling threatened. This means trusting each other enough to give spontaneous reactions. For instance:

Åse to Sue: 'What on earth were you doing making people work with a pre-formed cut-out mask? It did not give them choices.'

Sue to Åse: 'You're being too complicated – they'll never understand what you mean.'

as well as more reflective ones.

We use each other to express immediate 'discharge' as well as giving thought to the processes with which we are engaged both individually and together.

When we had discussed and written down this list, we realised that there was a lot more that we had yet to discover – rather like having found another way of being, of inhabiting another space where we continued to grow. Then we realised that we enlarge and expand each other's frame of reference without invading it or monopolising it.

This became very important, because we realised that it is possible to see, hear and listen to each other, so affecting our art and drama in artistic

* Embodiment – Projection – and Role: the dramatic paradigm of human development, as described in detail in Jennings, 1993b.

and dramatic ways. I do not become more of an art therapist because something that Åse does engages me and my drama. Neither does Åse become more of a dramatherapist because she finds a stimulating new way of looking at something from me. *What happens is that we become more of ourselves by being exposed to the other.*

This, of course, could take us right into theories of human development and we could look at these processes from the point of view of object-relations theory* (see also Chapters 2 and 3) or indeed symbol-interactionist theory†. However, what seems to be of crucial importance for us is the fact that this relationship is based on our art forms. It is through the art and the drama, the art therapy and the dramatherapy, that we can be both separate and together, distanced and close. We do not feel that this symbiosis and the individuation could exist without the transitional and in-between spaces of the art and the drama as well as *in* the art and drama.

This brings about a major question: could this work with *any* collaboration between art therapy and dramatherapy? On the evidence of the emergence of the two professions, it sadly seems unlikely. The places where they are used closely and trustingly together, whether in training or in practice, are very few and far between. The following report is of two meetings which took place *over twenty years ago*, and illustrates how little progress has been made in developing a truly collaborative approach in the arts therapies.

> Interim Statement from the Committee representing Drama, Music and Art in Therapeutic and Remedial work on suggestions for the formation of a professional body to represent the 'arts' in this work, and to suggest means of greater collaboration in this work. May 1971
>
> 1st Meeting between Sue Jennings, Julienne Brown and Diane Waller:
>
> The above met to discuss methods of co-operation between the different arts being used in therapy and remedial education. It was said that although there were different art disciplines, the needs of the workers in the field were the same, therefore co-operation and liaison would be to mutual advantage. It was suggested that an association to link and support the arts in therapy could be formed, but first other representatives should be approached for further discussion. Diane Waller, representing the art therapists, pointed out that they had their own professional body but

---

* Object Relations theories can be very narrow or extremely wide, depending on the orthodoxy or otherwise of the writer (see Appendix and Further Reading). However, people are beginning to agree that a more appropriate term is 'Human Object Relations' (Kernberg 1984).

† Symbolic-interaction is the name given to the process influenced by writers such as George Herbert Mead (1934) who suggest that the basis of human development is through the interaction of roles with self and other. See also Landy (1986, pp.79–82) for a discussion in relation to dramatherapy theory.

nevertheless were keen to link with others in this field. All parties agreed that the aims of such a recognition for arts therapists was a prime consideration. The discussion closed with the agreement to approach others in the field. Sue Jennings stated that she intended seeing Dr Mel Marshak to discuss the Remedial Arts Course at The Institute of Education and her feelings about such an association.

Before the second meeting, Sue Jennings saw Dr Marshak and discussed the formation of such an association at some length. Sue Jennings also invited Marion North to represent the movement therapists at the next meeting. Dr Marshak stressed the importance of such an association, especially for those candidates who had completed the forthcoming Remedial Arts Course, as well as an advisor with others to such an association.

2nd Meeting between Julienne Brown, Diane Halliday, Sue Jennings, Marion North, Diane Waller:

There was much discussion of a general nature on the whole question of the representation for therapists in the arts. One member suggested that it should take the form of a learned society within which all the arts were represented in their own sub-association. It was pointed out that the art and music therapists already had their own associations and there was no reason why approaches should not be made to them concerning affiliation to a wider association.

It was decided to form from the members present the 'Ad Hoc Committee to form the British Association for the Arts in Therapy'; this title for the association as yet only a suggestion.

It was agreed that various specialists should be approached in the fields of psychiatry and psychology and other allied disciplines to advise the Ad Hoc Committee in setting up this scheme.

All members realised that recognition in an art therapy where little formal training as yet existed, would prove a real difficulty, necessitating much further discussion. It was asked whether the needs of a teacher using the arts in a special school were different from those of an arts therapist working in a hospital. It was felt that this association would fill a large gap for practitioners both in schools and hospitals.

Some members felt that group therapy or individual psychotherapy was a pre-requisite for workers in these fields, particularly if they were working with adults in psychiatry day hospital clinics and psychiatric social clubs.

All members agreed that those taking the title of arts therapist and seeking membership of such an association, must have a full training in an art form to offer. It was suggested that other disciplines, e.g. O.T. nurses, doctors etc. who wished to make use of art forms in their work, would not be eligible for full membership (possibly associate members?). In any case they had their own professional bodies.

All members agreed that the art form must not be abused in therapy or the aesthetics of artistic experience distorted.

There was much discussion and variety of opinion amongst committee members as to the final definition of 'an art form in therapy'; for instance, it was asked whether an arts therapist should interpret.

This led to much discussion on work boundaries; for instance, it was asked whether psychodrama should be included in the arts in therapy or did it belong to another discipline. In addition, it was asked at what point does a drama therapy session become a group psychotherapy session communicating through drama?

All members said that they thought much clarification was needed for the aims and policy of such an association. At closing it was agreed that Sue Jennings should be temporary organiser/secretary during these initial stages as she had taken the initiative in approaching various bodies. She informed the committee that there was already interest being shown from other professions and several had shown their willingness to be advisors.

Before closing, the committee expressed the opinion that the title 'remedial' should not appear in the name of the association because of other misleading connotations.

It was agreed to call another meeting in the near future but after certain approaches had been made to other individuals.

During the Easter period, several committee members were very occupied, so Sue Jennings and Julienne Brown agreed to draft ideas on the association which would form the basis of the discussion at the next meeting.

Suggested Aims of The British Society for the Arts in Therapy (Association?):

1. To recognise and accredit workers in the field.
2. To negotiate status and salary with respective ministeries.
3. To publish a journal as well as papers from accredited practitioners.
4. To encourage and, where possible, finance research projects to further develop and investigate this work.
5. To advise, encourage and link with established training schemes to qualify members of this profession.
6. To organise seminars, conferences etc., where appropriate, linking the arts in therapy.
7. To form communication links with other professional bodies in 'therapy' and 'arts'.
8. To form links with similar associations abroad.

The following have already agreed to act where possible as advisors to this scheme:

Dr Charles Enfield, Psychiatrist, Tavistock Clinic

Dr Rosemary Gordon, Jungian Analyst

Mr Edward Hazelton, Psychologist, British Psychological Society

Dr Mel Marshak, Institute of Education

Dr Malcolm Pines, Institute of Group Analysis

Dr Robin Skynner, Group Therapist

This document is being circulated not only to members of the Ad Hoc Committee and advisors, but also to other interested parties for comment before the next meeting is held.

Julienne Brown, Music Therapist
Sue Jennings, Drama Therapist

We have no wish to get into the various 'politics of arts therapies' or to personalise here our various experiences with authorities and institutions both in the UK and Norway. However, we both feel a sadness that, after all these years, there is not more mutual trust and respect between the very professions that claim to be therapeutic and in the service of helping other people.*

The following is a 'free association' that we both did on this theme when we were discussing co-arts therapy in relation to our courses:

...difference of ladder yet you meet – sense of humour both in group and out – keep ourselves sane – share worries about work and life – but clarity of time boundaries – we may therapise each other but we are not each other's therapists [important boundary here of our own personal therapy and supervision] – embarking on a joint path can allow one to wander – the other then is map-holder – point of reference – specialism can cause alienation – 'little boxes' – (girl in the box or girl in the sea?) – society compartmentalises – can we avoid it?'

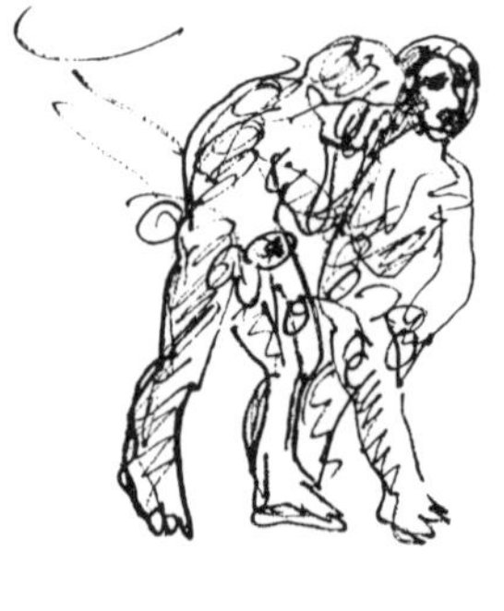

Masaccio's 'Adam and Eve's Expulsion from' Paradise

* It is a salient reminder that in Israel, a country with such strife, there is an umbrella organisation for all arts therapies, psychodrama and expressive therapy, within which each 'discipline' has an individual professional association.

We then did a 'free association' on our roles as women:

> 'We are both mothers, daughters, sisters and have careers – Åse is married and Sue has been married – we both had roles of 'nice little girls' – we both feel we are on the sane side of feminism.
>
> Sue feels she needed to 'climb out of herself' – to reconcile parental expectations that she should be only a wife and mother and make art more than a hobby.
>
> Åse felt how long she waited to become a mother – she never knew Sue as a mother of young children or indeed as a wife.
>
> We both reminded each other how we had been mistaken for sisters.'

To return to the theme at the beginning of this chapter of houses and shelters as a possible Summer School topic, it can be seen how the early discussion prompted a lot of other material and considerations. However, we have realised from this that there are three main processes that we were engaged in when we first explored the dominant theme, as in the first telephone conversation.

1. Allowing the theme to work on our own unconscious, knowing that some variant on what we have talked about will emerge. We must be careful not to tune it or try to make something happen, and also to be aware of our own competitiveness.

2. The necessary research on the theme we need to do at a cognitive level: what do Freud and Jung, for example, say about houses and bodies? Who has painted houses and shelters? What anthropological knowledge is there on houses and shelter, literature, poetry...?

3. Our own feelings about our past houses and where we live now. What are our feelings about our own bodies; What will this theme mean for us?

The conversation was continued in February 1984:

Åse: Sue, I have some news! I'm pregnant!

Sue: Wonderful! Will you be all right for the seminar?

Åse: I'm fine – the baby is due in October.

Sue: So what about bodies and containers now?

Åse: I'm the 'container' right now.

Sue: With the house theme, are we going to use myths or stories, or their own material?

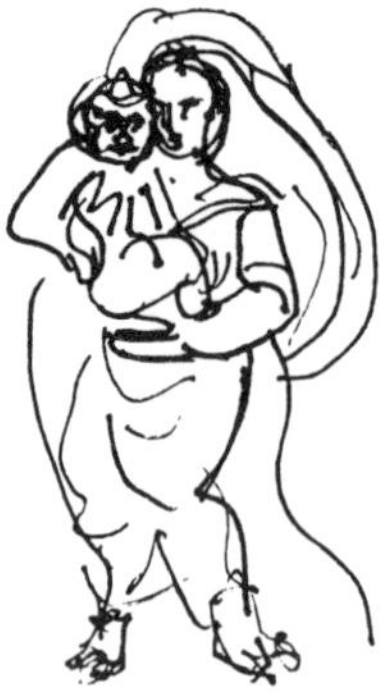

Raphael's 'Sistine Madonna' by Gro Finne

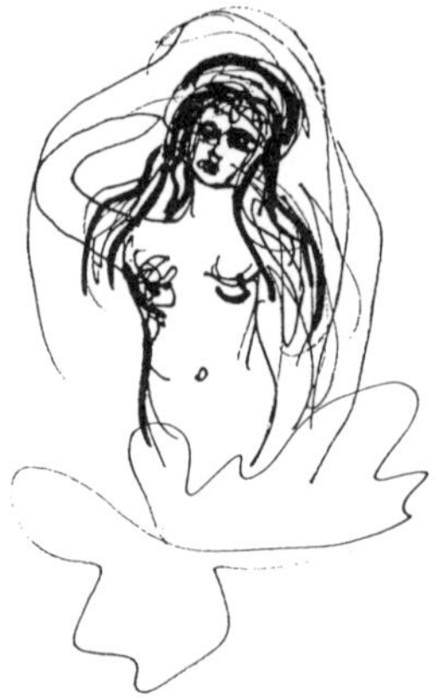

Munch's 'Madonna' by Gro Finne

Åse: If we are starting with the clay and then creating their own safe place, why don't we see where that will lead us?

Sue: And what about all the house-building rituals that most other societies have before and during the building of a house?

Åse: Let me read out to you House and Uterus from *The Symbol Dictionary:*

> *House* A world centre; the sheltering aspect of the Great Mother; an enclosing symbol; protection. The cult house, hut, lodge or tepee of tribal religions is the Cosmic Centre, "our world"; the universe; it is the *regressus ad uterum* of initiation, descent into the darkness before rebirth and regeneration.
>
> *Womb* The matrix; the Great Mother, the Earth Mother, hence "the womb of the earth" with the cave as its chief symbol, and Dying Gods being born in a cave as emerging from the womb of the earth. The womb is also the unmanifest; the totality of all possibilities; plenitude. It is symbolized by the well and all waters and all that is enclosing, such as city walls, caskets, etc. In Alchemy the womb represents a mine, with the ores as the embryo; minerals are born of the earth, and man's function is to aid nature and hasten the birth.'

Sue: And, of course, there is not only your pregnancy. Do you remember the woman who became pregnant last year after the work she did on her image of her uterus? (See Chapter 6, the work on body parts).

Åse: Uterus as container; a good one this time…

Sue: A safe place, a container; so we are working with inner image and outer image.

Åse: So we need varied media, clay as well as shelter materials.

Sue: Why don't we ask people to bring boxes – shoe boxes or other small containers that we can work with...?

Åse: So the container for the clay figure will not be so large.

Sue: Or overwhelming.

Åse: So the clay is their feelings about their body, and the box a safe place to be.

Sue: And the box also becomes the container for the private feelings, and the outside becomes their outside – 'can I allow anyone in?' – which takes us on to sexuality. Will we have a balance of men and women?

Åse: We have only just circulated the information, so we don't know. Last year it was about two-thirds: one-third.

Sue: And we are talking about doors and windows. What about *vagina dentata*?*

Åse: So, we've got a central theme. Let it float until we meet in June...

Pre-seminar meeting in June 1985

Sitting outside a cabin in the pine forest, with papers, colours and notes from last year's seminar and a list of participants. Gunvor, the dance therapist, is to join us later.

Stage One

Feedback from last year: how we felt about it; feedback from participants; what went well and not so well; feedback to each other about performance and role; any students that gave us concern.

Check students who are returning for the second or more year – any connections they may make with the material we used and their own process. (The previous year was also Body, but approached from another perspective – see Chapter 6).

Stage Two

Harness all the ideas that have been floating since the telephone conversations. Pieces of paper are covered with notes and images; do they have any order? Where do we put limits on all our expansions?

---

* *Vagina Dentata* is the symbol of men's fears of castration during intercourse. According to Barbara G. Walker (1983) these fears increase in relation to the level of patriarchy in society.

Stage Three

The reality of the participants: their background and occupations and experience. Their reaction to Åse's pregnancy?

Stage Four

The reality of the time-table and the demands on staff. Sue worries that Åse will get tired.

Stage Five

A working structure with enough flexibility for the participants to go where they want to go, for us to be able to contain it and for it not to overwhelm.

Åse: The diaries: are we going to use them again?

Sue: Yes, I think it's important to record and contain the experience.

Åse: And why don't we use the house to contain the experience that they want to keep private – things that they can admit to themselves and yet don't have to share...?

Sue: And their ordinary diaries for sharing at the end?

Åse: Which can be in words and pictures...

Gunvor arrives and we talk through our possible working structure.

It is important at this stage that the whole thing can be abandoned; that no-one feels they have to hold onto an idea so strongly that it can neither grow into something or be left. We call this 'creative generosity', i.e. that all the ideas come from a mainstream of creativity that we are both a part of; that the development of the ideas are sparked from the initial free association and improvisation between us, and may need to be left and directions change.

Gunvor starts to give her ideas, using the body as the container and the contained. As we sit, our own gestures start to grow and expand. Gunvor gets up and shows us what she means concerning the exploration through dance of the shelter and the sheltered; how people can grow in self-esteem by being able to shelter someone else with their own body.

Sue tells the story of the tired animals that come to the forest seeking shelter, and the trees there that create a safe place for each animal to shelter; they close their doors and their windows and the little animals fall fast asleep.

Åse: And it makes touching much safer.

Åse is heavily pregnant and we remark how this year she has been preoccupied in her theme of the safe container. Sue is able to share her ambivalence about Åse being small as compared to her own height and weight; and this is the first time that Åse has been large. The discussion moves on to the fact that all three have either danced or had longings about dance – how does that connect with the theme of bodies and perceptions?

We return to the theme of the group of students who will meet us at 9 o'clock the following morning – are we clear about the structure and sharing of roles? As always we start with a big group experience, the group then splits into introductory and advanced groups and then comes together again on the last day for another big group and closure. There is always the issue of whether people are ready for the advanced group, and several clinicians try to insist that they should be in the advanced group because they are advanced clinicians. If there is too much insistence, we arrange a meeting and talk it through with the person.

It is still difficult for people to see that it is the experience in Art Therapy and Dramatherapy that is important and, even more so, in art and drama as a medium. How far have people developed their own art form, or are they just seeing the art and the drama as a useful collection of techniques? We want to ban the word 'technique' for a year and talk about method and, therefore, methodology.

There are two people to see in the morning who feel they should be in the advanced group. As it happens, one does not turn up and the other is clear that it is helpful to her to be in the advanced group. She is very tense and says how many seminars she has been to. Yes, we point out, but none of them have been experiential sessions. All her learning has been at the cognitive level. We are firm and she has to accept it. We check the equipment, the folders for their work. No, we are not going to organise a party. If they want to, then that is another matter. We check the programme – are we giving them what we said we would? Is the timing of the lectures right? Is someone looking after the slide projector?

We feel it is important that all this planning – even points which seem trivial – is part of making a complete process. We have recorded the process leading up to the seminar in such detail because it clearly illustrates some basic points about the co-arts therapies process. It shows, amongst other things, how important the mutual trust becomes in order to be creative with each other and truly take risks. In addition, it points to a truly collaborative creative process based on our own experience of our art and life.

Workshop on houses and shelters

Participants were asked to bring with them lidded boxes about the size of a shoebox and also any scrap or junk materials that they might have at home. As Peer Gynt says:

> Our gold may seem scrap to you.
> You may think each crystal window-pane
> Is just a fistful of socks and rags.

Day 1: Movement and Dance

- Physical warm-up and expanding of physicality.
- Different 'moods of self' explored in improvisation.
- Create different sorts of shelter with the body.
- In small groups expand the shelter theme.
- Taking it in turns to be inside the shelter and calm.
- Repeat trying to break out of the shelter and not succeed.
- Repeat and you can succeed.

People closed the sessions by writing in their diaries any themes about houses and shelters. They were asked to look at their box and think about the possibility of creating a shelter or house that would be safe inside.

(*Teaching Point:* Note how through the movement we are planting the core themes of the workshop, remembering that the body, as we said earlier, is a primary means of learning.)

Day 2: Clay Work

- Write diary and consider again the box: What might be on the outside and what on the inside?
- Repeat physical warm-up from yesterday but in a different order – from groups to individual.
- Sit in a quiet place, close eyes and picking up the clay. Åse plants ideas about just letting the clay take shape, do not try to control it – they create a person or animal that can inhabit the shelter they will make.

People had half an hour for the creation in clay and then opened their eyes and looked at the figure: some had created people and others animal creatures. Everyone was surprised that, although the figure was not what they had thought it would be, they were nevertheless very pleased. However, there was a feeling of vulnerability hanging in the group which both the leaders felt should be grounded through the work on shelters:

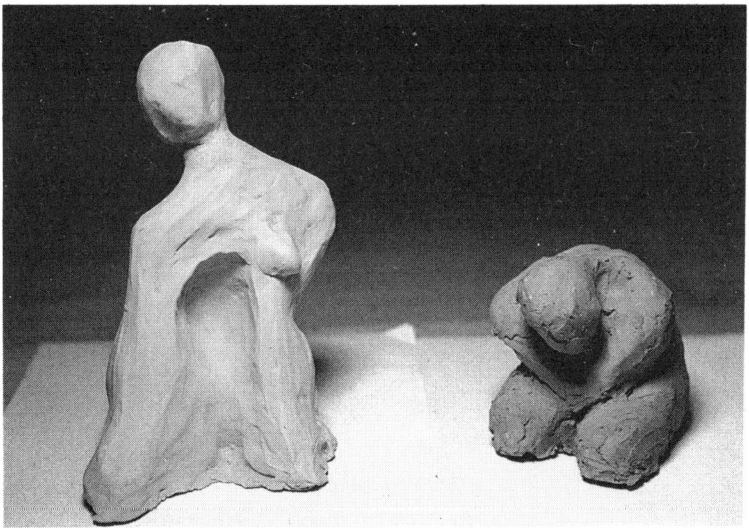

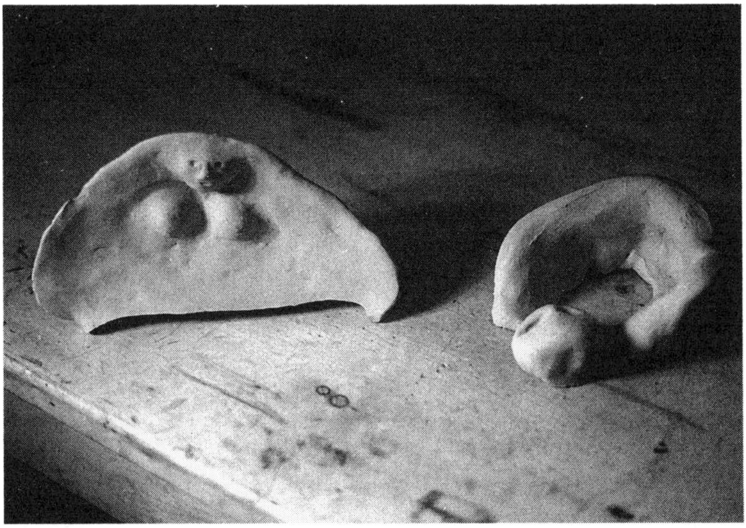

Sculptures by two women in a group, on becoming a mother, being a mother and feeling like an underdeveloped foetus.

- Place the clay figures in a place of safety while they dry.
- Close eyes and thinking about an actual house or shelter, or an imagined one, where it would be safe and contained.
- What is at the front? At the back? Tip-toe up and look in through a small opening.

(*Teaching Point:* It is important to consider the language used so that people feel they have choices – the important thing here is to make sure that 'a place of safety' is created (unlike one borderline patient who insisted in creating a house with no walls 'because I must be able to escape').)

- Use any of the materials, create the outside of the house or shelter. The box may be cut, but it must be able to be closed.

People spent the remainder of this session working on the outside of the houses and the energy was very focused. In the feedback we commented on the difference between the energy used on the clay figures and that used on the houses. People in the group shared how very vulnerable they felt about their clay figures. It brought up a lot of material about early childhood experiences of being abandoned; being left without knowing where adults were, being in dangerous spaces and being with dangerous people.

People placed their figures inside the safe box-container, then wrote a closing diary to end the session.

(We had a lengthy discussion after this session because we were both sure that there were themes of both child sexual abuse and violence in the group. We felt it was important to work with the themes in symbolic form since it was not a therapy group with a therapy contract. However, we also realised that we prefer to work in this manner anyway, although it is more difficult and makes more demands on the therapist).*

Day 3: Shelters and Dramas

- Write the diary and add any more to the outside of the house.
- Physical warm-up which gets people into small groups.
- Without using words, improvise the themes of safety and danger.
- Share the themes verbally and think of a fairytale that they relate to. (People chose a variety of tales which included *Red Riding*

---

* There is often an external perception that says: 'Aren't you lucky to be doing what you want'; 'How wonderful to be able to mess around/just play/earn a living doing what you do'. We cannot emphasise too strongly the importance of regular supervision of practice for all artistic therapists, whether or not they are full-time or just have a small case-load. Of course, all practitioners will have had their own personal therapy which, from time-to-time, they may need to return to.

Hood, Cinderella, Per Paul and Espen, Askelad, and *The Three Billikin Whiskers.*

- Create a drama based on the fairy story and perform it for the rest of the groups (maximum five minutes). (This process takes time, as people are encouraged to go through dramatic processes and rehearse and not just 'do a bit of role-play').
- Create a sculpt of the main theme in the story and then a sculpt of its resolution.
- Share the sculpts with the rest of the group.
- Return to the houses and decide how they will be inside. There is half an hour to create the inside of the house.
- Feedback and share in the small groups and look at the models – both inside and out.
- Close with the diary and shut the house shelter with the clay figure inside.

(*Teaching Point:* The use of fairy stories as containers for early life experience is an important part of both our work. We have included stories from both our cultures in most chapters.)

The little birds sang:

> Let the green one be
> Let the red one be
> Take the blue one, the blue one
> With crosses three.

CHAPTER 6

The Body-Self and the Body-Image

What I have been I have forgot to know;

(*Pericles*, II.i.71)

This chapter is about the primacy of the human body in the development of people both individually and culturally. Art and dramatherapy, which both work at a *primary-feeling level*, are very potent forms of intervention with clients and groups who have a variety of 'body problems'.

Extensive research has been done on posture, gestures and facial expression by psychologists and anthropologists,* and it is useful for us to remember that:

1. Although some body movements and expressions are universal, many more are culturally conditioned.
2. Metaphoric and symbolic statements are made both *about the human body*, as well as *through the human body*, which are important to the belief and life of the society.
3. Human beings experience sensation at a primary level through the human body: the body is a primary means of learning.
4. The way in which infants are handled when young, and the parental messages they receive about their bodies, play a major part in the way they mature and form relationships.

There is a constant ebb and flow between society and the images it creates. Does the society create the image, or does the image create the society?

For example, we can see how values are expressed using the body as a metaphor by looking at commonly used English phrases; nose to the

---

* Anthropologists from Mary Douglas (1966) onwards have developed extensive material in relation to understanding the human body. How far is the opposition between 'purity and danger' (MD's phrase) relevant to eating disorder? The opposition between the virginal pure body and the lustful impure body? Further suggested reading on anthropology in the Appendix.

grindstone; shoulder to the wheel; best foot forward; keep your head down.

Advertising and the media create images that we respond to that can be reduced to a few basic principles: Are bodies covered, or uncovered? If so, which part is to be uncovered – thus emphasised? Or, through covering and additional padding, which body part will be highlighted?

Human development

Although there is much debate on the external influences on the development of the foetus, there is no doubt that the way that infants are physically handled from birth is a major determinant in satisfactory maturation and the formation of relationships.

We can contrast the socially accepted ways of handling small children, from the carrying on the hip until walking in Africa to the swaddling in a Babygro in a pram in the UK. As technology enables us to distance ourselves more from primary experience – for example, rockers for babies instead of being carried – sufficient thought is not given to the impact of this on sensory and emotional development.

The paradox of child-handling is that the more the child is held and touched, the more it will mature physically. For example, the child that is breastfed for two years will not be more dependent, but more *independent*. Temiar children are breastfed for three to four years and it is not unusual to see a new baby on one breast of the mother and a toddler suckling on the other.* Yet Temiar children mature more quickly than their western counterparts. The oft-held western view is that a child who is cuddled and handled too much will become 'namby pamby' and, especially for boys, might become 'soft' or 'effeminate'.

Art therapy

Åse: Art therapy is a very bodily experience. When you are working with art materials, it is a dialogue between primary and secondary processes. Rhoda Kellogg, in *Analysing Children's Art*, describes how children's scribble, which occurs at two to three years, has several observable stages. The particular stage which interests her is where the child makes only vertical lines on the page. Whereas many adults dismiss this stage as wasting paper, or only movement or activity, Kellogg points out that it is an important transition for the child in discovering its individual body-self.

* Temiar children are breastfed until three or four years and if their 'real' mother is not nearby other mothers will provide instead.

> It has long been assumed that the primary pleasure young children derive from scribbling is that of movement, or 'motor pleasure'. It could equally well be assumed that visual pleasure is primary. Why does a child bother to mark paper or to make lines in dust? Why does he soon stop his scribbling motions if they do not produce marks – if, for instance, his crayon breaks into unusable pieces? Why is a steamy window attractive only as long as the steam lasts to show the lines the child's finger traces? The answer is that visual interest is an essential component of scribbling, whether or not it is primary (Kellogg 1969, p.7).

It is important that Kellogg draws attention to these early processes and that we remember that they are not random.

Ehrenzweig (1970) emphasises that the *undifferentiated* structure of the primary process is different from the *chaotic*:

> The undifferentiated structure of primary-process fantasy corresponds to the primitive still undifferentiated structure of the child's vision of the world. Piaget has given currency to the term 'syncretistic' vision as the distinctive quality of children's vision and of child art. Syncretism also involves the concept of undifferentiation (Ehrenzweig 1970, p.21).

All children go through the scribble stages, and gradually add to their drawings of body the 'contact organs', i.e. head with mouth, teeth, eyes, nose, fingers, legs – all the body parts to do with sensation and touch. It is later that the child differentiates, putting a separate body from the head. Early disturbance in small children often results in a lack of the sense and contact organs being drawn.

Many clients experience disturbance at different stages of their development, and this can be observed in their art work. Arthur Robbins, in his book *Artist as Therapist*, says:

> ...in therapy, patients and therapists alike are engaged in finding the artist within themselves. The therapeutic process for patients is an on-going struggle to find true inner representations and symbols, and give them form in terms of developing richer, more congruent living realities (Robbins 1986, p.21).

When working with art, you are both part of your art work and outside of it. It is a process of entering and being part of it, as well as leaving it and being separate. There are many experiences in life, which are not possible to verbalise, but often through art work they start to take form which later may be transformed to verbal language. Many of the clients with whom I have worked throughout the years have very little contact with their bodies; they have, for example, fears, low self-esteem and self-destructive patterns of behaviour. Their art work is a way of working through, and coming to terms with, these distorted experiences.

Clinical Example:

A young woman, aged 22, was a patient in a surgical ward after a self-inflicted accident.* For several months there was the possibility of her having one of her legs amputated. She was also anorectic and refused all nutrition, and consequently was being fed directly into her stomach. Her physical state deteriorated and for a long time she did not wish to talk or look at her own situation. In her art work, she never gave legs to the bodies, and she made a lot of pictures of 'poison' (her term), which she said infected and contaminated the rest of her – at one level this was medically the case, as she had a serious bacterial infection. She felt there was little hope in her life and did not want to live. It was a difficult therapeutic situation, since she was a 'captive' patient, confined to bed. I visited her rather than her visiting the art-therapy room. Many times she would refuse to talk or engage in any art work. Physically it also proved difficult since she had minimal movement in her arms and hands. After a long period of silence, at one session she peered from the sheets with only her eyes showing like an Egyptian mummy, looked directly at me and said 'What are you thinking about?' I replied that at that moment I had been thinking of a large green plant I had at home. I was very fond of this plant but had neglected it and it was losing its leaves as if it would die. I had given it plant-food and water and it had improved a little, but the leaves were beginning to fall off again as I had not taken regular care of it. She looked at me and said: 'You are not talking about your plant, you are talking about me.'

I was not immediately aware of the metaphor and it took me a moment to realise that the story of my plant was her story too. This was a big breakthrough for her, and she wanted to start work. She chose to work with Plasticine, which she put in the surgical dish which was placed at her bedside for throwing up. The dish became a symbol of all she was getting rid of and the Plasticine became a beautiful woman with breasts. The woman had no legs but she had form. The patient no longer wanted to vomit her feelings, but was able to transform them through her art.

Different materials are very important in art therapy, especially when working with the body – the different smells and textures put people in touch with a range of senses. Very often, people rigidly stay with the same materials because they are frightened of losing control. Sometimes the way forward is by giving them a new material to encourage them to take risks. Some people will move themselves into taking more risks through new material, or by changing their artistic style.

---

* It is unusual for art therapists and dramatherapists to work in surgical settings. However, Åse worked in a surgical ward and Sue works with gynaecologists in a fertility clinic.

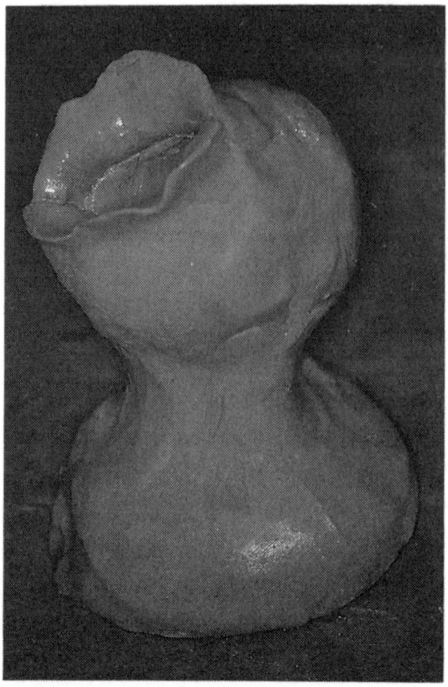

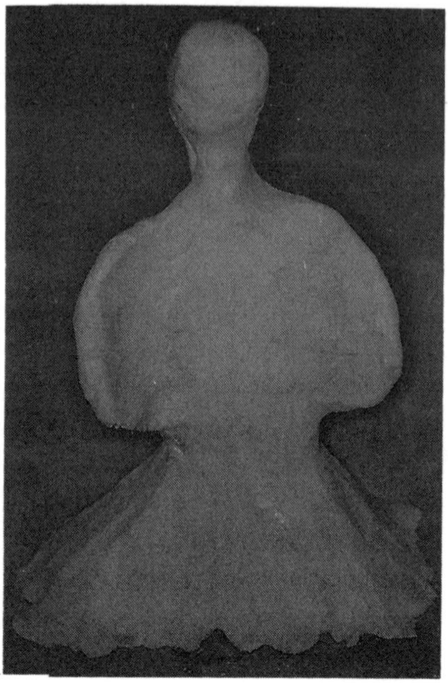

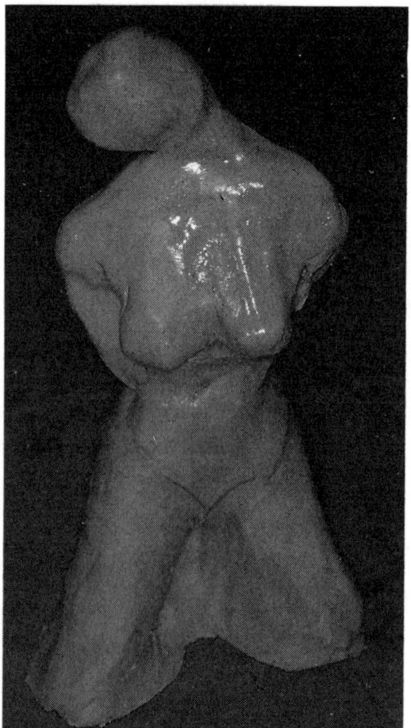

Three stages of a woman's development

Marie von Franz gives the following example in her book *The Way of the Dream*:

> ...I had for instance in my practice a painter whose predilection, as well as training, prepared him to paint very accurate renditions of things, and therefore he earned his living by very accurate old-fashioned, photograph-like portrait painting. This was his fashion and he had a violent resistance to what he called modern art. He despised its destructive and impossible ways. Night after night he dreamt that he had to change his painting style completely and paint inner things and abstract things. For instance, he always used dark colours, but he had clear dreams that said he had to paint in bright colours. And he had, among others, one very disagreeable physical symptom; he was impotent. But as soon as he began to obey the dreams, his physical symptoms including his impotence disappeared. He was cured by completely changing his artistic style. He did not have to change his vocation. He had only to change his style (Von Franz 1988, pp.101–102).

In this example, the patient was working through his resistance in everyday life by experiencing change in his unconscious life – in his dreams. Art therapy works in the waking state as dreams do in the sleeping state, or indeed can be linked to the dream life as well.

Clinical Example

There is only one psychiatric ward for deaf people in Norway. For many years I worked with a deaf young woman who also had many autistic characteristics. She had spent her whole life in different institutions. She used a little sign language, and very occasionally would try to speak. Her art work clearly could give her and the staff some understanding of her inner world. In periods when she was disturbed, her landscapes would be full of catastrophes, storms and violence. During part of my treatment with her I was pregnant and during this period she started drawing pictures of a black bathing suit and a green dress. She repeated these two images in about a hundred pictures. She refused to work in any other way. One day, I took a chance in working on her picture. My own impression was that the bathing suit was a girl and the dress was a woman. I drew a girl and a woman on the two garments, and she immediately responded and drew her own mother and herself. There was a change in the picture. She drew a toilet and her mother pointing to it and holding a packet of sanitary pads. She wrote the word 'dirty'.

I interpreted this to be confused fantasy and reality about what she had been told of her own bodily functions. Her understanding was that it involved a lot of shame, so I drew a picture for her which involved a row of women of different ages and told her that they all menstruated. After this, she never drew the image again and she saved the picture I had done like a treasure.

This again illustrates how art can work directly with the body and enable some clarity of experience.

Dramatherapy

Sue: As we said at the beginning of this chapter, the body is the starting point in all art and arts therapies and, indeed, in human development. It is often assumed that drama is to do with role, and that movement and mime are part of dance. However, we have established earlier in this book and elsewhere* that the body and its experiences are intrinsic to drama and dramatherapy. As human beings, we often 'know' something in our bodies before we can verbally articulate it. For example, the atmosphere when we go into a room is picked up by physical sensors before we are able to rationalise it.

If the body is the starting point in dramatherapy, this does not mean that we progress in a unilinear way from movement to role. What happens is that the movement dimension is carried forward in a multi-dimensional way and is part of the multi-faceted human being. Therefore, movement never ceases to be an intrinsic part of ourselves and wholesome expression.

Much of what is done in arts therapies is to assist people to reconnect with their bodies and to discover the hidden self – the body that is not seen. A dramatherapy session may well start with structured movement, comparable to an actor's training, that slowly starts to expand the person's repertoire of movement and their sense of their body in space. This expansion of movement also leads to an inner expansion, i.e. working from the outside–in. Alternatively, it may begin with a person discovering an image from a dream, story or picture, which starts from within and which they can then express through movement. What in fact happens is an inner/outer loop system, in which outer movement works on the inside, and inner experience influences the outside. The following two case histories illustrate the relationship between inner/outer dimension of the body and dramatherapy.

Clinical Example

A weekly dramatherapy group took place at a psychiatric day hospital for a mixed group of patients of various ages, diagnoses and stages of recovery. Since there was some coming and going it was necessary to structure each session, with the knowledge that the whole group would not be there the following week. Many people in the group paced, had

* Åse is currently preparing a book on art therapy and eating disorder entitled *From Chrysalis to Butterfly* based on original theory and case histories.

automated movement or had a drug-induced lethargy. I decided to structure the automated movement and use it creatively. We started with machine movement – pulling levers, typing – and developed into pair work where one person was the machine and the other the operator. Then, in small groups, we developed different sorts of machines – domestic, rural, air-borne. The topic fired the group's imagination and their co-ordination and concentration improved once we were creating the machines. They showed a high degree of inventiveness and attention to detail.

I suggested that as a whole group we could invent a machine of our own and after some deliberation one young man who had always seemed very agitated and would often break off from the group and pace or sit in a corner, asked if he could invent a sausage-making machine. The group agreed and he became very involved, placing people to be breadcrumbs, sausage meat, herbs and a mixing bowl with big paddles in which everything was mixed. He then directed them through a shaping machine that cut the mixture into sausage-shaped lengths. It shows the degree of trust in the group that the members were prepared to go through these procedures, not just as the machine, but also as the sausages.

Then, the young man suddenly stopped everything, smote his brow, and said 'We have a crisis! How do we put the skins on the sausages?' He paced up and down the floor saying the whole project was doomed, then suddenly turned to everyone and said 'I know what to do – we'll have skinless sausages!'

This same group, when they met a week later, asked if they could make a machine for chopping up psychiatrists and turning them into human beings!

Clinical Example

Many people who suffer from fertility problems have a poor concept of body-self. They experience their body as something that won't do as they wish; that won't *work* for them. As a result, they frequently have a punitive attitude towards their own bodies. One couple in a dramatherapy group used to arrive immaculately dressed; even at the end of a working day: it was as if nothing could be out of place. When I asked the group to wear comfortable clothing such as track suits, the couple turned up in newly-purchased designer outfits. We worked on a fertility dance that the group had evolved and then went on to create fertility masks.

The mask-making necessitated each couple creating the shell of the mask on each other's faces. First petroleum jelly had to be smoothed onto the face. This couple had an extraordinary reaction to this; the woman claimed that she could not have the jelly on her face and must use her own moisturiser, and that her husband must not touch her face and she would have to do it herself. The compromise was that she could use her own cream, but that her husband would smooth it on. Within three minutes of her eyes being closed she sat bolt upright and said she was going to be sick. Her partner propped her up with a cushion and began to treat her like a baby – the baby they did not have – cooing and gentling her along to finish the procedure, which she readily did – like a baby.

Up until now, this couple had only brought their outward, smart, clean and seemingly independent selves to the group. In fact, they were often looked upon by the group as the most mature and sophisticated. This was the first time they had demonstrated their private body relationship – that of parent and baby.

Integrated art therapy and dramatherapy

Throughout the years we have been exploring the body in different ways through drama and art therapy. An enormous range of symbols exist that people have in relation to their body. Bodily reactions to stress situations are very individual, but certain reactions appear to be common to a range of people. For instance, a very common theme is one of feeling invisible, or wanting to be invisible both at a conscious and unconscious level. This frequently occurs with people suffering from eating disorders and with those who have experienced early childhood abuse. In Chapter 4 is a synopsis of one of Tove Jansson's 'Moomintroll' stories called 'The Invisible Child', which we have both used in work with both these groups of patients.*

(*The Authors' Process:* While writing this chapter, S.J. dreamed about co-directing a play and there was a discussion as to whether she and her co-director should wear black clothes, and long-sleeved T-shirts instead of short-sleeved ones, in order to be invisible while they were waiting in the wings to change the scenery.)

Just as in the Introduction we looked at the therapeutic possibilities inherent in Botticelli's picture *Primavera*, we now wish to consider the relevance of the Greek myth of Demeter and Persephone, especially in relation to work with eating disorders and child abuse.

Demeter is a goddess who occurs in many stories and manifestations. She was married to both Poseidon and Zeus. She is a fertility goddess (compare with Inanna in Chapter 10) and had a daughter Persephone by Zeus, who promises her in marriage to Hades. Gaia approves the marriage and sends flowers for the ritual to a valley where Hades abducts Persephone. Demeter hears her scream but is too late to rescue her. She refuses to eat in her misery and searches the whole world with her ritual torches. In anger and rage she withdraws her gifts of the fruits of the earth, and stays in her temple. Zeus realises that there will be famine for the

---

* See Ann Cattanach's comments in *Play Therapy with Abused Children* (1992).

mortals and no sacrifices for the gods so, using Hermes as a messenger, he orders Hades to return Persephone to her mother. Hades gives Persephone a pomegranate seed to eat which means that she will return to him for three months in every year. Demeter is joyfully reunited with her daughter and obeys Zeus in making the earth fertile once again, despatching Triptolemus to teach men agriculture.

Even in the shortened version of this old myth we can see the possibilities of its themes for work with the body: the fertility goddess who refuses to eat, the daughter abducted into the underworld, the near famine caused through cessation of the growth of seeds and fruit, the symbol of the pomegranate and the three-month period 'underground'. In some versions of the story, Persephone was raped by Hades before being taken underground. In her book *Starving Women: A Psychology of Anorexia Nervosa*, Angelyn Spignesi (1983) says that it is essential for women to be able to relate to the underworld rather than be distorted by the concretism of the dayworld:

> This necessity that the psychic place of Mother be uncovered leads me to wonder: Who is struggling for Mother today? Who has Mother chosen to enact her relationship with Hades, with the underworld, the realm from which she has been excluded? I pause: my glance is held by the spectacle of the anorexic. Here we have a woman who explicitly enacts a war against aspects of traditionally binding a female to the material earth – food, body, reproduction (Spignesi 1983, p.5).

Spignesi develops a complex mythic structure through the use of Demeter and other goddesses to facilitate change in women with eating disorders. Her thesis is impressive and the following extract must suffice in this context:

> In her temple, Demeter stays far away from the other gods, still longing for her daughter, and now her longing breeds action. She conceals the seed in the earth. Zeus summons her first through the goddess Iris, then through the other gods, sending beautiful gifts to persuade her back to Olympus, thus to prevent the famine which might destroy all humans. Demeter refused (ibid, p.74).

She goes on to suggest that Demeter is involved in two very powerful statements – her withdrawal into herself and the concealment of the seed. The symbolism for people who suffer from problems of body-distortion are beginning to be clear.

We may choose to work with this myth in a group with people taking the different roles, or we may use it with individuals. In the roles of Demeter and Persephone we can see the split between Fertile Mother and Maid and the struggle to keep them separate. Just as earlier we saw how

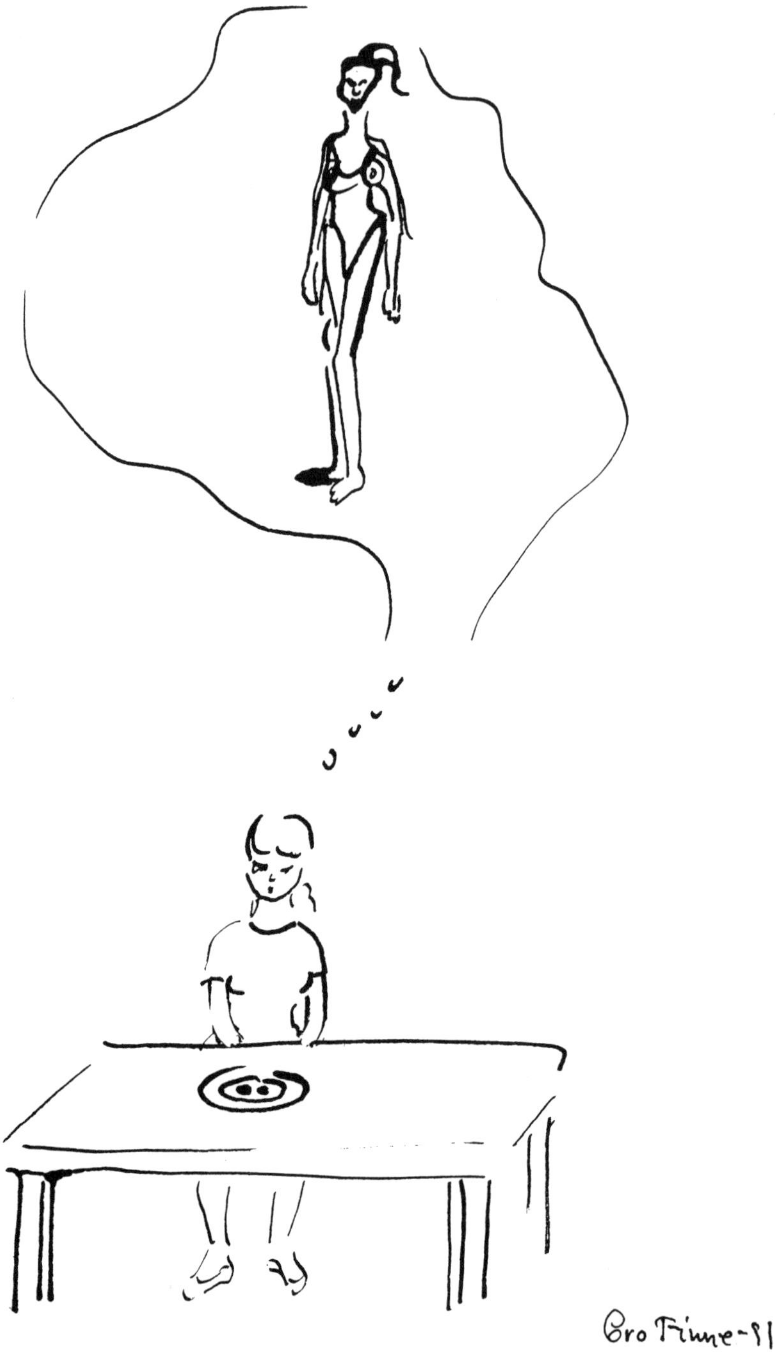

Chart on the body (by Gro Finne)

Chloris is transformed into the fertile Flora (see p.14), we can also see the possibility of transformation between Demeter and Persephone.

Art therapy with women with serious eating disorders

Åse: My long-term experience in working with this particular client group (including anorexia, bulimia and obesity) has convinced me that using art, imagery and metaphor in relation to women with eating disorders, gives them the possibility, in a symbolic way, to move away from the focus on their bodies and to see their problems with a new perspective.

Research in Norway shows that there are very few therapists trained to work with this particular client group and that many of the clients who suffer this affliction feel that they are not understood in therapy situations. As a female therapist myself, I naturally have an interest in the female psyche. One assumption about anorexia nervosa is that the relationship between mother and daughter is one of the main causes of the disorder. This is, of course, a very narrow view of a very complex problem. I believe that the cultural impact on women is far more important. It is certainly interesting that while some women starve and others gorge, both experience themselves as fat.

One of the problems in working with this client group is meeting the clients 'where they are'. Often, they feel they are struggling alone and a 'meeting' between themselves and the therapist does not occur. Many of the clients are verbally very articulate and can talk about their problems superficially, but are totally out of touch with their emotions. Many of the women I have worked with have been functioning very well in their jobs, in high positions with a lot of responsibility, while all the time they have an on-going inner war and are struggling to survive in other parts of their lives.

There seems to be no connection between the two worlds – of keeping up a beautiful outer image, handling a job, being on a restricted diet with rigid self-control – and gorging on food and vomiting. Emotional needs are starved, vomited up or gorged down with food. Because many of these clients are verbally very articulate they often hide their real fears and lack of self-esteem behind their words. It is easy to sit 'on the first floor' talking to the client, while they are actually 'in the cellar'.

The art work becomes a meeting place between the therapist and the client. They can go together on a journey to the underworld and understand the hidden meaning behind a struggle which can go on for years. Even after the clients feel they have a fairly normal relationship to food,

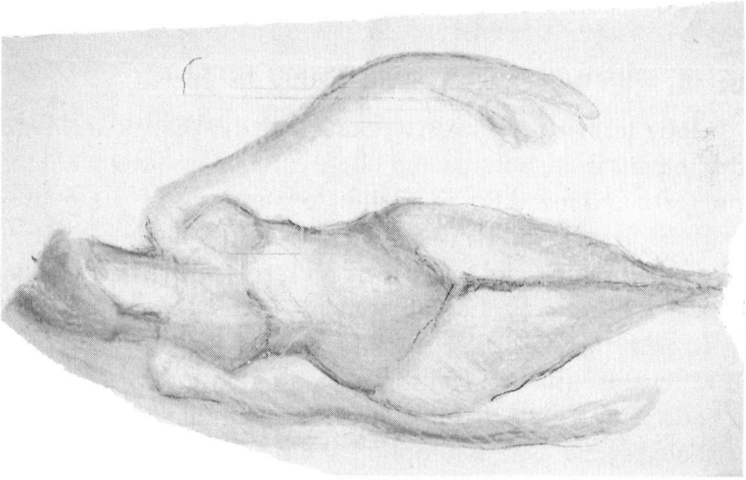

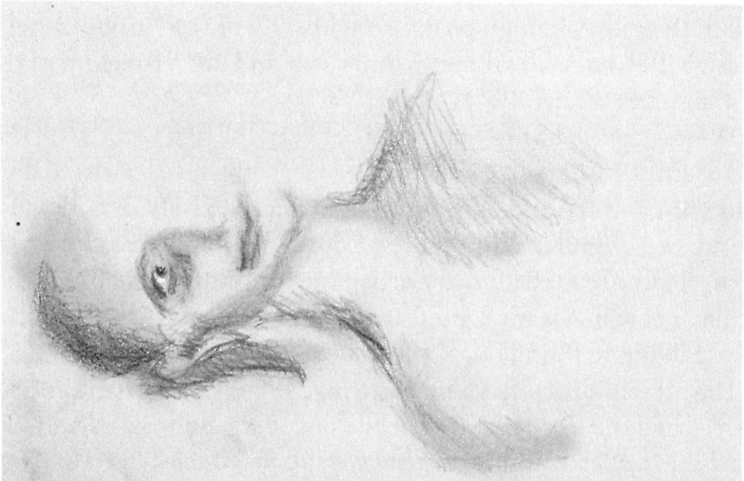

if the problems are not treated they will often occur in other symptoms. It is an on-going struggle in the search for personal identity.

In the art work of many women with anorexia, I have seen that they are struggling to work with the whole body. Many can draw only half a face or just parts of the body; the rest, they feel, they are not in touch with.

Different art materials can serve very different purposes in therapy situations. Many anorectic clients choose fine crayons to work with because they feel they are easy to control. However, it is important that when they feel safe enough in the relationship with the therapist and that the therapist is able to contain their fears and inner emotions, they can then move on to using different materials. Sometimes, I give materials because they will provoke the client to make an important move or to get in touch with the joy of play. Many of these women feel that they were never allowed to play as children and had to take on early responsibilities. Play can be threatening, but through art one can slowly get in touch with play again. In other situations, some of these clients lack boundaries and by trying out different art materials this can often help clarify their boundaries in relationships.

> 'I am struggling to be free, one part of me is always held back. After years on my journey to become free, I feel released?'

The art therapy and the dramatherapy, together with certain mythic structures, become the 'meeting place' where the client and the therapist can meet.

> Thus for the psychosomatic patient, owner of a fragile self-image, it is the stomach that is always 'nervous', the bowel that is 'irritable', and the 'nerves' that are weak or 'shattered' – but never the individual himself (Helman 1991, p.106).

Remembering the description of the creation of the 'forest of the group' in Chapter 1, it can be seen how it is possible to create the 'body' of the group as well as for an individual to dramatise the body-parts which, as Helman describes, are invested with emotion and separate existence.

The therapist's process

It was important in this context for Åse to introduce Sue to the Moomintroll stories which, although translated into English, are part of a common stock of stories such as those of, say, A.A. Milne. The use of the story would

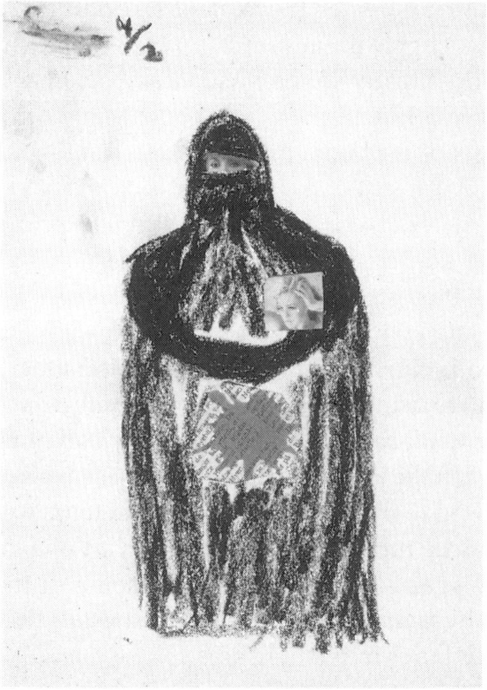

The woman within is well hidden away. the body parts the patient is most in touch with are the eyes, the heart and the stomach.

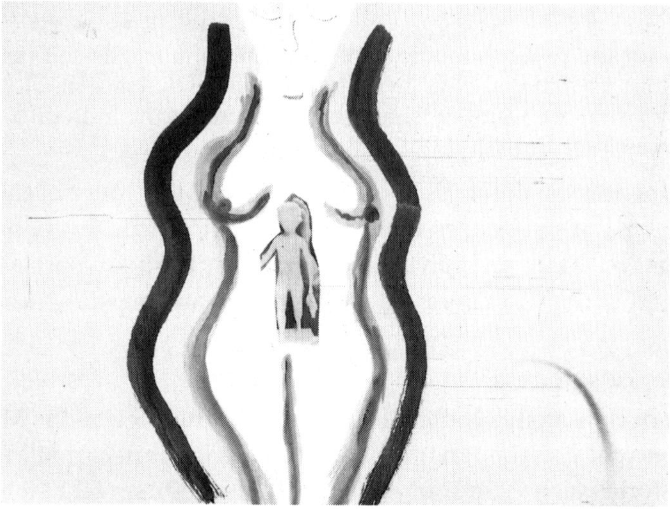

'I have a border outside my physical body border. I am afraid of anyone coming near. Inside is a hidden child.'

not have worked if it had not made a strong connection for both the therapists.

The starting point for both drama and art work must be a point of connection that the client can make and relate to. There is a wide range of methods, and it is the therapist's task to select appropriate material. It is important to know that the body is not a separate piece of the person and that throughout the therapy there is a connection with the person as a whole. Play and the interaction with others are also important parts of the development; some people have never been allowed to play or their play has, somewhere along their journey, been interrupted in negative ways, which has produced a fear of play in later life. As therapists, it is important to be able to sense where the journey has gone wrong in order to help the patients move on or navigate their lives in different directions. A person who has never played is not asked to get down on the floor and play, nor is a person with a fear of drawing asked to play with finger paints in the assumption that they will be able to do it. The patients must be met 'where they are' and then, together with the therapist, can try to build a 'room' where it is safe to play.

In one of the summer schools, a group of trainees worked with the Jansson story 'The Invisible Child'. Throughout the week they were working with this family in different ways; individually – small groups and big groups, by physically playing and using paint, crayons, play pastry (with which they created the whole family), and by dramatising it and playing the different roles of the family members. It was amazing how many people identified with the 'invisible child' within themselves but, after being allowed to play out the painful feelings of the child, were also able to identify with other members of the family. This identification with the family also occurred with those who, at the beginning, could not identify with the 'invisible child'. After playing a role they had chosen, they were later able to see that there was a part of all the characters in them.

One exploration was on the family dynamics before the story began and the whole group felt it was important to explore the 'frozen aunt'. They developed scenarios of her childhood and family and many people experienced their own feelings of rejection, or being controlled, which led to part of themselves being 'frozen'.

During the progression of the sessions the 'invisible child' was accepted for itself and more and more parts of its body became visible, first the feet, then the legs and slowly the remainder of the body. Alice Millar (1983) says that we internalise the projections of others, especially our parents, and make them parts of ourselves. What we have discovered through art therapy and dramatherapy is that this often has a physical manifestation. The internal and external body become models of the parents' ideal or control.

Through the art and drama, people discover how to play and, by being helped to explore different roles or re-shape the one they feel stuck in, they gradually start to build up their own self-image. Bit by bit, like with a jigsaw puzzle, the image becomes more whole. They learn to put aside pieces that do not belong to their picture. It is not only the picture that they have about themselves, but also the role they have in relation to that picture that leads to transformation and maturity. However, as human beings, they never have the total picture, and the journey of life is about discovering new aspects of both the self and the world.

Within the context of an intensive training group like a summer school it is important that people reach a safe plateau before they leave. In the story of the invisible child, it was important for people to connect with the internal wise grandmother who could be a source of wisdom and guidance.

The Moomintroll stories provide a rich source of material for working with individuals and groups, and should be part of the therapist's repertoire. As we said in Chapter 4, the art therapist and dramatherapist both need to have an extensive storehouse of material and experience from which they can draw to assist the patient move on. The detached therapist who cannot make a connection with the person in the therapeutic space, either through metaphor, media or life experience, is unlikely to make the invisible child visible and may well be experienced by the patient as yet another frozen aunt.

The well body and the unwell body

Another summer school had the underlying theme of health and illness to be explored through different art and drama media. It was our intention to explore the physical image people have of themselves – whether people accepted feeling unwell as a matter of course and whether they also denied being unwell.

We started with a body-self questionnaire:

1. If you had to describe your body on a job application form, how would you describe it?
2. What would you not include on the form?
3. What is your favourite body part?

4. What is your least favourite?
5. What body part do you regularly get ill or in pain?
6. If plastic surgery could be had by just wishing, which part of your body would you like to change?
7. In your family as a child, was a lot of attention paid to illness?
8. If yes, in what ways?
9. If not, how was health drawn attention to?
10. Who was allowed to be ill in your family?
11. If you had a medicine cupboard, what was in it?
12. What bodily descriptions can you remember being called as a child?

Through the questionnaire, people became sensitised to the fact that illness and health can be relative rather than absolute for concepts, individuals, families and cultures. Participants shared their questionnaires and discussed in particular who had the 'sick role' in the family or who was given 'weak' statements such as 'you are the delicate one'. These roles and images we are given become internalised and accepted into our false body-self.

We then explained to the group that in Greece they have small silver disks which are offered up on the altar when people pray for good fortune, health and so on. Many of these 'tamata' picture different limbs/body parts/babies and so on, which are offered up when people are ill. We asked the group to create their own tamata on a small piece of paper. They drew a body part they perceived as ill or weak and then a second one of a part they perceived as well.

It is important to create both these images so that people are able to acknowledge the 'well side' and so that they can create a bridge of healing energy that can be used from the strong to the weak. It is also possible that people will only try to create the strong and the well and will deny that there are any any aspects that are weak or ill.

People grouped in relation to their image – if they had a similar picture or area of the body that they felt was weak or ill. There were five groups in a whole group of twenty people: three had themes of the uterus, ovaries and vagina; and one was about the senses – ears and eyes and one was about limbs – hands, legs and feet.

Each group was asked to create a dance based on those parts and they developed very vigorous movements with a lot of stamping and clapping and pelvic thrusts (especially one of the uterine groups). It surprised us that these were the body parts that they experienced as weak and ill!

Each group then took two large sheets of paper which ran down the whole length of the room. One piece was the 'well' map and the other the 'ill' map. They were then asked to free-associate on the paper in relation to wellness and illness using colour, words, symbols, environments, weather and so on. Each person then went on a journey, saying how they felt at the different stopping points on the maps. What surprised many people was the strength they found in the 'ill map'. One woman, suffering from very debilitating pre-menstrual tension, said that although she felt very vulnerable, she actually felt very strong in the 'weakness'. Several people did not know how to cope in the strong 'well' map.

The purpose of both these methods is to enable people to bring into a relationship and dialogue both the well and ill parts of themselves and to leave outside those parts that do not belong to them. Although psychotherapists would say that this is the purpose of most therapy, our contention is that the body – the living body as an organism as well as a metaphor – needs particular kinds of attention. Many therapists themselves are out of touch with their own bodies and have difficulty re-discovering them and making use of their own medium in relation to their patients.

Many people find it difficult to give up a 'sick role' or being the invalid; they may only feel 'visible' if they are sick. This could go back to childhood when children are usually given their sick role and discover for example the strength in being weak. Many of our roles are learned in childhood and children discover that a 'sick role' brings its own rewards. So-called 'weakness' becomes very powerful and can be used to control the family.

(*The Authors' Process:* Åse and Sue shared that dance had been a fascination for them both as children, which seems to be their main body pre-occupation. It is said that the children of medical families are usually medically neglected, and Sue feels she was no exception!)

A recurring theme for many people is that of 'superwoman' – the woman who does not allow herself to be ill. It is part of her multiple performance of succeeding in the workplace and the family that she never admits that she is below par. This, of course, is a pretend role, and takes a lot of energy to keep up. If it is internalised and maintained for a long period of time, it may lead to eating disorders or body neglect or the suppression of medical conditions.

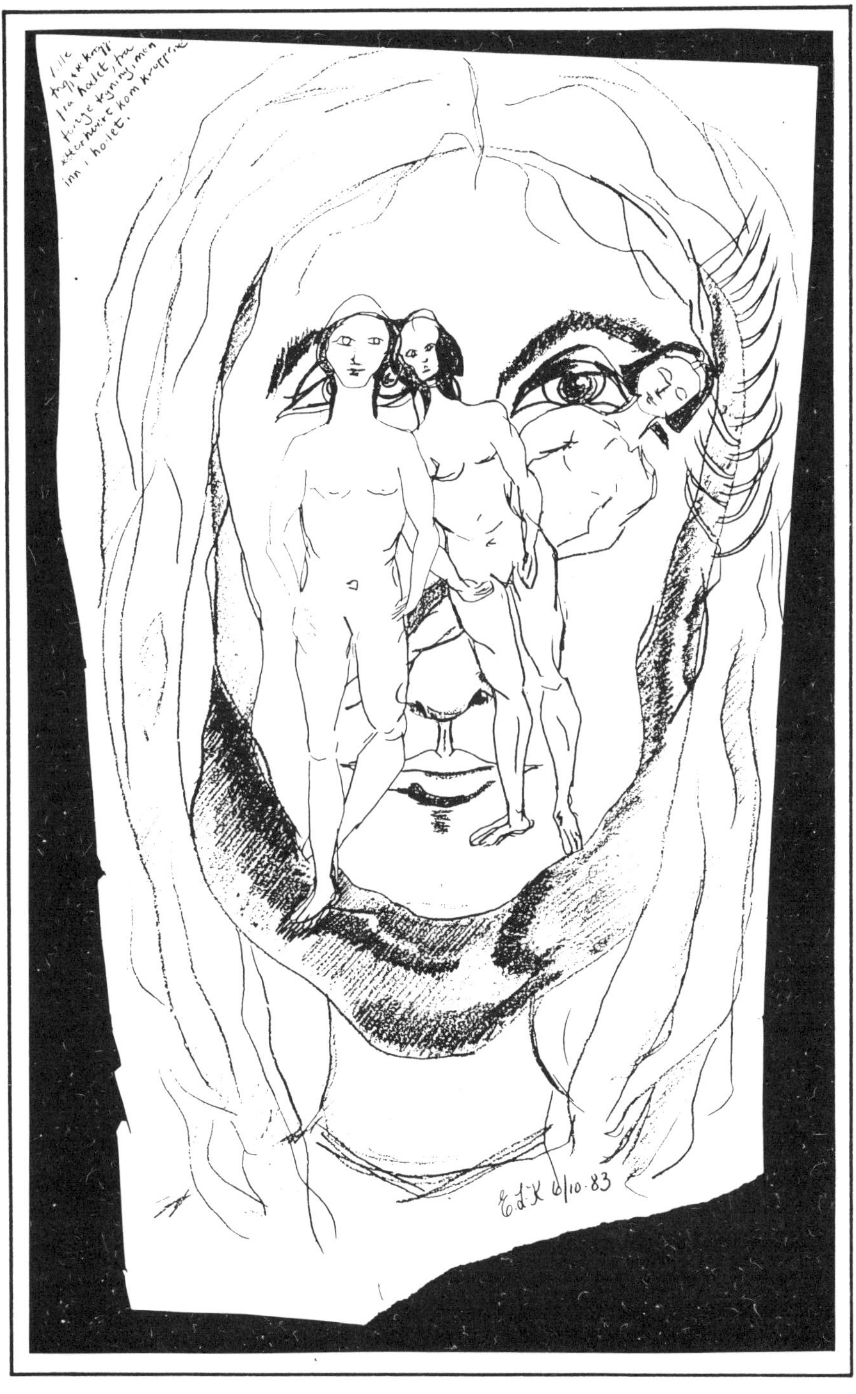

Our hidden faces

Because there are such physical demands made upon art therapists and dramatherapists, it is essential that professional people have time and space to re-experience art and drama for themselves. It is also important that they have sufficient 'time out' to allow their own bodies to regenerate. It is easy to become automotons without sufficient physical nurturing and replenishment.

> A man thronged up with cold; my veins are chill,
> And have no more of life than may suffice
> To give my tongue that heat to ask your help;
>
> (*Pericles* II.i.73)

CHAPTER 7

Transitions and Bridges
In-Betweens, Go-Betweens and Marginal States

OLIVIA: Of what personage and years is he?

MALVOLIO: Not yet old enough for a man, nor young enough for a boy; as a squash is before 'tis a peascod, or a codling when 'tis almost an apple....one would think his mother's milk were scarce out of him.

(*Twelfth Night*, I.v:150)

We have both been very moved and inspired by the writing of Winnicott and his emphasis on the importance of transitional* phenomena. In a chapter entitled 'The Location of Cultural Experience' (1971) he asks the question:

> If play is neither inside nor outside, where is it? (1971, p.113)

He then goes on to describe his main thesis which is summarised as follows:

1. The place where cultural experience is located is in the potential space between the individual and the environment.
2. The use of this potential space is determined by every individual's life experience.
3. Babies have maximally intense experiences between 'me and not-me' in this space.
4. All babies have their own favourable or unfavourable experience in this space, where dependence is maximal.
5. In order to study play and then culture, one must therefore study the potential space between the baby and the human mother-figure.

---

* Sue Jennings 1992 for a discussion of Transitional, transitionery and Trance

For Winnicott, the in-between, or transitional, space is essentially creative and contains the early play of the child – especially its experiences with the transitional object.

> I have claimed that when we witness an infant's employment of a transitional object, the first not-me possession, we are witnessing both the child's first use of a symbol and the first experience of play. An essential part of my formulation of transitional phenomena is that we agree never to make the challenge to the baby: did you create this object, or did you find it conveniently lying around? That is to say, an essential feature of transitional phenomena and objects is a quality in our attitude when we observe them.' (ibid, p.113)

We were discussing the possibility of an art therapy and dramatherapy course which included the exploration of transitional objects. However, curiosity about each other's early experiences of special toys, transitional objects and, indeed fantasy world took over. The following is what we recorded about our personal worlds, which we include before further developing theory and practice:

Sue: So, Åse – did you have a special toy or transitional object?

Åse: I can't really remember. I can remember when I was about five, I had a doll; it could close and open its eyes. My parents rented out a room to a student. This student used to talk to me with my doll. She made for me a red silk skirt for this doll, and when I woke up in the morning it was there – I have never seen anything so beautiful. And this student made me feel a very special person, especially when she made something for my doll. I kept the doll until my teens and used to write books for it, pretending that the doll was this student. Later, I gave it to my niece, which was a pity... Did you have a special toy?

Sue: Of course it was war-time. I remember sucking two fingers for a very long time – maybe until I was eleven years old.

Åse: I sucked my fingers as well...

Sue: I was given a furry rabbit in a doll's bed when my younger sister was born – it had very silky ears – and then a doll in a pram, which I used to put in the garden like my sister, until a girl from down the road stole it and ran down the road to her house. My mother and me, running after her – it made it very exciting! Much later, I had a teddy bear – after the war was over – and put scent in its ear so that I could smell it when I went to sleep.

Åse: This student's room was a magic place where I could go and visit. And writing for the doll was like a diary. I took photos from my parents' album and created something very beautiful – a history for the doll. It was very private, and I hid it. It was important that no-one else read it: it created a whole fantasy life for me, through the doll. This was just after the war and there were buildings and cannons still left around. It became important to me that I should be able to save people around me if there was another war. This was what the diary was about...

Sue: It was important for me to create spaces where I could hide. I had several places in the fields near where I lived and no-one else knew about them. I felt very responsible for other people. The war had done some sort of damage which was why no-one had any money.

Åse: There was so much anxiety after the war; people were always whispering about what had happened, and the toy was something safe and constant: also a silk skirt for a doll when there was such a shortage of everything was very important.

Sue: We seem to have some similarities; both being born near to the war and having families that had a lot of secrets or were very preoccupied. Magic or special places were important for feeling safe and also for having adventures – also, mine were very green; up willow trees or behind a pond or moss-covered bank. I also had strong feelings about justice: fierce loyalty was very crucial, and if someone let me down, at least I would know that the toys would be trustworthy.

Åse: So, we are talking about symbolic processes – imaginative processes – special places or objects representing something that we want them to – we can project our needs into it.

Sue: Not just our needs, but also our fantasy. We can be anyone or anything in the fantasy. My spaces were like a kingdom, both inside me and outside me.

Åse: We lived more in the fears of the war than in the celebration that it was over, so one way to get out of this was by creating the doll and having adventures. We travelled around the world together and met people who were different from the people around me. In those days people did not travel much. Going from Norway to Sweden was a major trip.

Sue: Yet both of us as adults have made major journeys around the world and met such a range of people, and both of us chose at the time very unorthodox ways of helping people. When we first started, art therapy and dramatherapy were not exactly well known. What did your parents want you to be?

Åse: My mother wanted my brother to be a priest. My sisters and I were encouraged to be carers of other people. It was important for girls to marry and have children.

Sue: Yes, I was told that marriage was a career anyway and that men did not like intelligent women! Adults' view of the world I found very boring, but also the pressure to conform was enormous. My preoccupation with special places, yes places that can contain a whole world, are very important. Grown-ups always thought that I romanticised the idea of living in a bed-sitting room, but for me it was a whole world in that magical space, rather like the theatre.

Winnicott states that there is a third space that is neither intra-psychic or inner space nor the real external world, but a space where playing and culture take place.

> I have used the term cultural experience as an extension of the idea of transitional phenomena and of play without being certain that I can define the word 'culture'. The accent indeed is on experience. In using the word culture I am thinking of the inherited tradition. I am thinking of something that is in the common pool of humanity, into which individuals and groups of people may contribute, and from which we may all draw *if we have somewhere to put what we find* (ibid, p.116).

He does not wish to devalue the other 'spaces', but suggests that in this third space we do things that we value in a special way:

> Nevertheless, playing and cultural experience are things that we do value in a special way; these link the past, the present and the future; *they take up time and space*. They

> demand and get our concentrated deliberate attention, deliberate but without too much of the deliberateness of trying (ibid, p.128).

The importance for the development of the art therapy and dramatherapy is this idea of the transitional space and the experiences that it contains, which links, or bridges the past, present and future. The art and the drama are part of this focused time and space that gets a unique type of attention – not our everyday attention, but the worlds of images, metaphors and symbols.

Whereas Winnicott suggests that the importance of transitional phenomena decreases as cultural interests increase, we maintain that the emergence of the creative process is central to the projective stage of human development which leads into children's play. For psychological health, it is not sufficient to have a cultural interest. Art and culture are deep-seated and ancient forms that reconcile and express unfamiliar experiences both for individuals and groups.

We mentioned earlier how small babies express what we term 'proto-art' before they can walk: it would seem that this early sensory experience of touch – as taste, sound and rhythm – focuses into transitional phenomena that must have the qualities of both sameness and difference. So, for example, the child who needs a piece of cloth to remain the same, and who is distressed if its mother puts it in the washing machine, also uses the same cloth to hide behind and frighten adults. Transitional phenomena allow the infant to express a range of emotions as well as being the means of creative development – creative development meaning that the child is exercising its imagination and creating, as Winnicott says, a world of illusion.*

In order to create this world of illusion, infants must be able to project their experience into symbols – a particularly human activity. Transitional phenomena represent the child's first attempts at symbolic action. These symbols, which increase in number and variety during the first three years of life, are used both dramatically and artistically. They create the symbolic world of the child, which is illusory in the sense that it is symbolic – *not* that it is not real. The creation *is* real within the boundary of dramatic and artistic reality, which is necessary for exploring our fantasy life as well as helping us to grasp our everyday experience. Thus, dramatic and artistic play are not just ways of learning about the world and developing motor skills, they are ways of grasping what is often the ungraspable, of

---

* see also Napier quoted in Chapter one

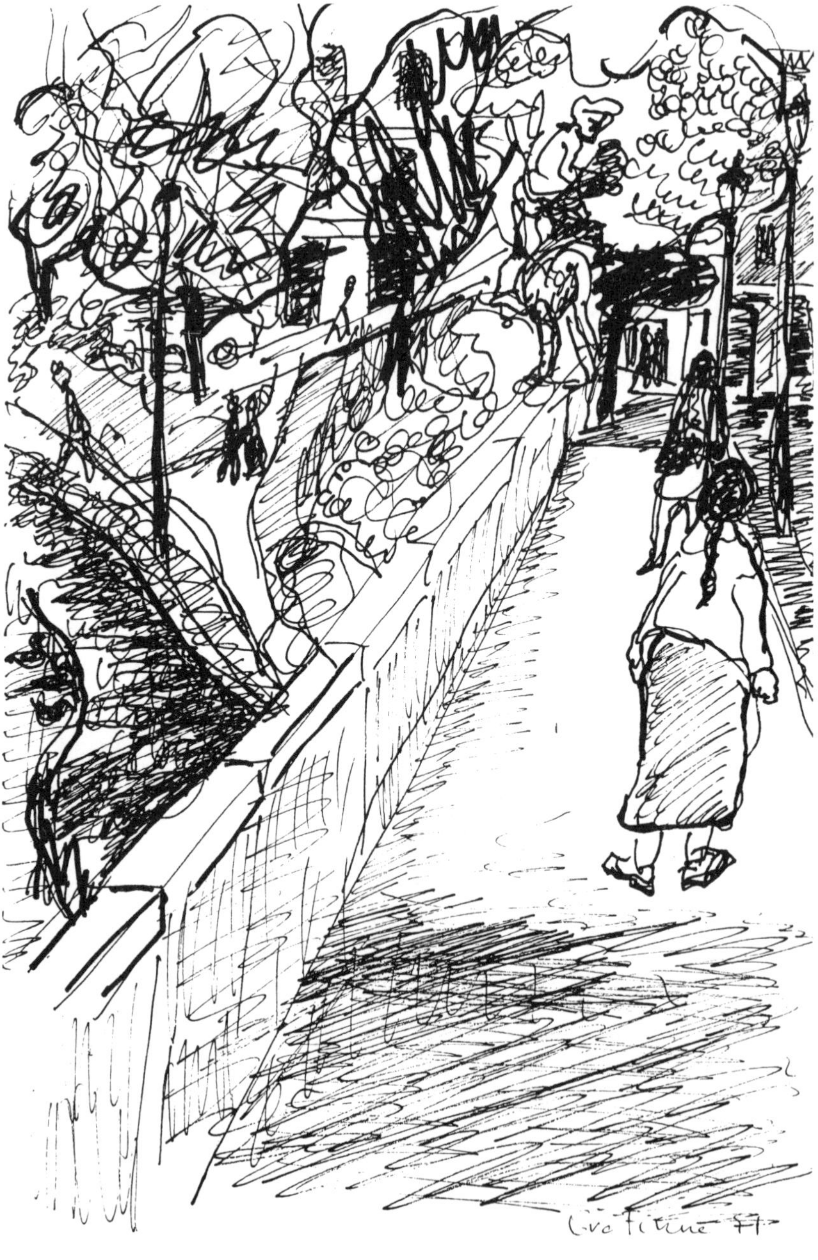

Patient and therapist meet on the bridge

expressing those human aspects that cannot be verbalised. The myth and fairytale are equally dramatic and artistic in their representation and allow children to experience and develop their imaginative selves.

Let us look at how this develops from the early experience of transitional phenomena:

> *Clinical Example*
>
> In an art therapy group, the theme was of transitional objects (TOS). A girl of twenty found it very difficult to express themes from her childhood and had difficulty remembering anything. However, the TO work enabled her to remember a doll; it gave her a lot of joy to recall it – she had recaptured her lost childhood and she made it in clay and cloth.
>
> Another patient, borderline, was obsessed by this doll. She was a patient who made demands in excess of reality on staff. Nothing was enough. She could remember a cat that was not hers but that she had to share with her brother. She was very jealous of the doll and said that she never had anything and no-one loved her enough.
>
> After the group, she took the doll from the first patient, having heard how important this doll was, the second patient wanted it too. The first patient was able to explore how she gave away important things – even herself.
>
> The second patient, however, was unable to make a connection between her needs and the taking of something so important. This patient was still trying to get her divorced parents back together, in a very manipulative way. Her mother wore young colours and also had had everything taken away. The TO work mirrored the early development of both patients.

Both painting and drama give us the chance to try out and test the possibility of difference. The transitional object(s) both integrate as well as enable exploration of the child's world. This balance between sameness and adventure allows the development of both dependence and predictability, as well as uncertainty and curiosity.

The rag doll that becomes the friend and confidante can also be neglected and stamped on and can also sail on the sea to a new land, as well as being 'role-reversed'; i.e. the child can talk to the doll and then become the doll and answer on its behalf. These diverse experiences are still proto-art and, rather than becoming less necessary for human beings as they develop, they become more necessary.

In art therapy and dramatherapy, it is important to bear in mind, that learning to work or play with 'the object' is an expansionist, not a reductionist, activity: it makes more possible that which was not possible before. Thus, the patient whose world is restricted to a narrow range of experience – the 'person in a box' experience – is able, through symbolic objects, to experience an awareness and understanding and find a greater degree of security in not knowing. The patient who has no containment or boundaries – the 'person in the sea' – through the dramatic and artistic structure can allow objects to take on their real function. For example, because a picture has a frame it contains certain experience and allows some phenomenon to become dominant. The person without a frame is unable to differentiate between experience. They are literally 'all at sea' – confused and chaotic.

In cultural terms, myths and fairytales serve as regulators of transitional materials – floods and loss of control versus castles and imprisonment; cast adrift without name, or trapped in a role and a name.

The following is a description of an extended workshop on the theme of transitional phenomena. It is important to remember that different people work within different time-frames. Winnicott again reminds us of the importance of waiting and of the primacy of the patient:

> If only we can wait, the patient arrives at understanding creatively and with immense joy, and I now enjoy this joy more than I used to enjoy the sense of having been clever. I think I interpret mainly to let the patient know the limits of my understanding. The principle is that it is the patient and only the patient who has the answers. We may or may not enable him or her to encompass what is known or become aware of it with acceptance ' (ibid, p.102).

The transitional object and its journey to find wisdom

A large group of twenty-five professional people are meeting together for three days:

Day 1

After introductions, names, stating of expectations and objectives, we ask everyone to write their diary and to focus on any childlike feelings they now experience. We warm up the group and physically centre the body.

STAGE 1

We set up a structured imagined journey in stages, back to people's own childhood:

> Sit comfortably. Start to think back in your lives. Think about college and studying. Then to your teens – where did you live?

...and so on.

> See if you can remember before you went to school. Can you remember your house? bedroom? anything special? in colours? toys? shapes?

textures? Can you recall your favourite toy or material? Did it have a name? What happened to it?

i. Focus on your earliest toy/beloved object.

ii. Paint the object.

iii. Walk around the group and see other people's pictures.

iv. Form small groups with people with similar object. Share how you feel about your toy/object.

v. Imagine you *are* the toy/object. Write the story in the first person of all the things that happened to you. Did you get abandoned? Share your story in the small group.

This stage took an hour and there was an atmosphere of complete focus and concentration. Many people shared similar toys and there was a group of very different ones.

STAGE 2

i. Let go of the youngest time and let your mind move around the time before you were ten. Choose an age and write it in the middle of a large piece of paper.

ii. Divide the paper into four with the following headings and include the various topics suggested below:

Rules Values Do/don'ts	**People** Family Friends
AGE	
Special Things Stories Toys Celebrations etc. Hobbies etc. Attachments	**Food/health** Anxieties Women's fears Losses

iii. Make connections between the different sections using colours.

iv. Underline anything that is still relevant in your life today.

v. Share what you have done in groups of people who have written about the same age as yourself.

vi. Paint a picture of *one* event at that age as a way of ending today's session.

Group members then wrote their diaries before session closing.

Day 2

Large group feedback and sharing of any dreams. Several people dream of their objects and scenes of childhood.

Physical orientation and focus.

STAGE 1

i. Comfortable position. We go on a guided imaginary journey through difficult terrain which leads to a forest where you meet…

ii. …a person with wisdom

iii. Hold the image of the wise person strongly in your imagination.

iv. You know that they are older than yourself.

v. Slowly wake up from the journey.

STAGE 2

i. With a partner, draw round each other's bodies on a large piece of paper.

ii. Using your own outline, create the wise person with paints.

iii. Place the picture on the wall, sit quietly and look at it.

iv. Write a story about this wise person: what struggles has he or she had? Where did the wisdom come from? What name has the wise person?…
[compare with the hero's journey in Chapter 9]

Think of a quotation or saying to bring tomorrow. Diary feedback and closure.

Day 3

Large group feedback – many dreams and scenes were shared.

STAGE 1

i. Re-read the story from yesterday.

ii. Sit in front of the wise person and read your story to the partner you drew around.

iii. Leave the person and story. Walk around the room, freeing yourself to be any age you want. Get 'into the skin' of the person at that age.

iv. Think of something you want to ask for – it's very important to you.

v. Slowly make the journey to the wise person through the difficult terrain with the transitional object and ask for what you want. Listen for the answer.

vi. Share the answers in your age groups.

STAGE 2

i. Go back to the wise person and look at them in detail. *Become* the wise person.

ii. Move around the room as that person, remembering all your experiences. Remember what advice you have just given. Remember the saying or quotation you brought in today.

iii. Meet other people as the wise person and share any words of wisdom you wish.

iv. Create a scroll with the advice, quotation and any symbols you want. Roll and tie it as a scroll and leave it at the feet of the wise person.

v. De-role from the wise person.

STAGE 3

i. Look at all the things you have drawn, painted, written and created. Make connections with them and yourself.

ii. Write down the connections.

iii. Open the scroll and read it to yourself.

iv. Feedback in your age groups.

v. In the large group, share the scrolls in Norwegian and English.

vi. Write your final diary before closure.

* * *

Another group with less experience developed the theme as follows:

Day 1

Share names/experience/expectations. Diary.

STAGE 1

i. Go back to childhood: think of early toys – what is the earliest memory you have? Toy? Object?

ii. Share these in a small group.

iii. Think of a favourite story from childhood and choose a character from it.

iv. Become that character – and play.

v. Find someone else to play with.

vi. Did you choose a character that could not play? Write a character analysis of it and read it out in your group.

STAGE 2

i. In small groups, create a story that incorporates all the characters.

ii. Enact the story to the other group.

iii. What did you learn – from your character?
– from the themes in the group/story?

Group feedback and diaries.

Day 2

Large group feedback and diaries.

STAGE 1

i. Go back to your childhood and remember early toy/transitional object. Did it have a name etc.?

ii. Share this with partners, and then in small groups; and anything else that comes to mind.

iii. Choose an incident when you *first* learnt something. Enact the scene to your group.

STAGE 2

i. If a story was written about your childhood, what would the main character be called? (e.g. 'the bad boy').

ii. On a piece of A4 paper, write 'once upon a time there was a little child called…who decided to go in search of a creative person.

iii. At the bottom of the paper write 'and this is how the child called…met the creative person'

iv. Write a story of meeting the creative person.

v. Share the story in the group.

Group discussion and diary.

(*Teaching Point:* We found that the child who is not allowed to play finds difficulty in playing and being creative and often becomes rigid as an adult, whereas the child who is left alone – who may be lonely or isolated – often has a rich store of creative ideas and fantasy situations.)

Childhood can be recalled through toys and re-creating playful times, whereas just talking about the past often blocks people in their recall. Play can reconnect a person with their childhood, as can sensory experiences. For example, a person can be taken back to childhood through a smell – fresh coffee, or bread, and so on.

Transitional objects are related to through the senses: they both feel and smell right as well as containing all the fear and insecurity, and so enabling risks and adventures to be taken, and providing friendship of an idealised kind.

We can see that although we are mainly working with projective material through the transitional object and the various art-forms, it is nevertheless a bodily and sensory experience. When, at a later date, these workshops were developed into pieces of theatre, one person brought along her grandmother's nightdress because it smelt right and another searched for the key from a former house because it became her imagined object.

The playroom and the sand-tray (as we described in Chapters 3 and 4), as well as art therapy and dramatherapy, provide the form as well as the content of this third space. Play and art are not alternatives in therapeutic communication, they both express what cannot be expressed in any other way.

The two workshop examples that we have described illustrate how the exploration of the transitional object enables people to get in touch with their own wisdom and creativity – indeed, their own wisdom *is* their creativity.

> For these transitions (those regarding art and therapy) to take place, however, the therapist has to be willing to feel the psychic fabric of the

> therapeutic communicative structure. Like the artist who must know the very texture and character of his material before he or she can create a work of art, so, too, must the therapist feel and touch the very substance of the patient's being, the quality of his or her presence, the very character of his or her armor, before an empathic transitional space can be created or maintained (Robbins 1989, p.9).

Arthur Robbins draws our attention to the responsibility, inherent in the transitional space, for the therapist to establish an empathic relationship. The relationship itself takes on an artistic texture 'to feel the psychic fabric' and is likened to the art work itself.

Through both art therapy and dramatherapy the transitional space takes on this sensory quality; the body itself and all the senses become receptors in an alive and vital way. This of course can be partly due to the 'regression in the service of the ego' when the sensory play awakens childhood memories and experiences. However, it is also important to say that creative play through art and drama needs to be positively encouraged in adults and not just seen as childish activity.

If we remember the developmental stages of artistic therapy intervention then we will not be surprised at the bodily experience of therapy; the human body is the primary means of learning – all other learning is secondary to the bodily experience – and yet there is a tendency to equate the physical with the infantile and disregard its importance in adult life itself.

> This is an interest in the biological base of art, not just in the sense of having a self-preservative function but also in how the artist works with body perceptions, an inner knowledge and experiencing based on the body's sensations. For instance, Milner writes of 'spreading the imaginative body around what one loves' as a way of dealing with separation and loss. She too felt an imaginative connection between this spiritual enveloping and eating. Milner also writes of this experience both in feeling oneself into the object one is trying to create while painting as well as using the deep body ego to enter imaginatively the experience of the analysand in analysis (Case and Dalley 1992, p.122).

The bodily experience of the art and the drama, if allowed to be expressed, may well lead both the client and the therapist into important areas of work. There is much discussion about 'physical touch' in therapy and the suggestion that it should be altogether avoided. Clients need to know that art therapy and dramatherapy may involve touch and the bodily messages must be clear and non-ambiguous.

It is through our bodies that we may be enabled to enter the transitional space where therapeutic growth and change is possible. The very physical nature of some of Åse's art and sand work has been described, and in

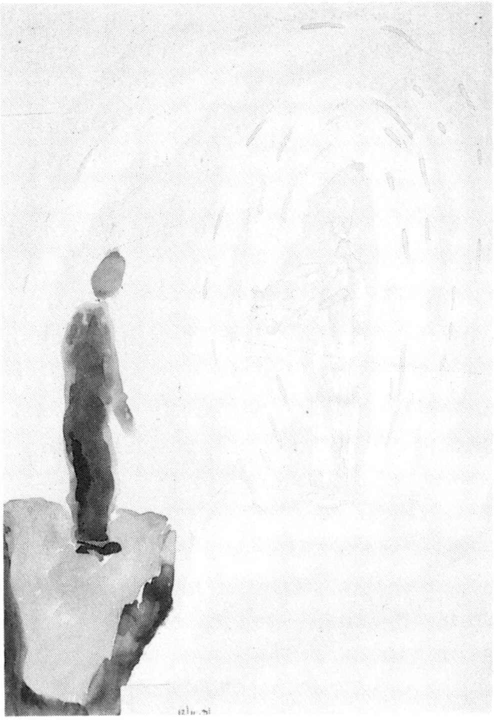

Transitionary space in which object and subject meet. The split object, the good and the bad, becomes one in the art work. There cannot be a meeting if there is not space for it. 'I can see the help is reaching out but I cannot take it'.

drama the physicalisation of characters is also relevant; i.e. to get into the body or 'into the skin' of the person in order to be able to understand the person.

Amongst Winnicott's prolific writing on matters transitional is the following description of what I would term 'stasis'. The question is whether this 'freezing' can become conscious and in what therapeutic mode is this possible.

> One has to include in one's theory of the development of a human being the idea that it is normal and healthy for the individual to be able to defend the self against specific environmental failure by a *freezing of the failure situation*. Along with this goes an unconscious assumption (which can become a conscious hope) that opportunity will occur at a later date for a renewed experience in which the failure situation will be able to be unfrozen and re- experienced, with the individual in a regressed state, in an environment that is making adequate adaptation (Winnicott 1958, p.281).

The art therapy and the dramatherapy are ideal media through which a 'frozen introject' may become conscious and thawed. There are schools of thought that suggest that this can only happen in lengthy psychoanalysis. However, perhaps there is also conjecture here, since it is frozen and unconscious we can only have a 'formless hunch', as Peter Brook would say, that it is there.

The deep bodily experiences of the psyche may be activated through artistic therapies and the therapist needs to be very clear of the levels at which they are equipped to work. It may be that the body itself becomes the transitional space through which there is an attempt to reconcile polarities.

Our closing quote from *Peer Gynt* surely suggests a human need to separate from the primary maternal object relationship.

[*They go, laughing and whispering*]

PEER [*looks after them a moment, tosses his head and half turns*]:
Let her marry whom she pleases!
It's nothing to me.
[*Looks himself up and down*]
Breeches torn. Tattered and filthy.
If only I had something new to wear –
[*Stamps his foot*]
I'd tear the laughter out of them
Like a butcher pulling the guts from a rabbit.
[*Looks round suddenly*]
What's that? Who was that sniggering?
I could have sworn – ! I suppose it was no-one.
I'll go home to mother.

(Ibsen, *Peer Gynt*)

CHAPTER 8

The Opening and Closing of Doors

'as safe as houses'

(old saying)

'three, four, knock at the door'

(nursery rhyme)

'The door of my childhood will always be locked'

(borderline patient)

'Shut up your doors, my Lord; 'tis a wild night:'

(*King Lear*, II.iv, 303)

Before you read any further into this chapter, we would like to take you through the following brief guided fantasy:

Have some paper and pencil near you and some crayons if you so wish; then, read the following instructions, close your eyes for a few moments and dwell on the following:

allow your mind to go blank from all images;

allow yourself to free-float with ideas;

allow an image of a door that *WAS* or *IS* significant to you to come into your mind;

when did you see this door?

why was it so important?

does this door exist or was it in a dream?

have you seen this door again?

Now open your eyes and make notes about anything that has come into your mind. Draw a picture or sketch of the door if you so wish.

We did this exercise together before embarking on the writing of this chapter, and the following is what we recalled. We both recalled actual doors that had been significant in our adult lives:

Åse: I am attending a three-day residential seminar for the staff group of a psychiatric hospital where I work. The seminar is to develop communication and to understand conflict in institutions.

In one of the lunch-hours we are to go on a guided tour. I am late and am locked out of the church where we are supposed to be. I call out and knock at the door, but it all goes unheeded.

Another member of staff comes along and, finding he is also locked out, starts to shout and bang; immediately, the door opens!

This event has proved very significant to me as it illustrates how easy it is to ignore my own needs and to look after the needs of others; how difficult it is at times to make my voice heard in certain situations. It showed me how I need to knock louder on certain doors!

Sue: I am in Jerusalem and have decided to visit the Holy Sepulchre. It is very windy and there are sharp gusts of wind biting into me and I am being pestered by the people selling souvenirs. When I arrive at last, the main door is open and I go inside with the other tourists and follow them around. I spend quite some time at the cave where the angel rolled away the stone (forced entries seems to be quite a theme!) and then go out of the cave and around the back of it where there is a sacred space overseen by the Copts. The back of the cave is their sacred space and a priest allows you to touch the stone for a donation.

I am so absorbed by all these anomalies and conflicts that I fail to hear the warning bell which informs people that the doors are about to close. As I turn the corner, these massive studded doors close with a resounding noise.

I am locked inside the Holy Sepulchre and am told that the doors will not open for several hours! I start to look for a way out through labyrinths of corridors and space and encounter all the religious groups there – even Ethiopian Christians on the roof*. Eventually I see a window and daylight and think that I have found a back door, only to discover that I am in the monks' somewhat smelly lavatories! I wait until the doors open – three hours later.

I felt dwarfed by these massive doors and quite powerless at being locked in. However, this was accompanied by a feeling of extreme sadness at the rivalry and competitiveness of all these Christian groups and their provocativeness towards each other. If the Greek Orthodox,

---

* I wondered what interpretation Bachelard might make of the various locations of these Christian groups and the fierce protection of territory between those who love their brothers!

> Franciscans, Copts and Ethiopians cannot find a way of being together, just what hope is there for the arts therapies? If these groups continue to squabble over spaces and artifacts that belonged to Christ is it really surprising that there are continued fights over the rights of arts therapists?

It was interesting for us to note that both these spaces were sacred spaces and that Åse could not get in and Sue could not get out. The incidents were also remembered as very sensory experiences as it was cold and windy.

There are assumptions made about therapists and patients alike in relation to the opening and closing of doors: 'therapists are the people who will open doors for their patients and will provide the magic key', or 'the main function of expressive therapies is to assist patients open doors'.

People's defence systems are seen as walls or barricades and the discovery of the doors or the key the obvious way of penetrating the defence system. It is very easy to adopt the language of sex or war in treating 'defences' – we talk about our 'breaking down barricades' or 'penetrating defences'. It is our contention that the therapists' function is to wait at the threshold* or doorway to assist people with the following possible choices:

> 'Do doors need to be renamed?'
>
> 'Is there a choice of doors?'
>
> 'Do people need to find a new door?'
>
> 'Is it the right moment to explore this door in particular?'
>
> 'Have I faced this door before?'
>
> 'If I knock on this door, will I be answered?'

You, the reader, may well find other preliminary questions to be considered. Indeed, it may well be that the discovery or the facing of a door – in itself – is the work that needs to be done. If, through the means of art therapy and dramatherapy, we are to assist people to knock on their difficult doors, we must be very clear that we understand the implications. *It should not be assumed that all doors are to be opened; indeed, one function of a door could be to lock certain experiences from consciousness.*

Traditional psychoanalytic thought claims that the opening of well-defended doors is at the core of therapy. However, as recent research with

---

* I have referred elsewhere (1990) to the notion that the dramatherapist is a frontiersperson; someone who waits at the threshold or doorway – a truly liminal person.

holocaust victims has shown,* total recall of the horrors does not necessarily mean the improvement of people's psychological states. Indeed, particularly in situations of post-traumatic stress disorder, the 're-living through' is not the most helpful way of working†. Rather, people's capacity to 'self-soothe' and the re-establishment of their belief system as part of the 'repair' is found to be more effective.

> Is there anybody there said the traveller?
>
> Knocking on the moonlit door.
>
> (de la Mere, 1936)

> Knock Three Times
>
> (popular song)

> Knock knock
> Who's there?
> Dr. Who
> Dr. who?
> That's what I said
>
> (modern joke)

The images of doors and their capacity to be closed or opened is also associated with knocking on doors and calling. Will I be allowed in? The following description of the central scenes in *Macbeth*, illustrates the powerful image conjured up by the repeated knocking on the door.

One of the most tense moments in theatre is the conflict that arises in Act II, scenes ii and iii in *Macbeth*. Immediately after the murder of Duncan, there is knocking at the castle gate. It is first heard by Macbeth, then Lady Macbeth, and then by the drunken porter:

> MACBETH: Whence is that knocking?
> How is't with me when every noise appals me?
> What hands are here! Ha – they pluck out mine eyes!
> Will all great Neptune's ocean wash this blood
> Clean from my hand? No, this my hand will rather
> The multitudinous seas incarnadine,
> Making the green one red.
> [*Enter Lady Macbeth*]

---

* Personal communication from University of Haifa with their research with Holocaust survivors.

† Whereas Inanna might need to appear naked and bowed low, many people need a cloak of protection. This is particularly so if we are working with post-traumatic stress disorder.

LADY MACBETH: My hands are of your colour; but I shame
To wear a heart so white.
[*Knock*]
I hear a knocking
At the south entry. Retire we to our chamber.
A little water clears us of this deed;
How easy is it then! Your constancy
Hath left you unattended.
[*Knock*]
Hark! more knocking.
Get on your nightgown, lest occasion call us
And show us to be watchers. Be not lost
So poorly in your thoughts.

MACBETH: To know my deed 'twere best not know myself.
[*Knock*]
Wake Duncan with thy knocking! I would thou couldst!
[*exeunt*]

(*Macbeth* II.ii.57)

Notice how Macbeth is terrified by the sound and Lady Macbeth responds calmly and with expedience. Both of them use very striking metaphors of colour and water (which are followed through later in the play). The very powerful image of the green *multitudinous* sea turning to red and a *little* water clearing away the evidence; and although they both have red and bloodstained hands, Lady Macbeth accuses her husband of having a white heart. It is as if the actual knocking at the gate has 'knocked' an awareness into Macbeth of what he had actually done. The last line illustrates his wish to reverse what has happened, i.e. if only the knocking could wake up the dead Duncan.

This scene is immediately followed by the Porter's scene where, in a drunken and bawdy interlude, he parodies himself as the keeper of the gate of Hell as he answers the gate:

[*enter a Porter. Knocking within*]

PORTER: Here's a knocking indeed! If a man were porter of
hell-gate he should have old turning the key.
[*knock*]
Knock, knock, knock! Who's there i'the name of Belzebub?*

The shock comes when the Porter alludes to hell and the everlasting bonfire in a comic scene which is placed immediately after the act of murder. There are links between the guilt, the expediency and the humour

* (The full text of this important scene is quoted in the Appendix).

through the knocking at the gate – multiple metaphor with multiple resonances.

Although at variance with traditional psychoanalytic thinking, which says that all areas of a person's life need to be brought into the conscious present and remembered and re-lived, it is our belief that some doors *need* to stay closed and that other doors can only be explored through the careful use of arts therapy. Words alone, without artistic structure and form, are unable to achieve the paradox of both containment and expression of some of our more shocking and painful experiences.

Although we would not disagree that many images of doors are linked with sexuality, we find it more helpful to put it in the following way. Doors are symbols of entry to, transition through and exit from, many areas of human experience, which include sexuality. In this way, we are working with 'both and' rather than 'either or'. With 'either or' it is very easy for meanings to become polarised and also very reductionist – if we work with 'both and' it assists the therapeutic process to be expansionist.

Doors, thresholds and gates are means of entry, experience or permission; doors and keys feature in ritual, myths and legends and the rites of passage through life stages.

We ask the reader to pause and think about a story or fairy tale that involves a door or a key that was significant for them as a child. Write down as much of the story as you can remember and create a picture of the door or the key as well.

Then think about the process that has happened to you; how did your own feelings become affected? What happened to your own concentration, body state, temperature, and perception? Write it down.

You may then like to write down as many key or door images as you can think of: did you have a 'coming of age' celebration? How many silver keys were you given?* The following is a quick list that Åse set Sue to do in a few moments of free-association:

Stigma of not having a key of your own door; gypsies and people of no fixed abode are treated harshly in courts; you cannot get hire purchase or loans if you do not have a permanent residence or if you are not on the Electoral Roll.

Brides are lifted over the threshold at marriage (in Africa they 'jump the broom'); fertility rite; opening doors of fertility.

'Open Sesame'; Arabian Nights; stories; keys of castles; the Laidley Worm and the keys being given to the daughter.

The gates of Heaven and Hell are both guarded and we journey to one or the other!

* The age at which we are 'grown-up' is purely notional – 17, 18, 21 – and, if you are a student – never!

The key to the 'Secret Garden', (a favourite book when Sue was a child).

Melanie singing, 'I've got a brand new pair of roller skates, have you got the key?'

The Temiar people do not lock doors and feel they can wander in and out of each other's houses freely. However, they shut their doors if they feel external danger is approaching such as tigers or dangerous strangers.

'I will give you the keys to Heaven; I will give you the keys to my heart'.

Alice in Wonderland and the miniature key.

We both have a vast collection of postcards which we use in our work: a whole section has doors, windows, keys, gates and various sorts of barriers and entrances. We may also ask patients to bring postcards and photographs that are important to them, as a starting point in therapy.

Doors and windows also feature in rituals of birth and death to ease passage into this world or the next – remember, it is only recently that we have stopped using the word 'confinement' when a woman gives birth and, indeed the 'lying in' period after both childbirth and death has traditionally been signifed on the front door with an announcement or bouquet or wreath. Both at birth and death there were appropriate times to 'open your doors' to visitors. In childbirth no-one should enter until the woman has been cleansed – several weeks after delivery. Many people do not visit where there is death because of a fear of the 'spirit of death' which may not yet have left the house.

> whether any mydwife within your parishe in tyme of weomens travill be knowne or suspected to use sorcerie, witchcrafte, charmes, unlockynge of chests and dores (McLaren 1984, p.15).

Certainly, in the nineteenth-century, nurses would open doors and windows as a person was dying in order to allow an easy death; some people thought it would allow the soul to escape and thereby prevent a person from 'dying hard'.

There is not space here to further elaborate in any detail the doors of birth and death,* however, it is important not to underestimate their significance in relation to the symbolism of entry to and exit from the world.

We need also to be aware of the impact of having doors locked against us or of being locked inside somewhere, and we should point out that this is in both literal and metaphoric senses. For example, a daughter may well have been locked out by an irate father or locked in a cupboard under the stairs; however, we may also feel locked out when we are rejected or

* In many of the birth and death rituals there is a similarity of symbols – for example eggs were found in the Egyptian tombs; we give flowers at both events.

indeed locked in when we feel trapped in a situation or a repetitive behaviour pattern.

In the Moomintroll story quoted in an earlier chapter, there is a storm raging outside when the kind aunt comes and knocks on the door of the Moomintroll's house. The impact of this story, when used therapeutically, is the transition from the raging storm outside, to the everyday calm of this family who are sitting around a table cleaning mushrooms (see Chapter 4).

> *Clinical Example – Åse:*
>
> In an art therapy group, members were taken on a guided memory journey down a pathway that was familiar to them and then asked to paint the door that each of them was standing in front of. After this exercise, a female patient said to me:
>
> 'I can't paint this door because it's not really a door – it's ... a coffin.'
>
> I suggested to her that she stay with this image and to paint it where it led her – what we call 'going with the flow'.
>
> She painted the 'coffin door' and then said it was next to two other coffins which contained her dead parents. She had a lot of resistance to engage further with the door, saying that she felt her grave had already been dug.
>
> In the group, we progressed to face the door that we had recalled and then painted. When this patient decided to face her door, she discovered that the 'coffin door' was indeed the door to her creativity and her creativity had been buried next to the coffins of her parents who symbolised all her loss and sorrow. In being able to face the loss and sadness in her own life, she also was able to discover a treasure in her creativity.

This illustrates very aptly the discrimination necessary when we decide which doors need to be addressed. It also illustrates how we 'bury' things, qualities, people who have not yet died or who do not need to die.

Sue: In preparing this chapter, I have been aware in my own notes of certain slips of the tongue and mixed metaphors as well as the curiousness of Åse and myself when translating into each other's languages. For example, I have just been making notes on *Åse in Wonderland*. Åse wrote and asked me to 'help put more meat and flesh on the bones and make the words more alive'. (Åse is a vegetarian and works with eating disordered patients).

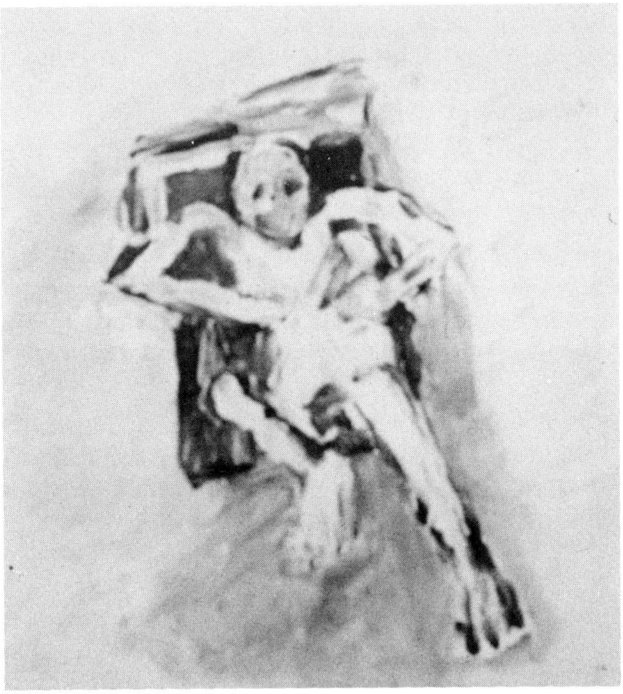

Coming up from the basement. 'The picture is dealing with birth and death. One dies to be born'.

In preparation for work in both art therapy and dramatherapy, the personal therapy of the therapists, as we discussed in Chapter 3, is very important. Within the context of this chapter is, of course, the theme of therapists paying due attention to their own doors – which of their doors needs to stay locked and which should be explored? Otherwise, we can fall into the trap (door) of imposing our door journeys on the people with whom we work and find vicarious experiences through people opening their doors on our behalf. Therapists can be guilty of invasion of their patients – do we break down their doors?

This is particularly important to address when we are working with the victims of abuse of different sorts – especially rape and sexual abuse. For people who have been sexually abused, their 'doors' have been broken down and repair is essential. However, repair, as we said earlier, does not necessarily mean re-experiencing the abuse – this could well result in the experience of secondary abuse rather than reparation.

Clinical Example

A young woman was referred for dramatherapy following a very vicious rape attack during which she was tied down, blindfolded and her mouth stuck with sticking-plaster.

Her preoccupation was with the 'sound and smell' of the experience: 'I have been defiled for ever. I will never be clean again, and there is not enough water to bathe night and morning.'

Her concentrated effort to wash away the experience and her own feelings of pollution were acute and real and she was very anxious about polluting other people. She was extremely anxious that the man in question would knock on her door again – a many-layered metaphor indeed.

In the session, we created a door in her life that had been safe and where she felt in control, and through this door she was able to discover a lot of healing energy to bring into the present situation. The door that had been violated – both the door of her house that had been broken down as well as the rape – could then be explored in the context of some doors being safe and some being dangerous.

During this time she explored in the general rather than in the specific, fearful and comfortable sounds and smells, which ended up with her dramatising her own version of *Alice in Wonderland*; being able to feel 'big enough' to deal with the world outside, and to hold onto the key which controlled her doors.

In our work we have sometimes asked people to imagine themselves as a house – 'If you were a house, what sort of house would you be?' – and then draw, paint and sculpt both in clay and through drama, the house. There is always attention paid to doors, windows, drawbridges, moats, and barricades. The well-defended house can be a statement from someone who has been abused. It also can be a quite different type of statement, as the vignette below illustrates:

Vignette – Sue

In a dramatherapy group we were exploring the house theme. Everyone drew an individual house having first closed their eyes and concentrated on the house as a theme, staying with the first image that came to mind.

This led into a 'mapping' exercise in which people placed their houses in relation to other houses. People were permitted to place their house as near or as far from other houses as they so wished, providing it was within the frame of the imagined 'map'. [It is important that the therapist makes these limits very clear at the beginning of the exercise].

We explored the group dynamics through the positioning of the houses – those that were in clusters and those that were more distant, and we eventually ended up with several clusters, one or two pairs, and a few that were on their own. We stood back and considered this 'map' of the group.

One young man had drawn a house with heavily mullioned windows and a studded front door. It was set in a large garden filled with flowering cherry trees. He was very ambivalent about where his house would be placed in the group's 'map', first placing it in the centre of a village and then placing it right outside. He looked very confused and was obviously struggling to 'place' himself. I suggested that he place it somewhere right now and that he could change it later if he wanted. He placed the house with the cherry trees at the very edge of the map and said to the group, 'The door of my childhood will always be locked.'

Later in the group's life, he was able to create a human sculpt of the door with different group members being different parts of the door. They were instructed not to let him open it however hard he tried. I asked him who was behind the door and he chose several people in the group to be his family. We created the sculpt again and he sculpted a family which looked very menacing. He was allowed to look through a crack in the door for twenty seconds before seeing and hearing how strong and bolted it was. This glimpse was enough for this extremely disturbed young man, who guided what he needed to do by saying that the door should be kept locked.

Summer school on the theme of doors

In 1987 we decided to focus on the theme of doors for a Summer School. We had developed many ideas and ways of working in a course two years' earlier in which we had focused on houses and shelters (see Chapter 5), and in which the motif of the door kept recurring as the metaphor, as the above case examples demonstrate. The brochure for the programme had a door on the cover that came from an old house in Trondheim.

The people were invited to bring with them anything that was important on the theme of doors. The response was amazing – it struck a chord with so many people. They had rummaged in their attics to find old keys and door-knockers and brought photographs and postcards of doors and keys; people had even started to dream about doors and pathways and gates.

As in previous years, we felt it was useful for people to keep a diary which, this year, would be in the form of a folder in which all their work could be contained. People arrived in a very excited state of mind with the door things which were all placed together in one part of the room.

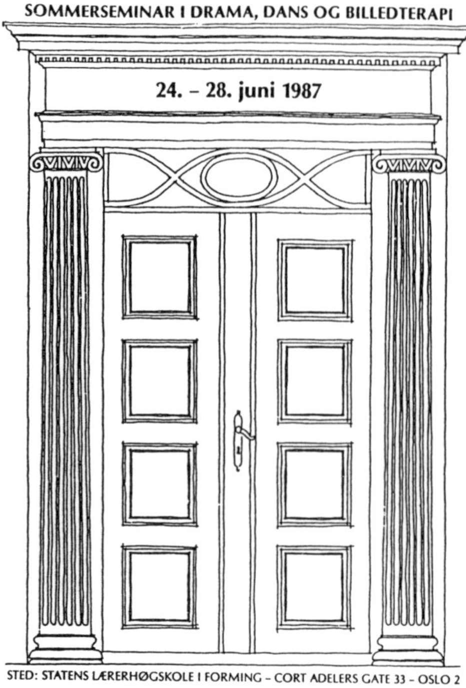

The Trondheim house

Day 1

We had the usual big group information session where the aims and objectives are clarified, practical information is dealt with and people are introduced. As before, everyone met in the big group on the first and last days and then worked in smaller groups (beginners, intermediate or advanced) for the intervening days. (This has become a rhythm of work for a Summer or Autumn School that we find works very well. The ritual shape of a course is important in its design, and participants feel secure to take more risks when they understand the ritual boundaries.)

Everyone took a piece of A2-sized card and folded it in half to make a folder. They found a space where they could be quiet and had paints and water with them.

(*Teaching Point:* The following exercise was done quite deliberately without a 'traditional' warm-up and we wanted to start with the 'doors' that people had with them at the outset of the course.)

We asked people to close their eyes and to think about what door they had brought with them to the course. Once the image was clear, they were to draw and paint it on the outside of their folders. After some minutes of reflection everyone became very absorbed in their first door – and the doors were so very different. Everyone had time to look at each other's doors and then they wrote their diary *as if* they were the door. For example:

> I am a large green solid door. I am the front door of a house that is near the fjords. I have some glass in the top quarter of myself and there is a little curtain there. I have been a door to this house for many years – maybe as many as eighty. I have seen people come and go in this house, although it has always belonged to the same family.
>
> The great-grandmother and father are now dead and so is the grandmother. In the house are the grandfather, mother and father and three children. The children are growing up fast and one is already away at the university – a son who is very clever. The daughter and the younger son both want to leave home and there are many rows.

(This person needed some help to stay with the story of the *door* rather than get too quickly and deeply into the story of this family. The family would prove a theme later in the School.)

> I am a very strong door and have stood up to the severe weather. There have been many gales and storms and when the wind comes in from the fjord it is very frightening. However, I have protected the family during all these years, even though I have been kicked and banged – especially when young Marit got locked out. Her mother locked her out when she wouldn't come in to do her school work.
>
> I know a lot about this family although I am a bit weatherbeaten and not a fashionable door. Some of the family want to move into a new house. There is security here – at least it is stable, but on the other hand some people are not very happy…

(She was prompted to describe the door more):

> I am made of solid wood – the outside is green and the inside is dark brown. The hall is very dark. I have two keys that open me: an old key that is kept hanging on a nail in the hallway and is only used if they all go away, which isn't very often; and another key that is a small modern key which is used day-to-day, except that people are always forgetting to lock me. In the old days people did not lock their doors and the back door of this house is always left unlocked.

(Notice how it is possible to establish the metaphor by guiding this person to 'stay with the door'. The door itself has a lot of possibilities for exploration: read through the above again, and write down possible themes for exploration.)*

---

* It is so important to stay with the chaos – the metaphor, until we know it is appropriate to move people on; however, usually people move themselves forward when they are ready.

(*Teaching Point* A character analysis can be written about anything or anybody; it is a way of people 'getting into the skin' of the part and developing some role boundaries. Although essentially a theatre and dramatherapy technique, it can also be explored through art – 'paint the character of this person; paint the side that they do not show; that the parents see...')

In the above example we assisted the person to create the necessary 'dramatic and artistic distance' to be able to establish a strong dramatic metaphor, i.e. the door. Because art therapy and dramatherapy can work very quickly – very often reaching the inner life of the person immediately – it is necessary for the therapists to be vigilant so that the person can measure the amount of disclosure they wish to make. Premature disclosure can be devastating for people and drive them to build up further defence mechanisms rather than allowing themselves to be freer.

People shared the stories of their doors in small groups and then wrote their diaries which they placed inside the folders.

The labyrinth

Day 2

After writing diaries and big group feedback, people went into groups of six or so. The aim was to look at their door of the previous day and consider whether it was a door that needed to be faced, a door they wanted to leave, or a door they wanted opened.

One young man became very distressed and said that he could not face his door – it was all too much and he was fearful.

We made a paradoxical intervention and got the other people in his group to become heavy doors that blocked his way to the fearful door. He was invited to try to reach the door and each time he removed one door another appeared. In the end this became a kind of labyrinth* with the fearful door at the centre.

He stopped and realised that it was not a one-dimensional issue for him of facing or not the door in question. He in fact was feeling quite lost in his life and the opening of *any* door felt frightening: 'I can't go forward and I can't go back' he cried (rather like the ram caught in the thicket in the I Ching who had to stand still and take joy in the standing).

This became a theme in the group, of issues such as:

'I take one step forward and then two back'

'I feel really stuck'

'I feel trapped'

'I feel too scared to move'

Everyone was asked to make an 'I' statement like the above and then in their group to body-sculpt the feeling. People created sculpts of being weighed down with people on their shoulders, being held by the ankles so that they could not move, being stuck in quicksand and sinking fast, being trapped in cupboards and attempting to scale a mountain and slipping back each time.

People had put a lot of physical energy into these sculpts and were very exhausted. We suggested that it would be useful to work with the theme of staying exactly where we were and not moving anywhere: if we do not struggle, then no-one needs to hold onto us.

We guided people into a relaxation exercise where they were able to do some deep breathing and replenish themselves. We then asked them to imagine a space that they go to in their dreams – it could be day-dream or sleep-dream – where they like to be. Whatever the place was, it was possible to have a fence or wall around it. Only they had the key to the

* The labyrinth represents a transitional space – the imagery appears on many ancient stone monuments. It contains as well as traps; it can hold you as well as lose you. However, it usually is a space for movement, though not perhaps what we expected.

door or gate in the wall to enter this place. When they shut the door behind them, they could rest and be calm, breathing in all the good things of this special place.*

Slowly, people came to again and we asked them to paint the door in the wall on the inside of their folder and then to write about the place inside in their diary.

An immense calm descended on the group and it was clear that they had found a way of being in the now and that they did not have to strive and struggle but could stay exactly where they were. The feelings of the shackles, traps and quicksand diminished although, of course, we knew they were not banished. However, the 'secret place' over which they had control gave a balance to the otherwise destructive place which existed in the now.

Day 3

We started again with diaries and feedback. People had a lot to say about the family themes that had begun to emerge: feeling trapped in the family and not being able to move; having a fixed role and feeling that they had to live up to the family's expectations.

(It was fortunate that we had both worked at length on our familial roles and the type of role-expectations that we had grown up with, because the themes in the group were very strong and powerful. Sue's family, in particular, believed in ascribing roles to all the children that persist into middle-age: 'so-and-so 'understands' wine or money or medicine (male roles)' and, by implication, no-one else in the family does!; so-and-so is good at mothering, writing, dancing, painting, acting (female roles) and, by implication, you cannot do more than one).

Each group worked on a family scenario where one member was trapped in some way, but where the characters were fairytale or mythic characters. We got into this by the 'character growing' exercise:

> Start naming characters in the family and then give them a mythic status: father and mother become king and queen and then weak king and wicked queen and then weak king in the green hat with a feather and wicked queen in the red shawl.

We illustrated how, on the first day, the door knew a lot about what was going on in the family; had lived with it for many years and could comment rather like a chorus on the situation. Each group decided what in the house, if not the door, could take on the chorus role: there was a clock, an old sofa, a door, a television and a family photograph. People

* My good friend and colleague Steve Mitchell always reminds me to 'breathe in the positive feedback or the insightful comments'.

rehearsed and presented these families in which they had to develop the role of the chorus-object who commented and made suggestions.

Each group presented their family to the whole group and there were strong themes about older/younger generation conflict, flexibility and rigidity, choices and favourites. People took comfort from the fact that each group had similar themes and that the chorus figure was so helpful, both in bringing some new observations to the situation as well as providing the security of the link with the past. Each group then had to create a sculpt of their family and speak their key lines.

The session closed with each person painting the door of their family and then writing their diaries.

(*Teaching Point* – Notice the pacing of people's experiences and how different images are taken into the general from the particular. The family exercise does not mean that the family necessarily changes, but it takes in the context of the family as a whole and not just the perceptions of one individual's perspective. In other words, what we have dealt with above is the family as a system and possible resolutions for the system as a whole, rather than change in a single individual.)

When a family system feels like a maze or a labyrinth, it is usually amenable to arts therapies. The maze is a trap, but is also chaotic, as people do not know where they are.

Day 4

On the final day of the Summer School we brought all the groups together again for an inter-group sharing and a closing ritual of the school as a whole. All three groups had been working in similar ways, although most of the material described above was from the advanced group. Everyone took their door folders, looked at their material and then shared it within the small group they had had on the first day.

People then created the door of their ending on the backs of their folders in answer to 'What door are you taking away from this course?' People then looked at their own journey through the four doors – the door they arrived with, the door to the 'secret garden', the family door and the ending door. People realised that they could take things from the second door into the third door; that the special place where they could be still could modify what went on in the family. Many people found that the difference between the first door and the last indicated areas in their own lives where they could start to work. For example, there were initial doors that were heavily barred or shuttered or with heavy hinges; doors that seemed like strong barriers or too heavy to move. Many of the final doors, although still secure, were less heavy and less like barriers; a variety of colours was used and door lintels were decorated.

We then asked everyone to stand their doors upright and wander around looking at the wide variety of doors. People were asked to create a small gift for themselves and another gift that they could leave on the 'doorstep' for their partner. When all the gifts were complete, people opened them, and they had included sayings and quotations.

The final session was inspired by the workshop in the previous year when the group had created a single person with all the 'junk' materials they had brought.

They said goodbye to the doors, walked away from them and re-engaged with the whole group in a vigorous physical warm-up. They then did 'spot' improvisations where everyone had to instantly *be* a door, a letterbox, a love-letter, a knocker and so on. We went through a whole range of 'door possibilities' and then asked them to choose one group to be in that was something to do with doors: there was the door itself; a hinges group, a knob and knocker group, a lintel group, a doormat group (!). Each group was asked to create a body-sculpt of their part of the door and we then attempted, amid much hilarity, to put the door together.

Then, each group was asked to create their part of the door from all the 'junk' materials. We both waited with baited breath, since the creation of this door was a rather different proposition from the hermaphrodite person last year. (Then, there had been arguments as to whether the person had breasts or not and how big was the penis and could you see inside the brain!) This group, however, was extremely industrious and set to work to create a strong door-part. Even a doormat had 'welcome' on it; there was a bunch of flowers to go on the doorstep, and a letter to go in the letterbox.

The moment of reckoning came when they decided to see if the door would fit together. The extraordinary thing was that it did! The door fitted the lintels and the hinges joined it together; there was a floral curtain at the window, and a door-handle, a knocker and a letterbox. Breaths were held as the door was lifted into position, suspended from a balcony by string, and it rose into position – a complete and decorative 16-foot door.

There was a moment of enormous silence as we all beheld what had been possible with a group of forty people and a room full of junk. The participants created a spontaneous folk-dance that went through the door and around it. Then each of us stood in front of the door and then behind it with our own silent final statements.

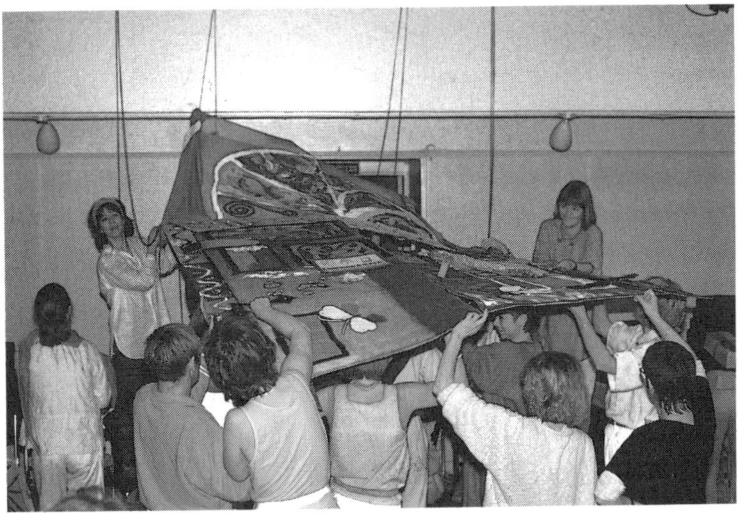

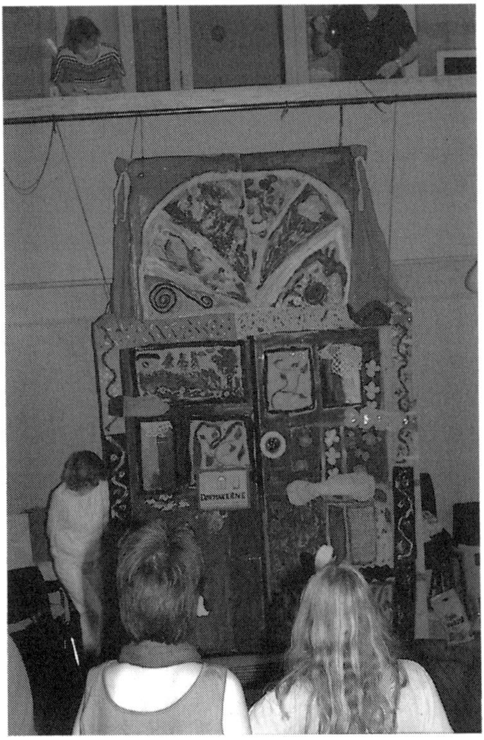

Group work

The door workshop has gone down in history of the art therapy and dramatherapy movement in Norway, it had such a profound effect on everyone; the leaders too were lost for words.

The photograph of this door speaks for itself, as the closing of the door of this chapter.

> **PEER GYNT**: There must be a bolt. I must bolt the door against trolls. Against men and women, too.
> There must be a bolt – a bolt that will hold against little goblins and all their spite.
> They come when it's dark, and they rattle and knock:
> 'Open up for us, Peer, we're as nimble as thoughts!'
>
> (Ibsens, *Peer Gynt*)

CHAPTER 9

Creative Journeys

HELENA: We must away;
Our waggon is prepared, and time revives us.
All's well that ends well; still the fine's the crown.
Whate'er the course, the end is the renown.

(*All's Well that Ends Well* IV.4:33)

PUCK: I'll put a girdle round about the earth
In forty minutes!

(*A Midsummer Night's Dream* II.i:175)

PEER: Well, I've reached one resting-place. Where's the next?
One must try them all, and choose the best.

(*Peer Gynt*, p.155)

Sue: In our lives as well as in our work, the theme of journeys is very important. We discovered, as we looked at a globe, that, between us, we had been round the world. Åse had journeyed west to the U.S.A. for a protracted period of work and study, and I had journeyed east in order to research a rain-forest tribe. Both of us had met in Scandinavia, the Mediterranean and the U.K. Despite a basic 'nomadic' quality in us both, we also realise that we need the 'base to return to' where there is calm and stillness as well as creativity and fertility. For Åse this is the wooden cottage in the pine forest, set all alone amongst wildflowers and animals, with water drawn from the well and a log-burning stove. For me it is my little house in Stratford-upon-Avon – right away from any tourist trail yet less than a ten-minute walk from the Royal Shakespeare Theatre – where there is both a wild and a cultivated garden, and the river and canal are only a short walk away. Both of us have journeyed to each other's spaces and found particular peace there.

As well as these 'bases', we find it is also important to continue journeying through our respective art-forms. It is easy for arts therapists to lose sight of their art-form for its own sake and be submerged in the work with clients and patients, so that it is always a direct form of therapy. Åse continues to weave, sew, knit and embroider, and I continue my theatre-art, drama and mask-making. Both of us find a sense of poverty and deprivation if we stay away from our art-forms for too long. We feel that our own art-forms complement each other and are aware that we only felt secure in each other's art after we had worked together.

All therapy can be described as a journey; all life can be thought of as a journey from birth to death. However, we are advocating the use of specific journey-structures to enable people to experience personal growth and to reappraise their current journey. Some people become 'stuck' in the journey, as we saw in the last chapter on Doors; others become trapped in a repetitive circle. Circular journeys become very demoralising and destructive for people who often enter therapy for other reasons such as depression, insomnia, repeated relationship breakdown, domestic violence and so on. Some people are permanently 'on the move' through friendships, jobs, religions and countries in an attempt to 'discover themselves'. We are not talking here of the pilgrim-philosopher on a journey-search who, although undergoing deprivation, nevertheless is content. We are talking of itinerant restlessness in which people continue the journey without having learned from the previous experience and everything is discarded.

In our discussions on this theme before one of the courses, I suggested to Åse that you could divide people broadly into two categories: those people who were 'settled cultivators' and those who were 'hunter-gatherers'.

Åse: I'm not sure which I am. With the children and family I feel like a settled cultivator at times, but I really think I'm a hunter-gatherer.

Sue: I've always felt I am a hunter-gatherer and yet all my brothers and sisters are definitely settled cultivators; one brother, actually, is a farmer.,
Maybe it has also to do with whether or not you are an artist or an artiste? All my actor friends that I've asked have seen themselves as hunter-gatherers.

Åse: Well, I have journeyed to many countries and been happy to stay where I found myself and moved on again when I felt ready. Having the children, especially as late as I have, has been a journey – or three journeys in themselves.

Sue: Yes – but look how well-travelled your children are already; like me when my three were young: you have given them a broad experience from a very early age. They are all still under eight years and are almost bilingual, like you and Fred.

Åse: Of course, travelling, in one way, in Norway, is almost a tradition; we go skiing or to the fjords or to a holiday cottage, quite apart from any travel abroad which is a more recent thing: I don't think that is the same in England.

Sue: I suppose, traditionally, we are a nation of farmers and industrialists, both of which you could call settled cultivators. We also are renowned for our explorers as well as sailors who of course are hunter-gatherers –

Åse: – though of course, travelling all over the world is more popular: have you noticed how some people want to keep things the same – food, hotels – settled cultivators on holiday!

Sue: Did you travel much as a child?

Åse: No, we lived in the same family house for all my childhood and my parents only left it quite recently when my father became seriously ill. I think my family – extended family – are probably settled cultivators.

Sue: I moved house as a child something like nine times before I was ten years old. I didn't understand why we moved so often; I knew it was the war and so on, but other families didn't move so many times! My father did not seem to mind the moving; he, ideally, was a hunter-gatherer and would have been happy in the Forces and moving from place-to-place, whereas my mother was a far more settled sort.

Åse: What journey-story can you remember from when you were a child?

Sue: 'East of the Sun and West of the Moon' in my Norse book of tales that my sister gave me when I was ten years old (and I still have it). And you?

Åse: I was going to say 'Askelad' who is a well-known person in Norwegian fairytales – many of my patients will mention him. Shall we use one of those stories on the course?

As it turned out, we didn't use either of those stories in this particular Summer School on journeys and transformation, but instead, used a journey-story structure adapted from Joseph Campbell* called 'The Hero's Journey'. We would like to make it clear that, in all our instructions, the hero is gender-free.

Because the hero's journey is the journey to encounter the dangerous unknown, it is essential that boundaries and limits are established within a very clear structure. Someone telephoned in panic after using this structure with a group of very disturbed patients in their second session. Half the group had left and the remainder were either very depressed or extremely agitated. No thought had been given to the therapeutic process that is engaged in such a structure – it is certainly not a method to be used with just any kind of group, let alone one where the disturbance level is high.

The ten stages of the hero's journey

1. The call to go on the journey.
2. Preparations for the journey.
3. What is in my knapsack to take with me?
4. Setting out on the journey – the landscape and terrain.
5. The encounter with the unknown or the danger.
6. The call for help.
7. Overcoming the danger.
8. Discovery of the treasure.
9. The journey on (to the new place) or the journey back (to the old place).
10. Reaching the destination and reflection on the journey.

This structure, which has various adaptations, may be used as we describe below in the context of an intensive Summer School over a period of a week, or it can form the basis of ten to twelve weekly/fortnightly sessions with a short-term group. It can also be incorporated into medium and long-term therapy when the group is ready to 'voyage'.*

* There are many variations on the journey of the hero as described in the books in the further reading section; the important thing to remember is that a primary mythic structure is essential if we are to explore these myths through active engagement with the themes—especially since most of them are taken out of their original context.

Most journey myths and stories incorporate variations on the above stages, and the reader is invited to consider their favourite journey story in relation to these stages.

Day 1

We started with the landscape that people would be journeying through and Åse took them through a guided fantasy about a terrain that they wanted to cross. Everyone then had an hour to paint their landscape. Following this, they spent some time in small groups with people who had similar pictures to themselves. There was a remarkable recurrence of bleak and empty landscapes that were difficult to traverse.

In the small groups people found that their pictures formed a complete map and one landscape joined onto another. Although there was a feeling of support for some people because they shared similar pictures, there was also a feeling of bleak depression which seemed to waft in the group.

Sue took the next part of the session and, through movement and drama, created some very difficult terrain. The mountain climb (Barker 1978), where the floor becomes the rock-face and people have to pull themselves up the mountain, seemed a very appropriate beginning. An environment was then created in the room of a very narrow ledge, stepping-stones in a raging torrent and an active mud-swamp (compare Chapter 8 and the quicksands). People traversed the terrain in pairs and assisted each other when necessary. The helper was instructed only to give help when asked and to give 'enough' rather than 'take over'. Sheets were then spread on the floor which made it very slippery, and people crossed the 'ice', finding their balance by themselves and also with a partner. They also experimented by doing this with their eyes closed.

People reflected on their landscape pictures again before deciding what they would take with them in their knapsack. The essence of the journey is to travel light and there was some discussion in the group concerning 'luggage' in real life. How easily we carry metaphoric burdens that are either unnecessary or do not belong to us. People also discussed whether they 'travelled light' when they went on holiday. Some people could not envisage a journey without their hair-dryer; others took a toothbrush and a clean shirt.

We returned to 'The Hero's Journey' structure and found that people had forgotten the title, though even it seemed to empower people to think what was necessary for their journey. The rule was that they could take two things that would either guide or comfort. People painted the contents

---

* If the individual or group is ready to voyage, then remember to establish where it is possible to lower the'anchor' and rest awhile.

of their knapsacks, which included maps, knives, family photos, drinks, seeds, sleeping rugs, compasses, and so on and, of course, the small 'photo' of the terrain that they had painted.*

We reflected that we had accomplished the first three stages of the journey – the call, the preparation and the knapsack, and that tomorrow we would be ready to set out.

Day 2

The first part of the workshop was spent in creating a complete landscape in the room that was to be traversed which incorporated all the things that had been talked about and worked with the day before. People chose their individual starting points and decided where they were aiming to get to. The terrain was less bleak than on the first day and, although there were ice-caps, there were trees with a river and some vegetation. People also created their knapsacks (from scrap materials with the help of a stapler) and symbolic objects to place inside.

The journey had a pause for rest and sustenance before the second part which brought them face-to-face with the danger. At this point we stopped the journey and created a painting of the danger. The dangers included fear of isolation, fear of the dark and the shadows, nightmares of monsters, fears of the world and not being able to compete, and fears from the family that imposed values and attempted to control. The pictures were an amazing set of rich images with a depth of fear and danger that could not be verbalised or communicated in another way. People then put their 'danger' picture alongside the landscape and wrote about the connections between the two. This was a very private diary that individuals wrote for themselves.

Day 3

In order to face the danger, people decided to create a 'cloak of wisdom' that is worn by a wise person who could help them. Again, we used materials brought onto the course – discarded sheets, curtains and scraps,† and people first created the cloak and then decided to either paint it or stick on motifs. They spent some time in reflection with their eyes closed on the symbols which for them, represented wisdom.

When the cloaks were complete and ready to wear people folded them up and placed them near their stopping place on the journey. They then went into the role of a wise person who is being asked for assistance, put on the cloaks and absorbed the wisdom before considering and writing

---

* Having worked with the big landscape picture people then painted its 'photo'

† It is possible to create the most elaborate artifacts from 'junk'.

down the reply. People shared their advice to themselves in both their small groups and the big group while still 'in role' . Many people surprised themselves with their capacity to reach out to themselves and to have some words of wisdom.

We then worked specifically on people's voices through breathing and amplification. People practised both their range the power of their voices in order to have more flexibility, with many discovering that they had a far greater range of voices inside them than they had thought of. They were then asked to create the 'poem of the wise person.'

They placed the poems and cloaks in their knapsacks and commenced the journey home. No-one this time was going to a new place; they said that they were going to the old place but seeing it as a new person – maybe they would be ready to leave it soon.

The session finished with people speaking their poems in their new-found voices, with the realisation that the voice itself could overcome fear. We talked about the different shields that we can wear and how each has a different voice to suit the particular situation we are dealing with. The poems read like epic tales of heroes on their journeys, and could well have been used by troubadours singing the tales of journeys that had been accomplished.

THE MEDICINE WHEEL WORKSHOP

The workshop on the shamanic medicine wheel took the form of a different type of journey. We had been impressed with the literature on shamanic symbols that enable people to move from their fixed points. According to Hyemeyohsts Storm:

> At birth, each of us is given a particular Beginning Place within these Four Great Directions on the Medicine Wheel. This Starting Place gives us our first way of perceiving things, which will then be our easiest and most natural way throughout our lives. (Storm 1972, p.6)

On the wheel, there are the four points of the compass each of which has a colour and an animal. The colour is associated with a quality and the animal with medicine. So, the North is White and has wisdom and its Medicine Animal is Buffalo; the South is Green, meaning Innocence, and its Medicine Animal is the Mouse; the West is Introspection which is Black and its Medicine Animal is the Bear; and, finally, to the East is the Eagle Medicine Animal and the colour Yellow, which represents Illumination.

Storm says that if we only stay at the point at which we are born, we shall only be a partial person and he gives the South as an example. He suggests that if we only stay in the South we will be too close to the ground like a Mouse and see only what is in front of us touching our whiskers! Therefore, it is our task to journey in all the Great Directions.

> After each of us has learned of our Beginning Gift our First Place on the Medicine Wheel, we then must Grow by Seeking Understanding in each of the Four Great Ways. Only in this way can we become Full, capable of Balance and Decision in what we do. (ibid)

In his book *Seven Arrows*, Storm talks about true experience which, according to him, consists of Touching and Feeling, through which we will overcome loneliness. He says that the Wholeness which is Total Being consists of Breath of Wisdom and Total Understanding. The Medicine Wheel can help us to journey in the different directions towards a state of wholeness.

In the workshop we told the story of the Medicine Wheel and asked people to create their own wheel from a large circle of card. They drew and painted the compass points and illustrated the colours and the animals. Then they created a smaller wheel which they fastened on top of the larger one with a wing-clip so that it could be turned round. The inner circle represents the individual and their personal journey within the bigger journey of the medicine wheel. People chose a symbol to represent their life's journey and painted in the small circle. During the workshop, people added to both the outer wheel and the inner wheel and turned them so that different constellations came together. The aim of the Medicine Wheel in the workshop was to integrate the various aspects of the journey alongside the personal revelation and insight that occurs within the personal wheel. All the work on the wheel was done through colour and image.

The Little Prince – Antoine de Saint-Exupéry

The journey-story that we worked with on this occasion is part of *The Little Prince* and his discoveries. There are people who do not work with this story since they say it focuses too much on death. However, there are some very important stages in the prince's journey which, if used with care, can provide an important voyage of self-discovery. The story is about the imagination and the nurturing of relationships – that one should waste time on something that really matters. The sections of the story that we use are summarised as follows:

Section I

This depicts the feelings of a misunderstood child whose imaginative attempts to draw the real world have to be explained to the grown-ups who then deny them as time-wasting. Disheartened, he gives up this creative side of his nature and eventually becomes a pilot. As an adult (as in childhood), whenever he tries to communicate his true feelings to another he feels that he has to pretend in order to fit into the pattern required by that person.

Section II

The narrator leads a solitary life, meeting no-one with whom he can empathise, until one day he crashes his plane in the Sahara Desert, a thousand miles from habitation. Here appears to him a prince-like child asking that he be drawn a sheep. Various pictures of sheep do not please until the pilot draws a box and says 'The sheep you asked for is inside.' The little prince is delighted, for here is someone whose imagination matches his own.

Section VI

In the prince's world his only real pleasure had been to look at the sunset, which gave him immense comfort in times of sadness. One day, using his sensitive powers, he was able to glimpse forty-four sunsets. Everyone needs something or someone to relate to in times of pain.

Section VII

Here, the little prince's feeling for the true meaning of life is revealed. Using the symbolism of the sheep eating the flower he shows the need to be aware of others, reaching out with a loving concern. However, this interaction between people depends on time being given for listening and communication and for true emotions to be expressed; otherwise inner pain and despair can result.

Section XX

The prince is saddened when he finds 5000 roses all alike, for he had thought that the one rose he had was special. He feels that unless something is unique it is not so worthwhile. He does not realise that we all have special qualities and interact with each other in different ways, however much alike we may seem.

Section XXI

Here the little prince is shown how a true friendship develops, not only from trust and responsible behaviour but also from a willingness to communicate honest feelings so that a shared understanding is built up.

> This the fox teaches the little prince when he says 'It is only with the heart that one can see rightly; what is essential is invisible to the eye.'
>
> Every relationship is unique and although when we open our hearts we make ourselves vulnerable to pain, the gain is the greater, for the memories live on in our hearts and become part of us. Relationships are the true meaning of life.

In the first two sections of the story the author gives us themes to address concerning adults and children. For example, how adults expect children always to be useful and not to day-dream – 'Satan finds work for idle hands to do' goes the saying. For the workshop, these scenes were taken from the story and the small groups created a family scene that involved children not being understood by adults. The groups work at their scenes and present them to the big group, and then before they de-role put something they had learned onto their wheels which moved them on in their journey.

In these families there were many children who chose not to explain to their parents what had been misunderstood and felt that it was easier just to let it go. In one scene, the child was scolded by the mother because she had dropped a cup. The reality was that the child had been locked out from the place that she normally went to after school and was frozen, which is why she dropped the cup, but she said that it would take too long to explain and it was easier to switch off. Several women in the group had wanted to follow careers that were seen by their parents as 'masculine' and men in the group had been laughed at for wanting to follow an artistic career because it was thought to be 'feminine'.

People also made comments that adults always want children to be busy, and that reading or drawing or dancing or singing are not considered busy. In particular being able to sit and think or be quiet in one's room and to 'just be' is prevented or diverted into more acceptable occupations.

With the next two sections of the story, we looked at the prince's pleasure and immense comfort in seeing the sunset and his concern for awareness of others and the capacity to listen.

Each person chose an image for themselves that gave them comfort and sustenance in times of pain and distress and spent an hour on painting it. Then it was shared with a partner who could demonstrate their capacity to 'really listen' and give full attention to the other. The instruction was to give full attention and to ask questions if they wished, but not to make interpretations of the other's painting. This image was then incorporated onto the inner wheels and the people continued their outer journey.

Finally, we read the full story of the 5000 rose bushes and the meeting with the fox. Here the true meaning of friendship can be found through being able to fully accept another: 'the taming of the fox'. This lead into a discovery about our own wildness and the need to understand it. The story was finished by the creation of the single rose bush to 'waste time with'; (remember the work of Violet Oaklander discussed on page 29; in particular her 'draw the rose bush' exercise).

The healing metaphor of the small tree that will blossom for us if we waste enough time on it enables us to create the final stages of the Medicine Wheel journey, and we place the rose bush on our inner wheel.

The points of the compass in the North-American Indian Medicine Wheel led us both into thinking about healing shapes from other stories and cultures. Similar shapes and images occur in rituals of birth and death in many cultures. Below is an image of a maze that can be trod in a fertility dance or that can be used to confuse spirits from finding the way to the grave of the recent dead. The stone circles in many forms are part of the earlier history of various parts of Europe.

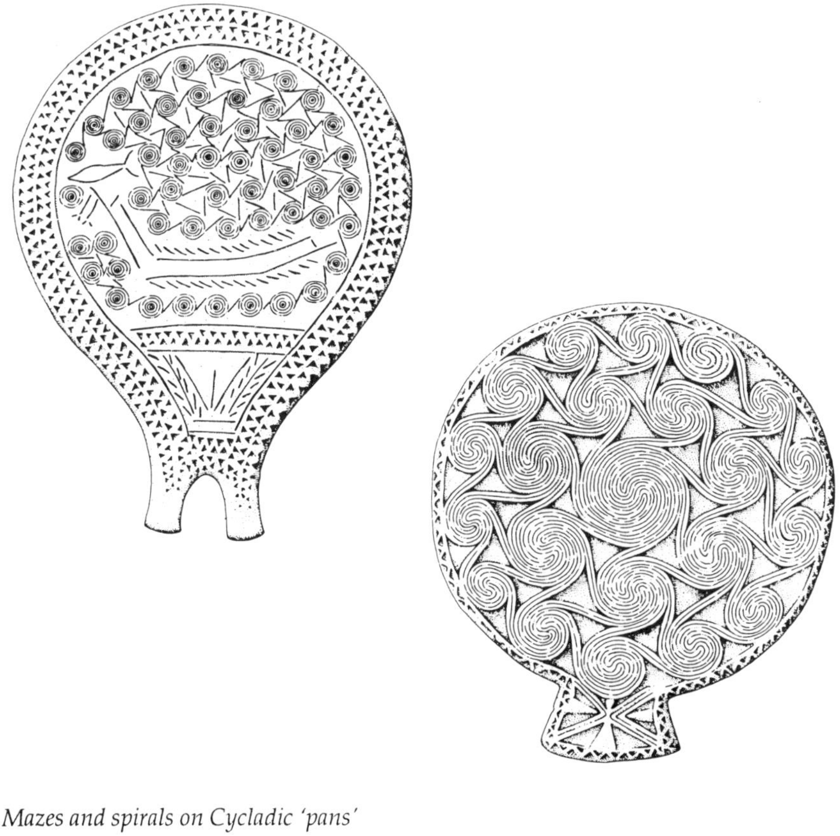

Mazes and spirals on Cycladic 'pans'

'East of the Sun and West of the Moon'

This famous Nordic story is very much linked to the themes of this chapter because it involves the North, South, West and East winds. It is a journey story that is to do with courage and trust as well as the triumph of good over evil. As is usual in troll stories, the troll bursts in the end. The following is a synopsis.

> The goodness of heart of the cottager's beautiful youngest daughter is shown when she agrees to go away with a large white bear who then rewards the poverty-stricken family.
>
> The bear takes the girl to a magnificent palace but, despite all the splendour and the fact that she is treated well, she is lonely for human closeness. Only at night does the bear come to her, although he remains where she cannot see him. However, she senses that he changes in form then.
>
> Recognising her sadness, the perceptive and kindly bear agrees to take her to visit her family on condition that she does not speak alone with her mother – this will result in unhappiness. Unfortunately, the girl is persuaded to be alone with her mother who suggests that it might be a troll occupying the girl's bed when she sense the changing form of the bear. She is advised to hide a candle which she can light to view the sleeping bedmate, but on no account must any of the wax drip onto him.
>
> Having lied to the bear, the girl disregards a second warning about unhappiness coming to them both and, overcome with curiosity, she lights the candle. When she sees the handsome prince sleeping beside her, she falls so deeply in love that she kisses him and three drops of candle-wax fall onto the prince's shirt. At this, the waking prince tells her that his wicked stepmother has cast a year's spell upon him, causing him to be a bear by day but a human by night. The cottage girl's actions mean that the prince must return to the stepmother's castle which lies east of the sun and west of the moon. There lives a princess with a long nose whom he will be compelled to marry.
>
> The girl is heart-broken when she finds the next morning that both prince and palace have vanished and in desperation she sets out on an arduous journey to find him. En route she gathers a golden apple, a golden reel and a golden spindle from old women who help her. All the four winds assist her too and eventually the North Wind, by causing a terrible storm, carries the girl to the castle walls.
>
> Here she is noticed by the long-nosed princess who begs for the golden objects, the cottage girl's reward being to spend three successive nights with the prince. However, having given the princess objects, she is devastated to find that on the first two nights she cannot wake the sleeping prince for he has been drugged. Hearing her tears some Christian prisoners speak to the prince about the events, so that on the third night he does not drink the potion he is given.

> When the girl enters he tells her that he can only be saved from marrying the next day if she can wash the three grease-spots off his shirt – he will only wed the one who can do so. Naturally all those who try to remove the grease find it impossible for they are wicked and avaricious, with the exception of the innocent cottage girl, whom the prince declares shall be his bride.
>
> At this all the evil ones are vanquished as they burst with rage. The helpful Christians are set free and, taking the gold and silver with them, the prince and his bride depart from the castle.
>
> Thus the cottage girl is rewarded for her kindness and by overcoming her own fears and showing a tenacity of spirit she finds true love and happiness.

This story lends itself to group exploration with people taking on the various characters and elements. It involves a girl who leaves her family, but she does not completely separate as she does what her mother says rather than her companion. She has to go through a lone and dangerous journey with much quick-wittedness, and the recurring image of the old women who guide her on her way give the story a ritual structure. Each of the old women say to her when she asks them if they can help her find the prince:

> 'All I know about him is that he lives in the castle that lies east of the sun and west of the moon. And you'll be there late or you'll be there never, but you can borrow my horse and ride to my neighbour.'

It follows the basic structure of the hero's journey with some repeated stages. The girl is given gifts by each of the old women (a golden apple, a golden reel, a golden spindle) which help her to outwit her troll rival. There are two families; her own family, and the step-troll family of the prince, with the intermediaries being the old wise women and the four winds. The girl has to submit to the winds to carry her in turn on her journey – certainly, a rite of passage on her journey to maturity.

In her book *Individuation in Fairytales* Marie-Louise von Franz points out that new meaning can be brought to the 'age-old words' of fairytales. She says:

> In interpreting fairytales as we do here, we try to bring out a new approach or understanding of age-old words which have always been told and understood in some form in their essential wisdom, but not understood in the psychological form in which we understand and interpret them now. We feel, with this clue of Jungian psychology, that is is possible to renew such a story so that it again has the living meaning which people had always formerly felt in it. Nowadays fairytales are only told to children and regarded from a literary and formal standpoint. Fairytales, as a whole, have undergone a process of becoming mere

> poetical words, no one even hoping that any meaning might be conveyed by them which we could understand in an adult way. So it can be said that the Jungian interpretation acts as a renewal of the words of the fairytale; the same thing can be done with any other representation. It can be renewed if it is linked again with its archetypal substratum, for then it becomes an emotional and feeling and intellectual total experience. You get again the reaction of, 'Ah, now I understand it,' with all its vivifying psychological effect (von Franz 1977, p.141).

In using the journey stories referred to in this chapter, we find that they all create the paradoxical structure whereby people are brought closer to their life experience by being distanced from it. These ancient journeys have the capacity to carry meaning across time and provide relevant themes to people here and now. These tales are able to structure people's energy that is diffuse, unfocused or without form, as well as provoking energy in those people who have allowed their energy to die or to stay frozen. As Robbins suggests:

> The core of the patient's self, therefore, consists of formless energy emanating from his center and moving toward form and structure. It is the essence of a personality, often observed at birth and sometimes lost in the various stages of growth. Development within this energetic perspective entails the building of forms that are fed from a center, radiating towards a grid that connects the inner and outer levels of consciousness (Robbins 1989, p.6).

Both in our clinical work and the seasonal schools we not only observe this move towards 'form and structure' in art, story and drama, but we are also aware of a struggle to change structures and forms that are unhelpful or imprisoning. Patients will ask for specific motifs from stories and plays, recognising connections with their own lives though not fully grasping the 'fine tuning'. We also find that what Sue terms 'the addiction to destructive forms' can be changed through experience from other forms drawn from art and literature.

For example, a patient who came for individual dramatherapy was trapped in a fusion with her dead mother. It threatened the breakup of her marriage and her wish to abandon her three children. She was a very articulate and literary person and could see much of her problem but felt powerless to do anything about it:

> I feel dead like my mother and I visit her grave and talk to her and ask her to set me free. When I try to be free all I do is cry and cry. Then it starts again and I freeze up and feel like death...

However, it became clear that she had always been 'tied' to her mother and, when she first married, her husband had enjoyed the additional female attention of more 'home-cooking' support and advice that his mother-in-law was able to provide. When she died he experienced a very powerful loss which he was unable to express because of his wife's traumatised state. Once his wife started in therapy he was able to get some bereavement counselling for himself and the couple were eventually able to acknowledge together their major loss and move forward into the capacity to 'parent' each other when the need arose.In the individual therapy we worked with the story of *East of the Sun and West of the Moon* and structured this journey over a period of some months, through which she was able to work through a process of separation. Although she knew the story, we took it a stage at a time, broadly divided up into the stages of the hero's journey, and usually spent two weeks on each stage. This formed her own structure of containing her story and the continuity in visual media that she created and asked me to contain. At the end of her work she asked for all the photographs back again because she felt that she could manage herself now. This patient recognised that, in the therapy, I had become the 'living-dead mother' for her while she experienced her separation. While I assisted her in her enactment and took on the role of the old women and the winds, she was able to experience:

1. the limitations of the wise women – they were helpers on a journey;
2. the loss of control when blown by the winds – she also played the winds;
3. the discovery of a new source of help, which can assist her, together with her own experience to resolve the difficulty.

It seemed a significant turning point for her came when she realised in the story that the North Wind is running out of energy, that he can only just blow on on the rest of the journey and that her feet are already beginning to get wet in the sea. This experience enabled her to understand people's limits – her dead mother's as well as her own (and of course mine) – which then enabled her to be more realistic about the expectation she placed on her husband and children.

Sue: A further example of a story that we have used both clinically and on our courses and which keeps returning to us again and again in several variations is the story of 'The Lady from the Stars' told by Laurence van der Post in *The Heart of the Hunter* (1961).

I was first introduced to this story by Alida Gersie who is well-known for her innovatory work in therapeutic story-making.* She and I have worked together for many years and it was with her that I made the well-remembered journey to Jerusalem and had the experience of the door of the Holy Sepulchre. I have used stories and myths in my dramatherapy work ever since I began, but Alida taught me her particular 'Storymaking Method' (Gersie 1990; 1991) which is an invaluable way of working in its own right as well as being able to be integrated into dramatherapy and art therapy.

> The Lady from the Stars concerns the story of a race of people who live in the stars but need to visit the earth with regularity in order to find milk, which is the one commodity they lack. The star women carry baskets on their backs that are quite unique and contain whatever is important to them (Stage 1).
>
> A lonely farmer notices that his cows are sometimes dry when he milks them in the morning. He decides to lie in wait, and one night he hears giggling and chattering. There, on fine silver threads, are a group of women coming down to earth with buckets in their hands and baskets on their backs.
>
> He runs towards them and they run away to their threads and are safely pulled back again to the stars, all except one who stumbles and does not reach her thread in time. The farmer says that he is lonely and asks if she will come to live with him. She agrees on the condition that he will never try to look inside her basket. This he readily agrees and they return to the house where she places her basket in a corner of the sitting room. Life settles down and she helps the farmer in his work and creates a garden outside the house.
>
> From time to time she gets a little wistful, especially around dusk when the stars are just beginning to come out and she thinks about her people and family and wonders whether they can see her and what she is doing (Stage 2).
>
> To start with, the farmer isn't troubled by the basket in the corner, but after some time it preoccupies him more and more. He keeps looking at it until eventually he cannot contain his curiosity. He waits until the Star Woman is busy in the garden and then creeps back to the house and looks inside the basket. He stands still in astonishment and then laughs. At that moment she comes into the room and stands in the doorway 'But you promised, never to look inside the basket' she said 'But there is nothing there' he said as he laughed. 'It is empty.'

* I must mention here my friend and colleague Alida Gersie and her innovatory work in Story Making as a therapeutic intervention. Although she works as a dramatherapist, her prime interest is in stories and she generously makes her extensive material available to those around her.

> At that point she turns away, leaves the house, walks down the front path that she had tended and opens the gate...(Stage 3). (In the original story she is spirited back to the stars again).
>
> The story is from the indigenous South Africans for whom stars are very important and contain a lot of wisdom. The important thing for them in this story for the bushmen is, not so much that the farmer broke his promise, but that he could not see anything and laughed.
>
> We have both used this story with individuals and groups, utilising the broad framework based on Gersie's work. For me it is surely relevant that the first time 'heard' this story (having read van der Post endlessly!)* was in a workshop at Haifa run by Alida on the same journey to Israel.

The first part of the story is told and then, at Stage 1, people are asked to create the Star Woman's basket, remembering that it is quite individual in design, that it has a tight lid and that is given to Star Women on special occasions by a significant person. After drawing the basket, people are asked to write down when it was given and on what occasion.

The next part of the story is told, and at Stage 2 people are asked to imagine that they are Star Women standing at the door of their house and gazing at the stars. They write a letter to their family and tell them what they are doing and then imagine they are a member of the family, write a letter to Star Woman, and say what they want her to hear.

The last part of the story is told and then, as the Star Woman stops at the gates, people are asked to complete what they think the ending is.

(*Teaching Point:* It is important to give people a firm time-limit for each of the stages, maybe twenty minutes for each stage. With this story it can easily get into very profound areas and people can get 'hooked' into writing their life stories.)

> It is the business of mythology proper, and of the fairy tale, to reveal the specific dangers and techniques of the dark interior way from tragedy to comedy. Hence the incidents are fantastic and 'unreal': they represent psychological, not physical, triumphs. Even when the legend is of an actual historical personage, the deeds of victory are rendered, not in lifelike, but in dreamlike figurations; for the point is not that such-and-such was done on earth; the point is that, before such-and-such could be done on earth, this other, more important, primary thing had to be brought to pass within the labyrinth that we all know and visit in our dreams. The passage of the mythological hero may be over-ground, incidentally; fundamentally it is inward—into depths where obscure resistances are overcome, and long lost, forgotten powers are revivified,

---

* I use the story of The Lady from the Stars as told in The Heart of The Hunter—yet I find that each time I tell it, there is elaboration!

> to be made available for the transfiguration of the world. (Cambell 1949, p. 29)

These Creative Journeys, both in our own lives and through myths and stories, illustrate not only the importance of the mythic structure and the hero's journey, but also the vast range of material that needs to be accessible to the therapist. We draw attention to this in Chapter 3 'The Storehouse'.

It may well be that we need to refresh ourselves and take a journey 'out there' across the land, or the seas or maybe we need to immerse ourselves once more in Conrad, Virgil, *The Pied Piper of Hamelin*, and *The Laidley Worm*.

CHAPTER 10

Mask, Myth and Metaphor

> In a mask you feel an ancient strength; in a mask you dare things that the mind cannot conceive. It is precisely behind the mask that I feel the intensity of things, and I feel the voice sounding out like a thundering volcano. Masks conceal, create, fall in love (Alekos Fashions Paris, 1978, quoted in Fotopoulos, 1980).

> What can I say about it? You start a mask and it carries you away, caught up in the mood. The enchantment of dreams begins – just try and stop it (conversation with Nikos Nikolaou in Aegina 1978).

> The mask signals to the audience that it is present at a ritual, that the natural world has temporarily been made static, heightened, formalized (Harris Smith 1984, p.51).

> If a mask gazes at the horrors, the terrors, it has to keep on looking...What does a mask do when it suffers or contemplates suffering? Words don't fail it, it goes on speaking (Tony Harrison, quoted in Taplin 1989).

The mask is where art and drama meet and, thus, where art therapy and dramatherapy meet. A mask may be seen as a piece of sculpture; a work of art that may be hung on a wall and contemplated and set in movement by the imagination. It may also be worn, inhabited and set in movement by the wearer.

We came together through the making of masks and for both of us it is the transition between our two worlds of art and drama. It was only after meeting Sue that Åse began to use masks in her own work in the clinical setting. She found that masks could help a person 'move on' when they had become stuck. After she met Åse and started working in a collaborative way in art therapy and dramatherapy, Sue felt affirmed in her own art form – that of mask-maker. Although she did not have the confidence to draw or paint pictures, nevertheless the mask-making and, later, costume design felt an important progression.

The therapeutic and religious worlds are at best ambivalent about masks and their use. Masks are often seen as 'the false self' or, indeed, as

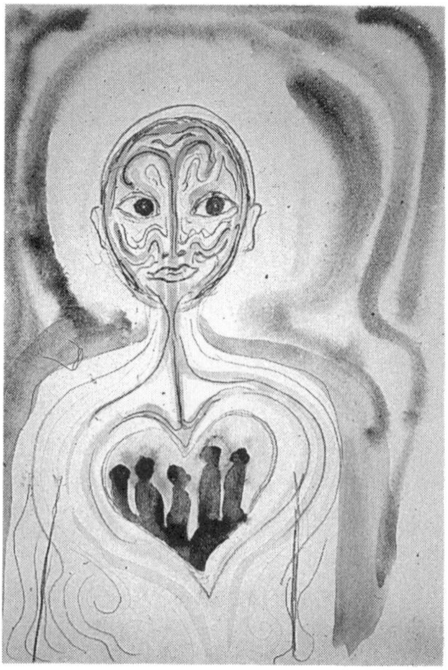

a

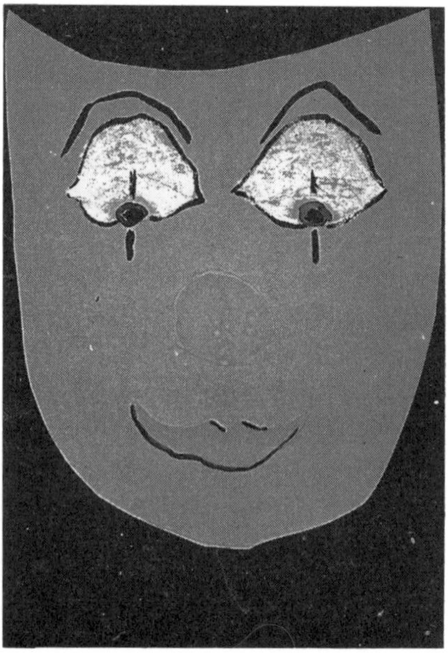

b

Figure a: The patient's words about this picture were 'The group is in my heart, the group is important to me.' The therapist also commented on the picture, saying that the patient looked very vulnerable without skin. The therapist wanted to guide the therapy in the direction of the patient building more boundaries and developing more 'skin'. A few weeks later, while on vacation, the patient committed suicide – he had a heart attack caused by drugs. He had been having to face up to having to make a choice about his life, but had too little 'skin' to make that choice.

the wicked self – the self that can go out of control, evoke demons and generally stir up unhelpful and unhealthy imaginings.

'Stop wearing a mask' or 'you only see the mask and not the person' or 'put on a brave face' are various ways of describing some notion of artificiality in relation to a human being's persona. The idea of removing the mask and being able to be 'honest and true' is a very prevalent idea in dramatherapy. For example, The Geese Theatre Company,* who specialise in working with offenders, maintain the convention that when the mask is taken off you have to speak the truth. Therefore, it is very important to establish with clients and patients the mask convention that is being established. The most usual one is to look upon the mask as having a function in itself of being able to expand, focus, develop, enlarge

* Geese Theatre Company specialise in working with offenders in a variety of settings and make use of the mask as the deceptive role – so the unmasking means that you have to be 'honest'.

or transform the character or role in the drama. The mask often forms part of the 'third space' described in Chapter 7 in the work of Winnicott. There is no doubt that masks enable feelings and perceptions that otherwise would not be able to be expressed by other means: as Harrison so rightly says, the mask continues to talk because it is made with the mouth open.

Sue: Although I work with pre-formed masks such as Commedia dell'arte or the masks from the Ramayana or Mahabhrata, most of the time I work with the mask that is created in the therapy. I see in mask-making – the slow evolution of the mask taking shape – a time of therapeutic process and transformation. Many of the masks I work with are based on plaster-of-Paris bandage being formed directly onto the face* and then shaped and painted. As the mask is being taken off the face, time and again people say it feels like giving birth. The period of withdrawal while the mask dries on the face, lying under a warm blanket, eyes closed and the closeness of the other person placing the bandage on the face, all contribute to the creation or re-creation or re-birth. I make use of a ritual of the person 'seeing and holding' the mask before it is put to dry.† When the masks have dried, people can work together in groups, talking as they trim and cut and paint, and they often find that the mask makes itself. There comes a point when the mask takes over and dictates to the maker how it will be. Sometimes, I deliberately put people into these groups in order to stop an over-identification with the mask. Some people cannot contain an individual, face-to-face encounter with the mask and need help to maintain the necessary distance.

(*Teaching Point*: Any mask-work needs to be carefully monitored, and if people are very fragile it can be more helpful to work with pre-formed masks or very small masks that only cover the eyes, for example.)‡

Åse: When I started to use masks in art therapy, I found an immediate use in my psychodynamic work: I used masks to express aspects of the self that usually could not be expressed. When a patient said to me 'I always wear a mask; I can't be myself', I asked her to draw the mask that is under the mask. Any mask is a part of the self, and what a person is saying is that there is a part of them that is kept hidden.

Just as through art people have the possibility to see things in different perspectives, through the use of masks we have the chance to see our-

---

* If you use plaster bandage, take care that people do not have over-sensitive skin and, in any case, use ample petroleum jelly to protect the face.

† Time and again people 'recognise' aspects of the self, through the judicious use of masks.

‡ For some people, the full mask is too frightening. See Jennings 1990 for a grading of masks for use in practice.

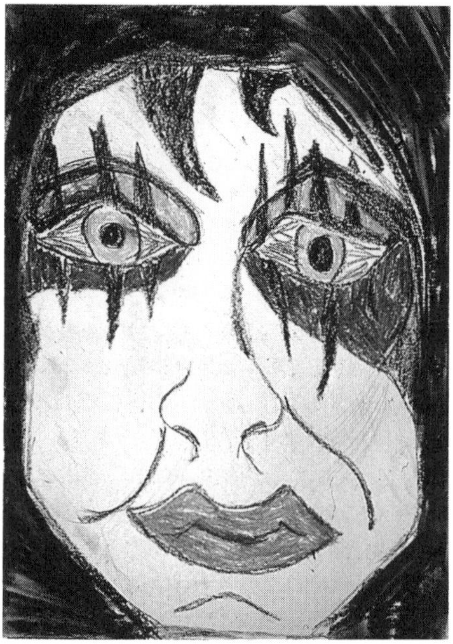

Mask painted by a young female drug abuser

selves in different perspectives. The mask is especially a safe container of the 'self that is dangerous', or the 'self that feels dangerous'.

Masks do not need to be simply face coverings, either part or whole. Masks can be for the whole body – quite literally a complete casing of the body. Furthermore, they can be created by several people; a total mask created by three or four people in itself is an achievement; the people have had to work together and co-operate in a creative endeavour. Group masks are also useful when you do not want an individual to go too deeply into the mask. In a forensic dramatherapy group, people created masks in groups of four which developed the theme of 'light and dark'. The struggle between the good and the bad had been their preoccupation in several improvisations, the dark being associated with their 'badness' but also the things that they liked. This, they felt, was the dilemma. The following themes were portrayed in the group masks:

1. 'All things glittery and of delight': a mask with dollar bills for teeth, hypodermic eyebrows, beercan ears, condom nose (with a hole in it to increase the risk).

2. 'The boil of badness and the ray of hope': all black with a 'scar of life' and one small blob of yellow in one eye. One group member insisted on this ray of hope, despite the pressure from his peers.

3. Confusion and feeling lost: a vertical split with half of the mask as a devil with a horn and the other half with a halo; the confusion felt in the middle of these two halves of the mask.

4. The cold side and the warm side: presented the two sides of a mask with the cold being associated with the dark and with badness, and heat with the light and being good. The group members said that there was a middle-time between the two states where things could change, so that the cold could change to warmth through approval.

These group masks show how profound feelings with their associated images can be struggled with probably more effectively in the group, rather than in the one-to-one settings.

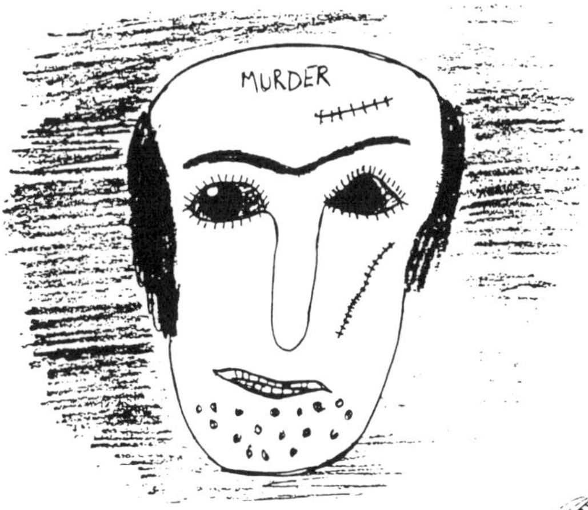

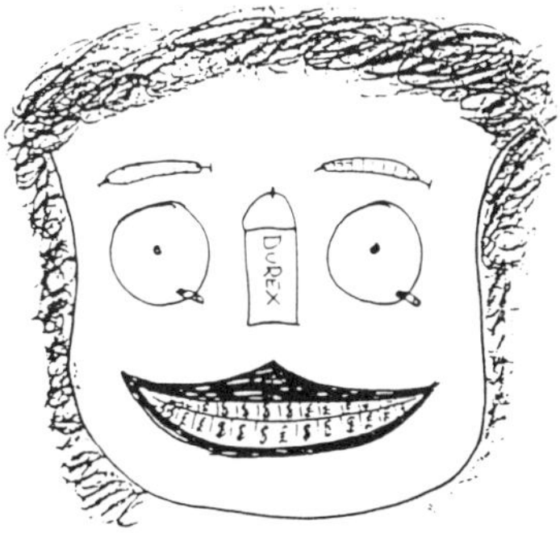

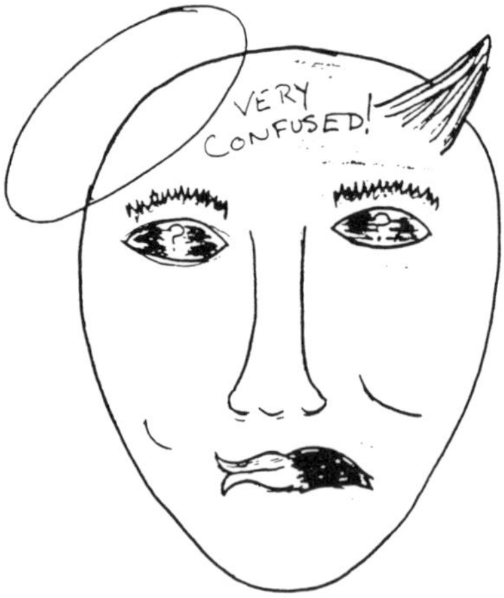

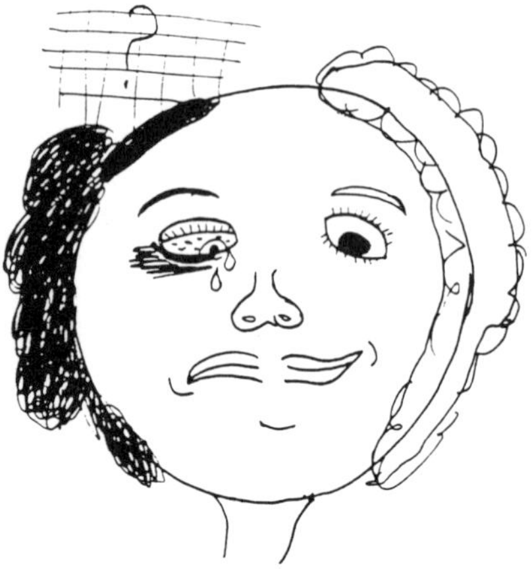

The following conversation took place in 1984 during the planning of a Summer School on masks:

Sue: We can start with the mask and create the character from the mask and lead into the improvisation...

Åse: Or we could start from the improvisation and find the character and then create the mask.

Sue: Do you remember that poem *The Eagle and the Mole*, and sheep come into it as well?

Åse: Like with *The Little Prince*...has the poem got negative or positive sheep?

Sue: Well, they're sort of group sheep; they need to be together, unlike the eagle or the mole. Could we work with the mole under the ground and the eagle all alone in the sky and the sheep on the ground?

Åse: Choose our animal and create the mask? Maybe we should draw all three – under/on/above the ground – and then choose one to explore.

Sue: That's just like the Temiar: everything is divided up into things that are on the ground and things that are off the ground, so houses and dancing and patients and children – things that are vulnerable or human or cultural – are kept from contact with the ground. The ground is associated with things that are dirty or dangerous; snakes are considered dirty because they crawl on the ground on their bellies.

Åse: So, when do children crawl?

Sue: They discourage crawling and encourage walking. A child cannot leave the house, unless it is carried, until it can walk, which is usually when it is first named.

Åse: The naming of the mask, the naming of the child. We could also work with names, drawing pictures of our names, finding out the meaning, who we were named after, maybe a family name, is it a burden to us, what would we really like to be called, and so on?

Sue: And then we could create the mask of the name we have chosen, or should we create the mask and then name it?

Åse: Do you remember the first mask workshop, where someone created a death-mask of the baby that she lost with a miscarriage? It was so powerful for the whole group. What about the mask of someone we want to say goodbye to? No, maybe that is too strong; maybe we could work at a mask we want to leave behind and a mask we want to find.

Sue: What mask do you want to leave behind?

Åse: The passive mask, the mask that keeps quiet – sometime it will explode! What about you?

Sue: I really want to shed the grief mask, the one that has cried long enough. I have done my mourning and I must move on, but there is almost a guilt at saying I'm not going to cry again.

Åse: But it's to do with permission: give yourself permission to give up the mask, and what mask do you want to find?

Sue: My theatre mask. That sounds strange, but these last few years I have been using masks in dramatherapy and when I'd made my own masks, my therapist wanted to interpret them. I want to both make my theatre masks and metaphorically be my theatre mask...

Åse: Well, I am discovering my mask of motherhood and that is very new...So, shall we work with the animal masks, maybe not with the poem, maybe everyone can choose their animal to make a mask. Why don't we use the toy animals first, the farm and wild animals. I've got so many lovely ones and people can make life stories...and then choose one for a mask they would like to explore...

This Summer School developed in broadly the ideas suggested above; from the small animals and sculpting of life here and now (which is similar to the sandplay techniques that we describe in Chapter 3) and then leading into the mask-making. Interestingly enough, the masks that people made did fall broadly into the categories of air, land and earth creatures, so we were able to explore the themes of social animals and isolated animals as well as using the metaphor of the space and terrain that they described, although in this particular group there were no water animals. However, some of the land animals chose to go on a voyage across the sea.

The Story of Inanna (Sumerian) or Ishtar (Semitic)

The story of Inanna and her journey to the underworld to meet her dark sister, Ereshkigal, is probably one of the oldest 'recorded' stories. It was written on clay tablets in the third millennium BC, of which some fragments have been discovered. The themes appear in many versions and in many cultures. Inanna is a fertility goddess as well as a goddess of war; this female deity from the time of the Great Goddess has many aspects.* Her two consorts, who compete for her, are described in detail. They are a farmer and a shepherd (which relates to Chapter 9 where we discuss settled cultivators and hunter-gatherers). The following is one version† of this story used in several workshops in Greece, Israel, Norway and the U.K. We mention this because it seems to have the power to 'speak' across cultures and also professions – one of the workshops consisted only of nurses who had not been involved in artistic therapies before.

> Inanna, goddess of earth and heaven, fertility and war, decides to visit her dark sister, Ereshkigal, queen of the underworld. Before leaving, she instructs her valued assistant, Ninshurbur, to rescue her if she does not return after three days. Inanna wants to mourn her dead brother-in-law, Erishkigal's husband.
>
> To the Land of No Return, the realm of Ereshkigal,
> Ishtar the daughter of Sin set her mind
> Yea, the daughter of Sin set her mind

---

* The sources I have used for Inanna are Cambell 1977 and Brinton Perera 1981, but also look at Gersie 1991.

† The Brinton Perera source is also discursive and very useful for therapists.

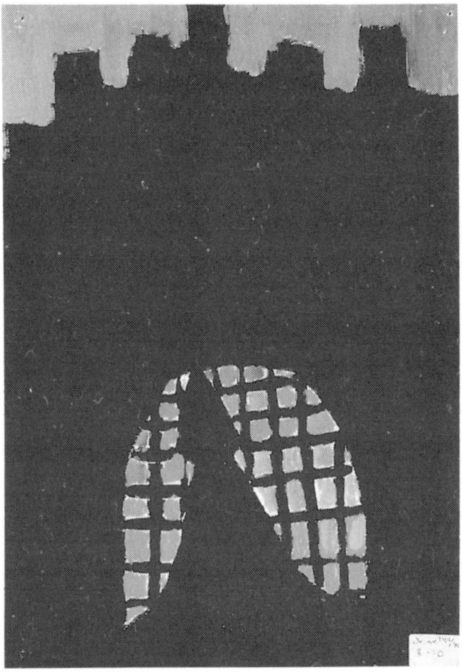

The journey to the underworld – facing the first gate

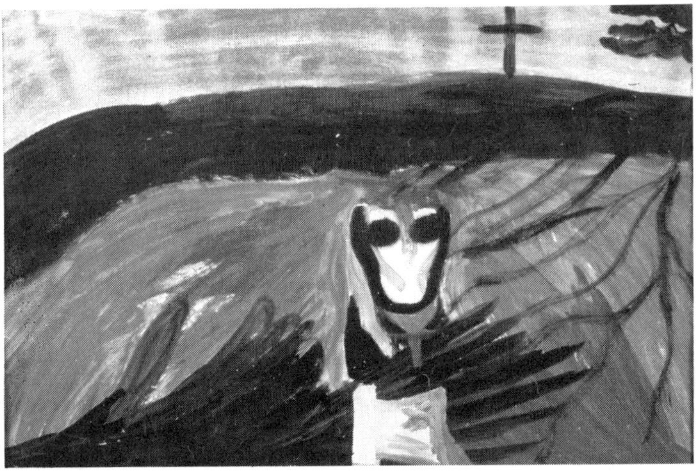

The underworld

To the dark house, the abode of Irkalla,
To the house which none leave who have entered it,
To the road from which there is no way back,
To the house wherein the entrants are bereft of life,
Where dust is their fare and clay their food,
Where they see no light, residing in darkness,
Where they are clothed like birds, with wings for garments,
And where over door and bolt is spread dust.

(Gray 1969, p.34)

Inanna descends to the underworld and her sister sends word to the gatekeeper that she must remove her garments at each of the seven gates. Inanna comes into her sister's presence, crouching and naked.

Ereshkigal kills her sister in jealous rage and hangs her corpse on a stake where it rots and turns green. When Innana's assistant, Ninshurbur, realises after the third day, that Inanna has not returned he takes action.

After three days and nights had passed,
Her messenger Ninshurbur,
Her messenger of favorable winds,
Her carrier of supporting words,
Filled the heaven with complaints for her,
Cried for her in the assembly shrine,
Rushed about for her in the house of the gods.

(Campbell 1976, p.283)

Her cries are heard by Enki, the god of water and wisdom* who creates two little helpers from the dirt under his fingernails. He sends them, with the water of life and the food of life, into the underworld, where they are able to slip in unnoticed. They rescue Inanna who returns through the gates and the land becomes fertile again.

The story can be developed in many ways, and we urge the reader to read the several versions of this story and to discover the themes and motives that are important for them.

Workshop one (1 day)

We tell the story, have some discussion and clarification, and then read the story again. People in the group decide which roles they would like to play in the story and then spend some time drawing and painting the character and its context and then writing about the character in the first person. It does not seem to be a problem for people to choose to be gates,

* The ancient 'gods' of wisdom can be usefully used in arts therapies groups, particularly where one needs to develop an 'anchorage' (see Chapter 9), and enable the development of inner strength.

trees, the sea and so on. Usually, this type of choice means that individuals will work on a theme that is important to them and it isn't usually a conscious choice. For example, one person who thinks rather resentfully that they will be 'just another gate' because there are not any other roles, later finds that the strength and sense of purpose that they gain from the gate is exactly what they had been looking for, as illustrated below:

> 'I am a gate. I am strong and frightening and I prevent people entering into this dark space. I am very necessary because if I was not here then the darkness would cover the whole of the earth. The queen of the underworld gives instructions when I am allowed to be opened, and usually it means a special password and ritual. In this story, the goddess had to remove her fine clothes before I was allowed to open and let her through. I feel very solid and powerful and am pleased that I have a function. I notice that more people pass through me on their way to the underworld than ever come out through it – though in this story it is a bit different and I felt glad...'

The following description comes from someone who has been gently encouraged to join the group and who wants to create 'the earth and pastures' through which Inanna passes before she begins her descent. The person is reluctant to choose a role for herself and is therefore asked 'If you paint a picture, which of the story will you choose to paint?', whereupon she replies, without hesitation, 'the field and the flowers'.

> 'I am part of the earth and pastures where things grow. There are flowers and grass here and many seeds have been planted. Inanna is walking past to go on her dark journey. I am glad I stay here in the light, but when she's gone I dry up and wither because the land isn't fertile any more and I can't grow. When she returns with the others, then everything is fine again and the land is even more beautiful than it was before because Enki decides to send even more water to nourish the dried-up ground.'

Compare this short piece of writing, which accompanies a picture of a field burgeoning with flowers, with the ideas described in earlier chapters of this book, especially when we talk about Primavera and the themes of fertility and fruitfulness in the seasonal schools.*

The other roles that the people in this workshop choose are as follows:

- Inanna (2 people)
- Ereshkigal (5 people)
- Ninshurbur (3 people)
- Enki and water (1 person)
- Two Little Helpers (2 people)

---

* The seasonal cycle or the four elements can provide a useful therapeutic structure.

- Fertile Pastures (4 people)
- Gates and Gatekeeper (5 people)

People divide into their role-groups and share their pictures and writing. They use this as a basis for improvisation on their contribution to the story. As we said earlier in relation to masks, there are some distinct advantages to working with small groups rather than individuals, and in this situation the contribution of everyone heightens the power of the images and the creation of an extraordinary piece of theatre where the full story is enacted. The pastures, the gates and gatekeeper, and also Enki and his helpers worked on ritual chants and movement, and the Fertile Pastures created a fertility dance for the whole group when Inanna returned to earth again.

The feedback after the theatre piece gives indications of the personal work that people can achieve in a single day. For example:

1. People become aware of their own creativity through the fertile earth and pastures.
2. People get in touch with strengths through the gates.
3. The character of Ereshkigal enables people to express jealous rage and violence.
4. Through the journey itself, people are able to descend into the darkness in order to meet their dark sister.
5. Enki and the Little Helpers stimulate people's awareness of their own creative potential even from dirt (see below).
6. People are reminded of the importance of friendship – especially same-gender friendship – which we discuss again in this chapter.

Sue: I am indebted to my art therapist friend, Jean Campbell, for showing me the version of this story which says that Enki created the two little helpers out of the dirt from under his fingernails; as she said, 'What an example of how you can create something out of nothing!' She and I went on to use this story in a Spring School in Art Therapy and Dramatherapy for nurses and embryologists who were training to be fertility counsellors. The story itself gets in touch with the participants' own fertility through the art-form as well as being an important journey of self-discovery. When I used the same story with both Greek and Israeli students, they commented on how it is common for parents to say to their children 'Are you mourning? Your fingernails are dirty.' Dirty fingernails are a sign that someone is in mourning in most Mediterranean countries.

Workshop two (3 days)
In this workshop, the version of the story that appears in the book *Descent to the Goddess* by Sylvia Brenton Perera, Chapters 1, 2, and 8 forms the basis of this more extended exploration of the Inanna story. The focus in this group is on the garments we need to remove at each of the gates before we can meet our dark sister.

Day 1
After the initial reading of the story and a discussion, the whole group improvises in movement on the theme of wanting to get out and wanting to get in. We struggle physically with the gates and doors and the fertile ground itself and our own growth. We reflect on the garments we wear that we would like to shed – that trap us or in which we feel uncomfortable or stereotyped. We then read the story again.

Day 2
Improvisation on the essential stages of the journey (compare with The Hero's Journey in Chapter 9), and the structure of the myth, moving from one stage to another. Each person considers the seven garments that they need or want to remove, together with the additional question 'Who gave you this garment?'There are people who struggle with the task and say that do not want to remove garments but other things such as depression. They are encouraged to consider what sort of garments depression might be (for example we refer to a 'blanket of depression'). Most people readily enter the metaphor, though concrete thinkers generally find it more difficult.

Once people have chosen their seven garments, we then re-tell the story with people enacting each stage with the symbolic removal of each garment, saying to themselves what it is as they remove it. (Jean Campbell created with her group the seven garments through art therapy and then people pinned them to themselves and removed them at the gates.)

We then look at whether we will clothe ourselves in the same clothes on our return, whether we will modify them or whether we desire new garments.

(*Teaching Point*: It is crucial to remember that people have metaphorically removed their defences and have arrived 'naked' in the underworld. Therefore, the issue of re-clothing must be addressed in both the pre-planning as well as the workshop itself.)

The story is read again and there is a feeling that not one bit of detail must be missed; not one crumb or one bit of fingernail-dirt to go unused.

Day 3

It is the morning of dreams – material about people's childhoods that had lain buried for years came to the surface in dreams. We set aside the morning to use the dreams *as if* they are our own personal myths and dramas and paint and enact them in groups where there is a similarity in theme. This is especially strong for those people who have played the character of Ereshkigal and there is some work done on her character in its own right.* We again enact the replacement of the garments we choose to wear as we return to the land of the light and the living. We then spend some time to consider what gift our dark sister has given to us.

The workshop closes with the celebration of the return to the fertile land with the creation of fertile pictures, the fertility dance, and chants and songs. It is a return to the light with the knowledge that we have journeyed to darkness and have survived.

The following are examples of people's seven transformations:

I.

1. The cloak of fear for not being liked by everybody, from my mother.
2. Clever-shoes, from mother and father.
3. A jacket of kindness, from mother and father.
4. Corset of self-judgment, from mother, father, mother's family and women's history.
5. Jeans/trousers denying my sexuality, from my mother and women's history.
6. Gloves, denying my trust in my own creativity, from my mother.
7. A hat of ambivalence/anxiety from mother and father.

II. This person introduced her 'gates' in more detail:

> At the first gate I stand fully dressed and take off my shoes that, for me, are a symbol of aggressiveness. Aggressiveness is something I took from my father.

* The work on a character can be extensive – especially if one explores the various aspects of the character. Because there are negative connotations of the 'dark sister' it is also important to look at her other aspects; rather like in Chapter 6 when we explored the ironical aunt and her childhood.

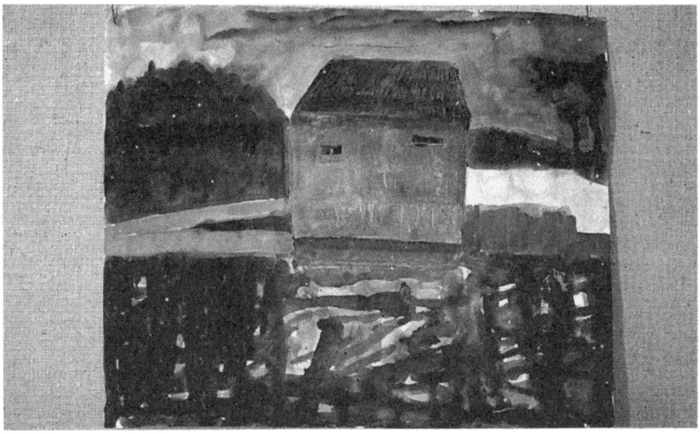

The house shelter. 'It is an old boathouse. It contains everything

At the second gate I take off my trousers, a symbol of control. This is also something that I took from my father.

At the third gate I remove my belt, a symbol of fear. This too I took from my father.

At the fourth gate I remove my shirt, a symbol of security. This I took from my mother.

At the fifth gate I remove my bra, a symbol of my fear of exposing myself. This I took from my mother.

At the sixth gate I removed my underpants, a symbol of control, violence and the fear of the exploitive. This I took from my mother. It is also a symbol of helplessness.

At the seventh gate I removed my spectacles, a symbol of the fear of seeing and being seen.

III. This person included more members of the extended family:

1. The hat of self-denial/despise (from mother and father).
2. The dress of miserliness/stingy (from my mother and one of my old aunts).
3. The coat of self-judgment (my three old aunts (aunts of my father) living in the same house as my family).
4. The bag of mistrust (from my mother).
5. The scarf of control (from my father).
6. Too small, high-heeled shoes of responsibility (from my father).
7. The glove of fear (fear of life), (from my father).

IV. Here, most garments came from Mother:

1. A cloak of vanity – belonging to my mother.
2. A belt of jealousy – belonging to my mother.
3. A bracelet of enviousness – belonging to my mother.
4. A glove of revenge – belonging to both my mother and father.
5. A black hat with some of the colours of the sun – my mother shadowing for my father (I wanted some of the sun).
6. A black stole – bounded – rolled together like a spider.
7. My aggression. I did not give it a piece of clothing. It belongs both to my mother and father. My mother shared it. My father suppressed it.

The gifts that people received from their dark sisters were very many and varied, and below are some examples taken from different groups:

> A new and deeper meeting with my need for someone who understands and accepts all of me and can meet all my needs.
>
> Social creativity, courage, faith, positivity, not to give a damn in the world around.
>
> If I don't run away but stay with the bad feelings, I have helpers to guide me and help me further on my journey. I have resources that I can count on – and they can count on me!
>
> That I could cry so much together with the others.
>
> Her demands on proper clothes for the ongoing situation.
>
> A burgundy-coloured rose. A rose that doesn't wither for days after being picked. This is because of the help she gave me in becoming aware and in renewing my growth.
>
> *The power* – the power to stay with the living life and stay with my strength. And the source of the water of life.
>
> The permission to let my sun shine.
>
> I have received a sword within a sheath.
>
> I received from my *dark sister* a little white clay figure, which means the acceptance of the very small steps that come out of myself – trust.

Another group created 'The Book of the Seven Gates' and illustrated the garments and the stages. Three examples must suffice to illustrate this:

1. The 'shield of rejection and projection',

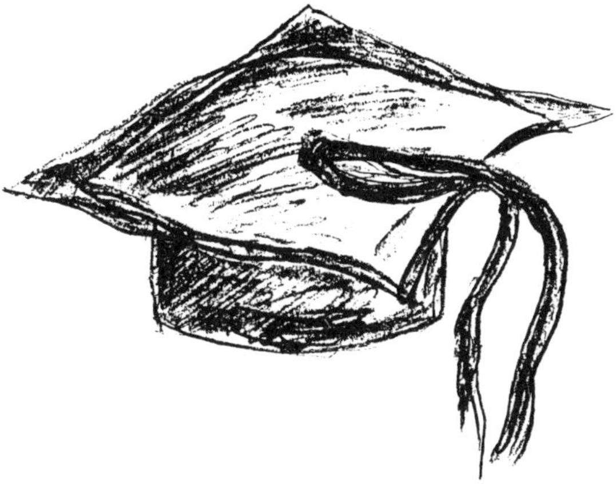

Hat of terror of obscurity

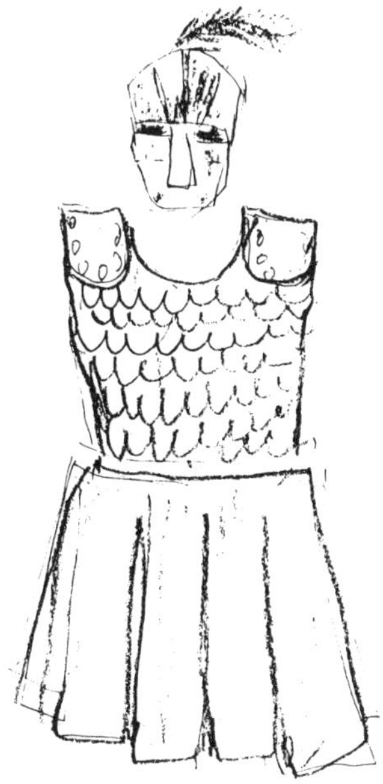

Shield of protection against rejection

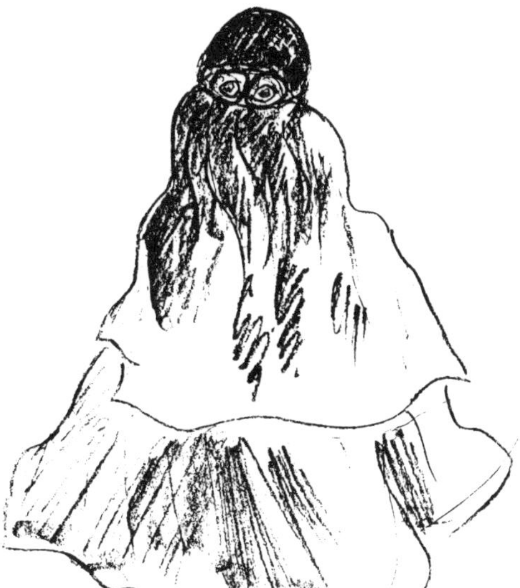

Fear of criticism

2. The 'cloak of fear of criticism'

3. The 'hat of terror of obscurity'

all given by a father.

So far in this chapter we have illustrated how art and drama come together in the mask and how this can be a very powerful medium when it is used in therapy and for personal growth. It must now be clear that a similar process takes place when we are using myths in therapy. The healing metaphors contained in myths and stories enable people to both hear the story they need to hear and tell the story they need to tell. In the above examples it is clear that however a therapist may structure the therapeutic session, individuals and groups will take a story where they need to take it. The importance of working with myth is that usually it is the greater story that will contain our individual stories; the myth resonates towards both individuals and groups. The structure of the myth in question, therefore, is as important as the content.

For example, with the Inanna journey it would be very easy to get diverted into the emotions expressed with people's defencelessness when they enter the underworld 'crouched low and naked', encounter their dark sister and are subsequently killed. It is important to experience becoming alive again through 'the water of life and the food of life' and the return to the fertile earth and, in fact, to realise that the world has become fertile because of our return (this story has many parallels with Demeter and Persephone which we discussed in Chapter 4).

It is also relevant to remember that Inanna is the goddess of storehouses, where grain, dates and livestock are kept – an interesting synthesis of settled cultivator and hunter-gatherer. Her story describes how grains and legumes pour forth from her womb. She moves between different worlds as goddess of earth and heavens and is considered to influence the rain as well as the flood. Because she moves between these different states, she is important as a goddess who manages boundaries and limits. She is known for her appearance both at dawn as well as dusk – the in-between states, or times of transition, where there is often vulnerability and danger as well as the potential for the creative act. Inanna is both an in-between as well as a go-between symbol and in her final attempt to 'go-between' she had to rely on her helper being able to rescue her.

Enki, as god of water and wisdom, brings several more healing metaphors to this story. We have discussed the important imagery of the dirt under the fingernails and the reassurance of these little nondescript people being able to outwit the larger forces of good and evil.

Enki has an equivalent in Poseidon and has many sides that appear in a host of stories and myths. Of course, he would be affected by Inanna's absence from the earth and the resulting period of sterility, so her return is important to him for this reason as well as his feelings of compassion. One of his aspects is depicted as the water-jar, which connects him with images of the female vessel and the 'kettle of transformation' that we mention earlier in the book.

Enki is a trickster and therefore also a god of borders and limits: he is creative rather than static, as he demonstrates through his playfulness and improvisation. As well as the seas and rivers, he is also connected to body-fluids, both of semen and amniotic fluid, so he embraces both the male as well as the female principles.

Brinton Perera suggests that Enki is the patron saint of therapists because, through his wisdom, he can

> meet the dark primal goddess in the consciousness of her suffering, in the suffering of her becoming aware of her outside and inside-of herself (Brinton Perera 1981, p.73).

She suggests that he is able to

> accomplish a basic restructuring of psychic inertia by using whatever is at hand – hidden under the fingernail (ibid).

Finally in this chapter, we would like to draw attention to the therapeutic themes as well as the personal themes that have permeated both our work and our personal lives – that of the importance of same-gender friendship. In Chapter 3, we saw how the basic structure of the 'Journey into the Forest…' made a wide variety of therapeutic journals possible. In particular, we drew attention to the old tale that is re-told by Shakespeare in *A Midsummer Night's Dream*. Relevant to the present discussion is the speech by Titania when she is talking to Oberon in the forest about why the little Indian boy is so important. Be aware of the language she uses:

> Set your heart at rest.
> The fairy land buys not the child of me.
> His mother was a votaress of my order,
> And in the spicèd Indian air by night
> Full often hath she gossiped by my side,
> And sat with me on Neptune's yellow sands
> Marking th'embarkèd traders on the flood,
> When we have laughed to see the sails conceive
> And grow big-bellied with the wanton wind;

> Which she with pretty and with swimming gait
> Following – her womb then rich with my young squire –
> Would imitate, and sail upon the land
> To fetch me trifles, and return again
> As from a voyage, rich with merchandise.
> But she, being mortal, of that boy did die,
> And for her sake do I rear up her boy;
> And for her sake I will not part with him.

(*A Midsummer Night's Dream,* II.i 122–137)

Titania is describing the companionship of women as she and the boy's mother talked and shared together 'women's mysteries':

> Full often hath she gossiped by my side

They talk and laugh together, especially when they see

> the sails conceive
> And grow big-bellied with the wanton wind

Similarly, in the story of Inanna, it is her trusted friend who sets the alarms going about her disappearance. It is Ninshurbur, her 'carrier of supporting words', who

> Cried for her in the assembly shrine
> Rushed about for her in the house of the gods.

(Cambell 1976, p.283)

> **PEER**: You mean I could have stayed where I was,
> Living in peace and luxury in the Ronde?
> You mean all this worry and toil has been for nothing?

(Ibsen, *Peer Gynt*)

> At sunrise the next morning I went to see how he was, hoping he would be well enough for us to start immediately after breakfast. His bed on the floor was empty, but from behind the hut an extraordinary sound was coming. There was in the wall a square opening which served as a window, and I went to it at once to see what caused the sound. It was Dabé, standing sideways on, fully dressed, his hat in his hand and head turned over his shoulder, eyes fixed on his own shadow which in that light lay like ink on the crimson sand and stretched to just beyond the far end of the compound. The voice which made the noise was not at all Dabé's normal one but hoarse, oddly authoritative, and deep, as if it came with the beat of an incantation from the pit of his stomach.
>
> 'Who is he,' the voice chanted, 'who stands here in the morning sun?'

> 'Who is he with so tall a shadow beside him?'
>
> 'Whose shadow is this that starts at sunrise and ends at sunset'
>
> 'Who is he who travels so far from his shelter and people?'
>
> 'Who is he who fears neither police nor kaffir nor red stranger?'
>
> 'Who is he who has an ostrich feather in his hat?'
>
> 'Who is he who puts the hat on the bare head of the shadow?'
>
> The voice paused while Dabé clamped firmly on his head the ridiculous European hat he insisted on wearing. Then he resumed deeper than ever on a big drum-like note:
>
> 'Why, Dabé, you child of a Bushman, you! It is you!' And with that he pranced a sprightly step or two, as a child might on release for play after hours of detention at school.
>
> He could not ever have known how this little shadow show at sunrise moved me (Van der Post 1965, pp. 88–89).

This delightful extract from Laurence Van der Post's book *The Heart of The Hunter*, illustrates so simply the deep healing that has taken place in the heart of the bushman Dabé who was near death. Please read the description through slowly and see how all the important images are brought together, and Dabé is wearing his mask, ('that ridiculous European hat'). Dabé is addressing his emergent 'well self' in his own private dramatic and artistic ritual.

References

The New Penguin edition has been used for all Shakespeare texts cited in the book.

Ariel, S. (1992) *Strategic Family Play Therapy*. New York: John Wiley.

Bachelard, G. (1964) *The Poetics of Space*. Boston: Beacon Press.

Barker, C. (1978) *Theatre Games*. London: Methuen.

Bateson, G. (1958) *Naven*. London: Wildwood House.

Bollas, C. (1987) *The Shadow of the Object: Psychoanalysis of the Unknown Thought*. London: Free Association Books.

Cambell, J. (1964) *Creative Mythology*. London: Penguin.

Cambell, J. (1977) *The Hero with a Thousand Faces*. New York: Bollingen.

Carroll, L. (1946) *Alice in Wonderland*. London: Puffin.

Case, C. and Dalley, T. (1992) *The Handbook of Art Therapy*. London: Tavistock.

Cattanach, A. (1992) *Play Therapy with Abused Children*. London: Jessica Kingsley Publishers.

Conrad, J. (1946) *Heart of Darkness*. London: Dent.

Cox, M. (1978) *Structuring the Therapeutic Process: Compromise with Chaos*. London: Jessica Kingsley Publishers.

Cox, M. (ed.) (1992) *Shakespeare Comes to Broadmoor: 'The Actors are Come Hither'. The Performance of Tragedy in a Secure Psychiatric Hospital*. London: Jessica Kingsley Publishers.

Cox, M. and Theilgaard, A. (1987) *Mutative Metaphors in Psychotherapy: The Aeolian Mode*. London: Tavistock.

Craik, Mrs (1991) *John Halifax, Gentleman*. Stroud: Alan Sutton.

Dalley, T. (1984) *Art as Therapy* London: Tavistock.

Dasent, G. (undated) *Tales from the Norse*. London: Thomas Nelson.

Douglas, M. (1966) *Purity and Danger*. London: Routledge and Kegan Paul.

Dundas, M. (1978) *Symbols Come Alive in the Sand*. Private publication.

Duvignaud, J. (1972) *The Sociology of Art*. London: Paladin.

Ehrenzweig, A. (1970) *The Hidden Order of Art*. St.Albans: Paladin.

Exupery, A. (1945) *The Little Prince*. London: Piccolo/Heinemann.

Fotopulos, D. (1980) *Masks Theatre*. Athens: Kastaniotis Editions.

von Franz, M. (1974) *Shadow and Evil in Fairy Tales*. Dallas: Spring Publications.

von Franz, M. (1977) *Individuation in Fairy Tales*. Dallas: Spring Publications.

von Franz, M. (1988) *The Way of the Dream*. Toronto: Windrose.

Freud, S. (1916) S.E. **XVI** *The Paths to the Formation of Symptoms*. London: Hogarth Press.

Gersie, A. and King, N. (1990) *Storymaking in Education and Therapy*. London: Jessica Kingsley Publishers.

Gersie, A. (1991) *Storymaking in Bereavement*. London: Jessica Kingsley Publishers.

Gersie, A. (1992) *Earth Tales*. London: Green Press.

Goffman, E. (1969) *The Presentation of Self in Everyday Life*. Harmondsworth: Penguin.

Gray, J. (1984) *Near Easten Mythology*. Feltham: Hamlyn.

Grotowski, J. (1968) *Towards a Poor Theatre*. London: Eyre Methuen.

Hall, P.N. (1987) 'A Way of Healing the Split'. In T. Dalley et al. *Images of Art Therapy*. London: Tavistock.

Halliday, A. (1987) 'Peak experiences: the individuation of children'. In T. Dalley et al. *Images of Art Therapy*. London: Tavistock.

Harris Smith, S. (1984) *Masks in Modern Drama*. University of California Press.

Hart, F. (1987) *History of Italian Renaissance Art*. London: Thames and Hudson.

Hellman, C. (1991) *Body Myths*. London: Chatto and Windus.

Hill, A. (1945) *Art Versus Illness*. London: Allen & Unwin.

Hill, A. (1951) *Painting out of Illness*. London: Williams and Northgate.
Hillman, J. (1983) *Healing Fiction*. New York: Station Hill.
Hobson, R. (1985) *Forms of Feeling: The Heart of Psychotherapy*. London: Tavistock.
Holland, L. (trans.)(1962) *Poems of the Elder Edda*. University of Texas Press.
Ibsen, H. (1958) *The Master Builder*. Trans. V. Ellis Fermor. London: Penguin.
Ibsen, H. (1963) *Peer Gynt*. London: Rupert Hart-Davis.
Ibsen, H. *The Lady from the Sea*. Trans. P. Watts. London: Penguin.
Jansson, T. (1962) *Tales of Moominvalley*. London: Puffin.
Jennings, S. (1986a) *Creative Drama in Group Work*. Bicester: Winslow Press.
Jennings, S. (1986b) *Dramatherapy and Group Analysis*. Paper presented to the Group Analytic Society Spring Conference.
Jennings, S. (1988) 'The Loneliness of the Long Distance Therapist'. *British Journal of Psychotherapy*, Vol 4, iii.
Jennings, S. (1990a) *Dramatherapy with Families Groups and Individuals*. London: Jessica Kingsley Publishers.
Jennings, S. (1990b) *Ophelia: Image, Projection & Madness*. Paper presented at The European Symposium on Dramatherapy & Shakespeare, Elsinore, Denmark.
Jennings, S. (1992b) 'The Nature and Scope of Dramatherapy: Theatre of Healing'. In M. Cox (ed) *Shakespeare Comes to Broadmoor*. London: Jessica Kingsley Publishers.
Jennings, S. (1993a) *Drama, Ritual and Transformation*. London: Routledge.
Jennings, S. (1993b) *Playtherapy with Children: A Practitioner's Guide*. Oxford: Blackwell Scientific.
Jennings, S. (ed)(1987) *Dramatherapy: Theory and Practice for Teachers and Clinicians*. London: Routledge.
Jennings, S. (ed)(1992a) *Dramatherapy Theory and Practice 2*. London: Routledge.
Johnson, R. (1992) 'The dramatherapist "in-role"'. In S. Jennings (ed.) *Dramatherapy Theory and Practice 2*. London: Routledge.
Jung, C. (1960) *The Structure and Dynamics of the Psyche: Collected Works Volume 8*. London: Routledge.
Kalff, D. (1980) *Sandplay*. Santa Monica: Sigo Press.
Kellogg, R. (1969) *Analyzing Children's Art*. California: Mayfield.
Kernberg, O. (1984) *Object Relations Theory and Clinical Psychoanalysis*. New York: Jason Aronsen.
Kramer, E. (1971) *Art as Therapy with Children*. New York: Schocken Books.
Landy, R. (1986) *Drama Therapy: Concepts and Practice*. New York: Charles C. Thomas.
Landy, R. (1992) 'One-on-One: The Role of the Dramatherapist Working with Individuals. In S. Jennings (ed.) *Dramatherapy Theory and Practice 2*. London: Routledge.
Lewis, G. (1982) *Day of Shining Red*. Cambridge University Press.
Lightbown, R. (1989) *Botticelli: Life and Work*. London: Thames and Hudson.
Lowenfeld, M. (1979) *The World Technique*. London: Allen and Unwin.
May, R. (1975) *The Courage to Create*. Stockholm: Bonnier Fakta Bokforlag.
McDougall, J. (1986) *Theaters of the Mind*. London: Free Association Press.
McDougall, J. (1989) *Theaters of the Body*. London: Free Association Press.
McLaren, A. (1984) *Reproductive Rituals*. London: Methuen.
McMahon, L. (1992) *Handbook of Play Therapy*. London: Routledge.
Mead, G.H. (1934) *Mind, Self and Society*. University of Chicago.
de la Mere (1936) in W.B. Yeats (ed) *The Oxford Book of Modern Verse*. Oxford University Press.
Miller, A. (1983) *For Your Own Good*. London: Virago.
Moreno, J. (1947) *The Theatre of Spontaneity*. New York: Beacon House.
Napier, A. (1986) *Masks, Transformation and Paradox*. University of California Press.
Naumberg, M. (1966) *Dynamically Oriented Art Therapy*. New York: Grune & Stratton.
Neumann, E. (1963) *The Great Mother*. London: Routledge and Kegan Paul.

Nielsen, (1988) *Godt Sagt*. Oslo: Kurer Forlag.

Oaklander, V. (1978) *Windows to Our Children*. Utah: Real People Press.

Perera, S.B. (1981) *Descent to the Goddess*. Toronto: Inner City Books.

van der Post, L. (1961) *The Heart of the Hunter*. London: Penguin.

Potter, B. (undated) *The Tale of Jeremy Fisher*. London: Frederick Warne.

Røine, E. (1979) *Psychodrama – psykoterapi som eksperimentelt theater*. Norway: Aschehong Forlag.

Reisby, J. (1981) 'Agripa'. *Journal of Psychiatry*.

Rilke, R.M. (1989) *The Selected Poetry of Rainer Maria Rilke*. Trans. and ed. S. Mitchell. New York: Vintage Books

Robbins, A. (1987) *The Artist as Therapist*. New York: Human Sciences Press.

Robbins, A. (1989) *The Psychoaesthetic Experience: An Approach to Depth Oriented Treatment*. New York: Human Sciences Press.

Ryce-Menuhin, J. (1992) *Jungian Sandplay*. London: Routledge.

Rycroft, C. (1985) *Psychoanalysis and Beyond*. London: Chatto and Windus.

Schaverien, J. (1992) *The Revealing Image*. London: Routledge.

Scheff, T.J. (1979) *Catharsis in Healing, Ritual and Drama*. University of California Press.

Schindler, M. (1964) *Goethe's Theory of Colour*. Sussex: New Knowledge Books.

Showalter, E. (1985) 'Representing Ophelia: Women, Madness and the Responsibilities of Feminist Criticism'. In P. Parker and G. Hartmann (eds) *Shakespeare and the Question of Theory*. New York: Methuen.

Spignesi, A. (1983) *Starving Women: A Psychology of Anorexia Nervosa*. Dallas: Spring Publications.

Stanislavski, C. (1980) *An Actor Prepares*. Trans. E.R. Hapgood. London: Methuen.

Storm, H. (1972) *Seven Arrows*. New York: Ballantyne Books.

Taplin, O. (1989) *Greek Fire*. London: Jonathan Cape.

Turner, V. (1968) *Forest of Symbols*. Cornell University Press.

Ullman, E. and Dachinger, P. (1975) *Art Therapy* New York: Schocken Books.

Waller, B.G. (1983) *The Woman's Encyclopedia of Myths and Secrets*. San Francisco: Harper.

Weinrib, E. (1983) *Images of the Self*. Boston: Sigo Press.

West, J. (1992) *Child-Centred Play Therapy*. London: Edward Arnold.

Willett, J. (1964) *The Theatre of Bertold Brecht*. London: Methuen.

Wilshire, B. (1982) *Role Playing and Identity: The Limits of Theater as Metaphor*. Indiana University Press.

Winnicott, D. (1971) *Playing and Reality*. London: Penguin.

Winnicott, D. (ed.)(1958) 'The Antisocial Tendency'. In *Collected Papers*. London: Hogarth Press.

Woodman, M. (1985) *Pregnant Virgin*. Toronto: Inner City Books.

Further Reading

Artaud, A. (1977) *The Theatre and its Double*. London: John Calder.

Bachelard, G. (1942) *Water and Dreams*. Dallas: Pegasus.

Betensky, H.G. (1973) *Self-discovery through Self-expression*. Springfield: C.C. Thomas.

Birkhäuser-Oeri, S. (1988) *The Mother*. Toronto: Inner City Books.

Bloch, D. (1978) *So the Witch Won't Eat Me*. New York: Grove Press Inc.

Brook, P. (1968) *The Empty Space*. London: Penguin Books.

Cook, R. (1974) *The Tree of Life*. London: Thames and Hudson.

Grainger, R. (1990) *Drama and Healing*. London: Jessica Kingsley Publishers.

Haugsgjerd, S. (1990i) *Grunnlaget for en psykiatri*. Oslo: Pax Forlag.

Haugsgjerd, S. (1990ii) *Lidelsens Karakrer i ny psykiatri*. Oslo: Pax Forlag.

Kramer, E. (1973) *Art Therapy with Children*. London: Elek.

Kramer, E. (1979) *Childhood and Art Therapy*. New York: Schocken.

Kwaitkowska, H. (1978) *Family, Therapy and Evaluation Through Art*. Springfield: C.C. Thomas.

Landgarten, H. (1981) *Clinical Art Therapy*. Bruner Mazel.

Miller, A. (1990) *The Untouched Key*. London: Virago Press.

Milner, M. (1977) *On Not Being Able to Paint*. London: Heinemann.

Naumburg, M. (1966) *Dynamically Orientated Art Therapy*. New York: Grun Stratton.

Naumburg, M. (1973) *Introduction to Art Therapy*. Teachers College Press.

Read, J. Pruyn (1975) *Sand Magic*. Albuquerque: JPR Publishers.

Robbins, A. (ed) (1988) *Between Therapists*. New York: Human Sciences Press.

Rodenburg, P. (1992) *The Right to Speak*. London: Methuen Drama.

Rubin, J. (1984) *The Art of Art Therapy*. New York: Bruner Mazel.

Steinberg, D. (1989) *Interprofessional Consultation*. Oxford: Blackwell Scientific.

Wadeson, H. (1980) *Art Psychotherapy*. New York: Wiley.

Woodman, M. (1982) *Addiction to Perfection*. Toronto: Inner City.

Shakespearean Scenes Cited in the Text

ROMEO: I dreamt a dream tonight.

MERCUTIO: And so did I.

ROMEO: Well, what was yours?

MERCUTIO: That dreamers often lie.

ROMEO: In bed asleep, while they do dream things true.

MERCUTIO: O, then I see Queen Mab hath been with you.
She is the fairies' midwife, and she comes
In shape no bigger than an agate stone
On the forefinger of an alderman,
Drawn with a team of little atomies
Over men's noses as they lie asleep.
Her chariot is an empty hazelnut,
Made by the joiner squirrel or old grub,
Time out o'mind the fairies' coachmakers.
Her wagon spokes made of long spinners' legs;
The cover, of the wings of grasshoppers;
Her traces, of the smallest spider web;
Her collars, of the moonshine's watery beams;
Her whip, of cricket's bone; the lash, of film;
Her wagoner, a small grey-coated gnat,
Not half so big as a round little worm
Pricked from the lazy finger of a maid.
And in this state she gallops night by night
Through lovers' brains, and then they dream of love;
O'er courtiers' knees, that dream on curtsies straight;
O'er lawyers' fingers, who straight dream on fees;
O'er ladies lips, who straight on kisses dream,
Which oft the angry Mab with blisters plagues,
Because their breaths with sweetmeats tainted are.
Sometime she gallops o'er a courtier's nose,
And then dreams he of smelling out a suit.
And sometime comes she with a tithe-pig's tail
Tickling a parson's nose as 'a lies asleep;
Then he dreams of another benefice.
Sometime she driveth o'er a soldier's neck;
And then dreams he of cutting foreign throats,
Of breaches, ambuscados, Spanish blades,
Of healths five fathom deep; and then anon
Drums in his ear, at which he starts and wakes, And being thus

frighted, swears a prayer or two
And sleeps again. This is that very Mab
That plaits the manes of horses in the night
And bakes the elf-locks in foul sluttish hairs,
Which once untangled much misfortune bodes.
This is the hag, when maids lie on their backs,
That presses them and learns them first to bear,
Making them women of good carriage.
This is she –

ROMEO: Peace, peace, Mercutio, peace!
Thou talkest of nothing.

MERCUTIO: True. I talk of dreams;
Which are the children of an idle brain,
Begot of nothing but vain fantasy;

(*Romeo and Juliet* I.4. 50–98)

LADY: There are two lodged together.

MACBETH: One cried 'God bless us' and 'Amen' the other,
As they had seen me with these hangman's hands.
Listening their fear I could not say 'Amen'
When they did say 'God bless us.'

LADY: Consider it not so deeply.

MACBETH: But wherefore could not I pronounce 'Amen'?
I had most need of blessing, and 'Amen'
Stuck in my throat.

LADY: These deeds must not be thought
After these ways; so, it will make us mad.

MACBETH: Methought I heard a voice cry, 'Sleep no more!
Macbeth does murder sleep – the innocent sleep,
Sleep that knits up the ravelled sleave of care,
The death of each day's life, sore labour's bath,
Balm of hurt minds, great nature's second course,
Chief nourisher in life's feast.'

LADY: What do you mean?

MACBETH: Still it cried 'Sleep no more' to all the house;
'Glamis hath murdered sleep, and therefore Cawdor
Shall sleep no more, Macbeth shall sleep no more.'

LADY: Who was it that thus cried? Why, worthy thane,
You do unbend your noble strength, to think
So brain-sickly of things. Go, get some water,
And wash this filthy witness from your hand.
Why did you bring these daggers from the place?

They must lie there. Go carry them and smear
The sleepy grooms with blood.

MACBETH: I'll go no more.
I am afraid to think what I have done;
Look on't again I dare not.

LADY: Infirm of purpose!
Give me the daggers. The sleeping and the dead
Are but as pictures. 'Tis the eye of childhood
That fears a painted devil. If he do bleed,
I'll gild the faces of the grooms withal,
For it must seem their guilt. [*Exit*]
[*Knock within*]

MACBETH: Whence is that knocking?
How is't with me when every noise appals me?
What hands are here! Ha – they pluck out mine eyes!
Will all great Neptune's ocean wash this blood
Clean from my hand? No, this my hand will rather
The multitudinous seas incarnadine,
Making the green one red.
[*Enter Lady Macbeth*]

LADY: My hands are of your colour; but I shame
To wear a heart so white.
[*Knock*]
I hear a knocking
At the south entry. Retire we to our chamber.
A little water clears us of this deed;
How easy is it then! Your constancy
Hath left you unattended.
[*Knock*]
Hark! more knocking.
Get on your nightgown, lest occasion call us
And show us to be watchers. Be not lost
So poorly in your thoughts.

MACBETH: To know my deed 'twere best not know myself.
[*Knock*]
Wake Duncan with thy knocking! I would thou couldst!
[*Exeunt*]
[*Enter a Porter. Knocking within*]

PORTER: Here's a knocking indeed! If a man were porter of hell-gate he should have old turning the key.
[*Knock*]
Knock, knock, knock! Who's there i'the name of Belzebub? Here's a farmer that hanged himself on the

expectation of plenty. Come in time! Have napkins enow about you; here you'll sweat for't.

[*Knock*]

Knock, knock! Who's there in the other devil's name? Faith, here's an equivocator that could swear in both the scales against either scale, who committed treason enough for God's sake, yet could not equivocate to heaven. O, come in, equivocator.

[*Knock*]

Knock, knock, knock! Who's there? Faith, here's an English tailor come hither for stealing out of a French hose. Come in, tailor; here you may roast your goose.

[*Knock]*

Knock, knock! Never at quiet! What are you? – But this place is too cold for hell. I'll devil-porter it no further. I had thought to have let in some of all professions that go the primrose way to the everlasting bonfire.

[*Knock*]

Anon, anon! I pray you remember the porter.

[*He opens the gate. Enter Macduff and Lennox*]

MACDUFF: Was it so late, friend, ere you went to bed,
That you do lie so late?

PORTER: Faith, sir, we were carousing till the second cock; and drink, sir, is a great provoker of three things.

MACDUFF: What three things does drink especially provoke?

PORTER: Marry, sir, nose-painting, sleep, and urine. Lechery, sir, it provokes and unprovokes: it provokes the desire but it takes away the performance. Therefore much drink may be said to be an equivocator with lechery: it makes him and it mars him; it sets him on and it takes him off; it persuades him and disheartens him, makes him stand to and not stand to; in conclusion, equivocates him in a sleep and giving him the lie, leaves him.

MACDUFF: I believe drink gave thee the lie last night.

PORTER: That it did, sir, i'the very throat on me. But I requited him for his lie and, I think, being too strong for him, though he took up my legs sometimes, yet I made a shift to cast him.

MACDUFF: Is thy master stirring?

[*Enter Macbeth*]

Our knocking has awaked him; here he comes.

(*Macbeth* II.2. 25–74)
(III.3. 1–40)

Current Addresses

Association for Dance Movement Therapy
99 South Hill Park
London NW3 2SP

British Association of Arts Therapists
11A Richmond Road
Brighton BN2 3RL

British Association for Dramatherapists
The Old Mill
Tolpuddle
Dorchester
Dorset DT2 7EX

British Association for Music Therapy
69 Avondale Avenue
East Barnett
Hertfordshire EN4 8NB

Dramatherapy Consultants
PO Box 32
Stratford upon Avon
CV37 6GU

The Institute of Dramatherapy
PO Box 32
Stratford upon Avon
CV37 6GU
Telephone (0789) 268558

Norwegian Art Therapy Association
Norsk Forening for Billedterapi
PB. 1 Gaustad
0377 Oslo
Norway

Norwegian Association for Psychodrama
Norsk Forening for Psykodrama
P.B. 5641 Briskeby
0209 Oslo
Norway

Norwegian Music Therapy Association
Norsk forening for musikkterapi
Toftes gt. 69
0552 Oslo
Norway

Education in Expressive Therapies in Norway

Music Therapy
2 years full-time post graduate training
Østandets Musikkonseravtorium
Vetlandsveien 45
0685 Oslo
Norway

Dance and Art Therapy
2 years full-time post graduate training starting fall 1993
Information about training:
Senter for Billed og Danseterapi
Sognsvannsveien 21
0372 Oslo
Norway

Expressive therapy 3 years part-time
Norsk Institutt for Uttrykksterapi
Nordengveien 1
1367 Billingstad
Norway

Psychodrama Training
Norsk Psykodrama Institutt
Treidene 3145
Tjøme
Norway
2 years part-time to become psychodrama assistant
5 years part-time to become psychodrama instructor

Subject Index

Name Index